The Wisconsin 3,800

Our Men and Women Buried or MIA in the Lands They Liberated in World War II

TOM MUELLER

First published by Dog Ear Publishing
4010 W. 86th Street, Ste H
Indianapolis, IN 46268
www.dogearpublishing.net

ISBN: 978-160844-085-6

This book is printed on acid-free paper.

Printed in the United States of America

This book is made possible through the generous assistance of:

American Family Insurance

Marcus Theatres Corp.

Dedication

For Tech. Sgt. Wilferd J. Mueller,
an Army combat engineer who fought in the war in Europe,
came home to Madison, Wis., and had two sons

Table of Contents

Chapter 1:

Our lost men and women

More than six decades after the end of World War II, this book has plowed some new ground and found some new wrinkles amid the long lists of those who died and were MIA or buried overseas, and it also tells in intricate ways the stories of those who probably have not been written about since their own brief obituary.

For example:

• Chapter 2 reveals that the first Wisconsin man buried overseas is a Merchant Marine from Milwaukee who died on March 29, 1940 – long before Pearl Harbor – on a ship carrying war supplies off the coast of Africa; he is buried in Tunisia. The last Wisconsin case was from July 21, 1948, and is an Army man who was MIA and is on the Honolulu Memorial.

• Chapter 3 declares, possibly for the first time, what was the worst day for Wisconsin in the war – 49 dead; 47 of them were killed aboard a prisoner ship in the Battle of Leyte Gulf on Oct. 24, 1944. They are on the MIA wall in Manila. Overall, there are 36,285 names on that wall, and 5 percent of them are from the very ship involved.

• Chapters 4 and 11 reveal the highest-ranking Wisconsinites killed in the war among those MIA or buried overseas, including an Air Force general and the commander of a submarine. This determination was made after two kinds of reviews of the records of the American Battle Monuments Commission.

• Chapter 8 shows that the only Wisconsin woman killed by enemy fire in the war was 2nd Lt. Ellen Ainsworth of Glenwood City, and she is buried in Italy. I first revealed this fact in the Memorial Day story published in the Milwaukee Sentinel in 1986, but now it is getting a wider and more permanent forum. Chapter 12 discusses the case of another nurse, from Rock County, who died soon after the war ended and is buried in Honolulu.

• Chapter 10 reports that Christmas Eve and / or Christmas Day saw death tolls in 1941, 1942, 1943, 1944, and even in 1945, of far more Wisconsin men than in many other days of the war over the years.

All in all, this research adds substantial new information to Wisconsin's record.

"This book is a valuable new resource for everyone interested in Wisconsin's contributions to World War II, from historians to enthusiasts to relatives of the veterans," said Russell Horton, reference and outreach archivist at the Wisconsin Veterans Museum in Madison. "It is clear that Tom Mueller has researched the topic very thoroughly and his analysis has unearthed some interesting facts, including the first and last Wisconsinites to die in the war and the deadliest day for Wisconsin soldiers. 'The Wisconsin 3,800' is a must-read for anyone exploring the role of the Badger State in World War II."

Many of the people in this book have not been written about since their obituaries ran in 1941, 1942 or later years. Most of their obituaries were only bare-bones, and did not report much, if anything, about their unit's fighting or the historical context of their deaths. There are many facts about the event that have come to light in the following decades, as well as multiple human-interest angles involved, whether they be irony or tragedy or something else. This book reveals those facts.

The men and women in this book sleep in foreign graves thousands of miles from home, or are on MIA walls in foreign places, and may not have had a relative visit in decades, if ever. The man on the cover, for example, had his first visitor 40 years later, and only one since then. Another soldier did not have a visitor until the 60th year after his death.

More and more World War II service people are little-known to their relatives of the next generation, and it gets worse for each generation that passes. For a few of the men in this book, it was impossible or very difficult to even dig up a photo, and for many more men, even their siblings are gone. This book helps preserve the historical record, not only for their families but also for their hometowns, counties, and the state as a whole, as well as for the United States.

The entire generation – the men and women who were there, and their siblings who survived – is leaving the stage, and it passes faster with each year.

Young men and women who were age 18 on VJ Day in August 1945 are 82 on that day in 2009, and sailors who were age 18 at Pearl Harbor will be 86 on that anniversary. In eight years, all of them will be in their 90s, and the vast majority of World War II vets will not be around in 20 years.

An estimated 900 such veterans per day are dying, according to the U.S. Department of Veterans Affairs. Nationally, there were about 2.58 million remaining as of 2009, and about 43,000 in Wisconsin. The state loses an average of 100 veterans per week, according to the Wisconsin Department of Veterans Affairs.

You, the reader, may have bought this book because you have a faint memory of a relative who was killed in the war and was buried overseas "somewhere." Use the how-to-search section at the end of the book to figure out where, and then go on your own voyage of history to find out more about what was going on at the time. Also, you can grill your relatives as to what the soldier was like, and all about his or her life. Start gathering the material today, and you will be surprised in a couple weeks how much you have.

For me, the road to this book began in a cemetery in France in 1984, and took many twists and turns through a newspaper career, graduate school, and a hobby.

I was the world and national news editor of the Milwaukee Sentinel, and was assigned to fly with the Milwaukee-based Air National Guard refueling tankers on a Cold War mission to Germany. In the event of a Soviet invasion, these planes would escort Air National Guard anti-tank planes based in Madison to the battlefield, nonstop. We were going to be in Germany for a week, so I talked my bosses into letting me go to France to find the grave of my soldier uncle, Pvt. Martin Miller, and write a Memorial Day story. He is the man on the cover of this book.

Little did I realize that he had been killed in Normandy, and the story grew into a series of articles marking the 40th anniversary of

D-Day. I started that day at Omaha Beach and then traveled through the back roads of the French countryside to his cemetery in St. James, which is in Brittany. Those peaceful-looking, back-country roads were the scene of weeks of fierce battle between D-Day of June 6, 1944, and the Breakout from Normandy, which began in the final days of July. My uncle was killed on Aug. 1, and his story is told in this book along with four other men killed in the same place on the same day.

Those other four were found because of an amazing coincidence and the fact that the American Battle Monuments Commission had put its records on-line, making the database searchable to an extent. The amazing coincidence was that after seeing the grave of my uncle, I walked one way in the cemetery and then another, deciding to look over the wall to see whether there were cows because the landscape resembled the farming area he came from. It also was raining, lending a surreal quality to the scene, like a painting. Quite by accident, I looked down at the exact moment I was passing the grave of another man, and found that he, too, was from Wisconsin, had the same last name, was in the same regiment, and was killed on the same date as my uncle.

Many years later, I checked on-line for other men from the 28th Infantry Division, and found the three others from Wisconsin who were killed on that date.

Over the years, I had started doing Memorial Day stories for my newspaper, selecting a soldier or two from World War II, Vietnam, or Korea each time. All the World War II service people that I wrote about were buried overseas, which was just a coincidence, but turned into a major reason why this book is being written. The database of overseas burials and MIAs is one of the most solid there is.

Their individual stories are the stories of typical young men and women from the Madison area, Appleton, Milwaukee, Baileys Harbor, Plymouth, Kewaskum, Menasha, Rice Lake, Glenwood City, La Crosse, Merrill, Augusta, Rice Lake, and many more. They were farm boys, sons of bartenders and salesmen, among other everyday professions.

This story will help readers understand what is behind each war death. Beneath each military cross and Star of David in all those cemeteries in Europe, Africa, the Philippines, and in Honolulu lies the sadly abbreviated story of a son, a brother, a cousin, a nephew, a neighbor, a schoolmate, a friend, or a co-worker.

We can read about D-Day, Pearl Harbor, Iwo Jima, Midway, Saipan and any other battle in all sorts of history books, and not fully realize anything about the individuals, who were killed by the tens of thousands. Conversely, we can read about an individual veteran in his own book, and not fully realize the many aspects of the average life – a 20-year-old having lived little more than 7,300 days. This book tells about those soldiers, whose DNA and lives make up the fabric of this country. They were in uniform, but their richly varied backgrounds also made them a khaki and olive Chorus Line of sorts, who all would have a spot in the play called of real-life history, as well as a revered role in keeping America a free nation.

So overall, this book uses both a microscope and an airplane to look at the fine details and the broad contours of the war, and such a picture leads to a better understanding of it.

Overseas cemeteries

The American Battle Monuments Commission runs 17 World War II cemeteries and large memorials, plus smaller memorials for sites like Guadalcanal, Saipan and New Guinea in the Pacific, and Utah Beach and Pointe du Hoc in France. It also has World War I cemeteries and other memorials around the world, such as the Panama Canal and the Spanish-American War memorial in Mexico City.

Here are the facilities, listed alphabetically, along with the general battles which are represented in them. The number of soldiers and the number of Wisconsinites are listed in the accompanying box. Videos and the complete information booklet about each facility and its unique design can be downloaded from the commission's Web site at www.ABMC.gov. This site also has information about sending flowers overseas to the cemeteries – it is easy to do, but you have to wait about two or three months before you get a picture of the grave.

ABMC cemeteries and memorials			
Cemetery	Wisconsin	Total bodies	MIA wall
Ardennes	111	5,329	462
Brittany	120	4,410	498
Cambridge	178	3,812	5,127
East Coast Memorial	94	0	4,609
Epinal	137	5,255	424
Florence	111	4,402	1,409
Henri Chapelle	224	7,992	450
Honolulu	636	national cemetery*	18,096
Lorraine	254	10,489	444
Luxembourg	142	5,076	371
Manila	1,035	17,202	36,285
Netherlands	208	8,301	1,722
Normandy	185	9,387	1557
North Africa	104	2,841	3,724
Rhone	30	861	294
Sicily-Rome	225	7,861	3,095
W. Coast Memorial	3	0	412
Total	3,797	*run by U.S. Department of Veterans Affairs; not solely a WWII facility	

They are:

• Ardennes, Belgium: Most of the dead are from the Battle of the Bulge.

• Brittany, France: Most are from the Normandy and Brittany campaigns of 1944.

• Cambridge, England: Most are from the Battle of the Atlantic or from the bombing raids against northwest Europe.

• East Coast Memorial, New York City: This commemorates soldiers, sailors, Marines, Coast Guardsmen, Merchant Marines and airmen killed in the Western and Northern Atlantic.

• Epinal, France: Most are from battles across northeastern France to the Rhine River, and beyond into Germany.

• Florence, Italy: Soldiers here are primarily from battles following the capture of Rome in June 1944.

• Henri-Chapelle, Belgium: This facility commemorates soldiers from two major efforts, one covering the U.S. First Army's drive in September 1944 through northern France, Belgium, Holland, and Luxembourg into Germany; and the second covering the Battle of the Bulge.

• Honolulu Memorial: Most are from the Pacific, excluding those from the southwest Pacific. The National Memorial Cemetery of the Pacific, commonly known as the Punchbowl, is next to the memorial and is run by the U.S Department of Veterans Affairs, but the ABMC site includes their burial information.

• Lorraine, France: Most were killed while driving the German forces from the fortress city of Metz toward the Siegfried Line and the Rhine River.

• Luxembourg: Here we find more troops from the Battle of the Bulge and the advance to the Rhine. One of the dead here is Gen. George S. Patton.

• Manila, Philippines: This facility commemorates people from the vast expanse of the Pacific, plus New Guinea and the Philippines.

• Netherlands: Most servicemen are from fighting and bombing raids in the Netherlands, as well as bombing raids in Germany.

• Normandy, France: Most are from D-Day landings and the weeks-long battle there.

• North Africa, Tunisia: Those who fought from North Africa to the Persian Gulf are remembered here.

• Rhone, France: Soldiers are from the liberation of southern France in August 1944.

• Sicily-Rome, Italy: The majority died in the liberation of Sicily in 1943, in the landings at Salerno on the mainland, at Anzio, and beyond, and in air and naval support in the regions.

• West Coast Memorial, San Francisco: Personnel killed in the American coastal waters of the Pacific are remembered here.

Research methods

To compile this book, I downloaded the entire 118-page list of Wisconsin names from the Battle Monuments Commission and then cut them out individually, sorting them first into half-years, then into months and eventually into days for the heavy periods. With nearly 3,800 names, this made for heavy use of a scissors and a near-encounter with repetitive stress injury. But it was interesting to note how few deaths there were in 1942 and most of 1943, relatively speaking, compared with the second half of 1944 and into 1945.

As each pile grew, story ideas started popping up and became chapters or parts of this book – such as how someone could have died in March 1940, how so many people were killed on Christmas Eve and Christmas Day, what the title "Ch/Capt" meant (chaplain), and why large clusters of Wisconsin men were killed on certain dates in 1943, non-famous dates in 1944, for example.

The ABMC database is one thing, one type of database, compiled in a specific way. The second and third databases used for this book are the lists of Army / Air Force deaths and Navy / Marine / Coast Guard deaths that were published in 1946. Each service compiles statistics in its own way, though – thus, the Army / Air Force list goes county-by-county, but has no dates, and the book of

Navy / Marine / Coast Guard deaths is alphabetical and gives home addresses, but likewise has no dates.

The fourth database used for this book is the Army enlistment records at the National Archives (all these databases are on the Web, and the Appendix to this book tells how to use them). However, the site notes there were 9 million computer punch cards, and that if the card was messed up, the Army did not fix it. So, if a particular soldier or airman is in there, the information is good, and includes birth year, enlistment month, education, and more. It is searchable by serial number, too, which is quite handy. But this collection does not include any officers, because it is from enlistment records.

There is no similar database for the Navy / Marines / Coast Guard.

The ABMC list is well-defined and needs no explanation by me. Furthermore, it is searchable by state and by cemetery. For Wisconsin, the list is 3,797 names.

This is 45 percent of the roughly 8,400 people from Wisconsin killed in the war. Various sources give various death tolls, ranging from 8,390 (Wisconsin Blue Book) to 8,149 (Web fact sheet from the Veterans Museum) to 8,432 (list compiled for Wisconsin Public Television).

Several of the men and women in this book were from my earlier work at the Milwaukee Sentinel newspaper, stretching back to 1984. The successor to my former newspaper has granted permission to re-use parts of those stories. In all of those cases, there were face-to-face interviews with family all over the state. However, people became harder and harder to find after the turn of the century as time marched on. For the new people in this book, there was a mixture of telephone interviews and a few personal visits in places like Appleton, Horicon, and Augusta. Before the interviews, people were sent the summary of the book a couple weeks ahead of time in order to think about the soldier.

The result of all of this is a book with multiple research methods, which provides the reader with a rich texture of facts and feature details. The Wisconsin information is supplemented with material from the Internet – many Army and Marine groups have their own Web sites, and some even list battle casualties – and information about any Navy ship can be found on the Web. And of course, there are books galore about almost any big battle; the titles of which are easily found on the Web and copies are easily found in a large library system or at Amazon.com.

But along the way, I found that no list is perfect.

Second Lt. Ellen Ainsworth, the only Wisconsin woman killed by enemy fire in the war, did not get put on the list for her county, St. Croix County, in the Army book. In addition, a member of the Women's Army Corps appears on the list for Wisconsin's Marquette County, but she was actually from Marquette County in Michigan, according to relatives of the next generation in the Upper Peninsula.

For that matter, as fine as it is, the ABMC list is far from perfect. One Wisconsin soldier was identified on it as "Clayton R. Smtih," an obvious transposing of letters in the last name, and a further search revealed that seven other men from other states had their names spelled this way. I flagged that to the attention of the commission in April 2008, and Martha Sell, chief of public programs of the commission, promptly sent her thanks for pointing this out, and the typos were corrected within a few days. The same thing happened when I noticed that the date of death for one of the men on the crew list of the Coast Guard cutter Escanaba, which sank on June 13, 1943, said "July 13."

Sell also said "I remember the correction to 'Wisconsin' vividly " – a decade ago, in the early days of the database being on the Web, I sent a letter noting that our Badger State was spelled as "Wisconsen" in every usage – obviously a database entry error. That was repaired ASAP.

Specific difficulties with specific names are detailed in the discussion for that particular soldier later in this book.

For the sake of simplicity, this book refers to the Air Force, when original books and burial records variously say men were in the Army Air Corps, and sometimes the Army Air Forces, or and sometimes, for example, the 20th Air Force within the Army Air Forces. The Air Force itself was formally established in 1947.

Lastly, I offer sincere thanks to the inventors of Google and to all of the people who helped or tried to help track down names, starting with those who did not think I was strange to be calling them about something from 60 or more years ago. County museums and historical societies searched for obituaries and sometimes had them, libraries did not mind a research question, the cemetery in Merrill gladly checked its records, local VFW and American Legion officers appreciated the work even if they had no information, and later generations of families referred me to the few surviving members of the older generation who lived as far away as California. For this assistance and much more, I offer my thanks.

Tom Mueller

Oak Creek, Wis.

July 2009

Merchant Marine member Charles Coffey, 50, died in March 1940 while at sea off the southern coast of Africa. He was born in Milwaukee and was the first Wisconsin man to die in World War II, according to the database of overseas burials and MIAs. He also is one of the first deaths of a Merchant Marine in the war. He is buried at the American North African Cemetery in Tunisia.

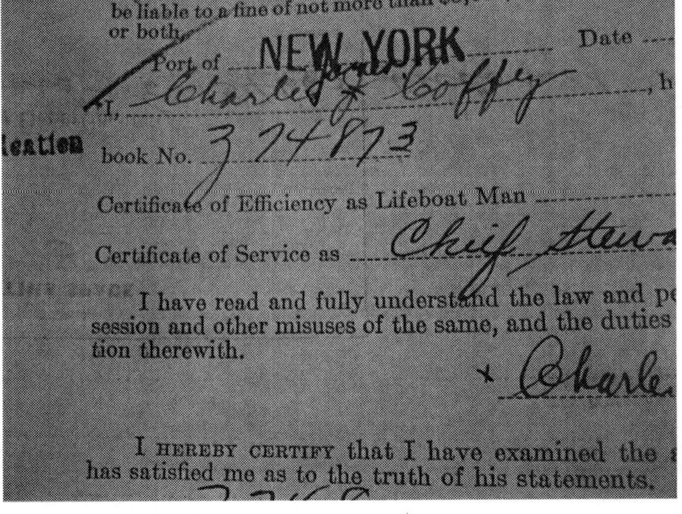

any blank form thereof, or aids or ...
be liable to a fine of not more than $5,000, or imprisonm...
or both.

Port of NEW YORK Date ...

I, Charles J. Coffey, h...

book No. 374873

Certificate of Efficiency as Lifeboat Man ...

Certificate of Service as Chief Stew...

I have read and fully understand the law and p... session and other misuses of the same, and the duties ... tion therewith.

x Charle...

I HEREBY CERTIFY that I have examined the ... has satisfied me as to the truth of his statements.

This is part of Coffey's certificate of identification as a chief steward in the Merchant Marine, bearing his signature. It was dated Feb. 14, 1938.

Chapter 2:

Mysteries of the first (1940) and the last (1948)

The first Wisconsin death in World War II that is in the database of those buried overseas or lost at sea is from long before Pearl Harbor. And the last entry in the database is from nearly three years after the war ended.

Charles J. Coffey, 50, who was born in Milwaukee, died on March 29, 1940, and was a member of the Merchant Marine, civilian seamen who were utilized by the Navy and government to transport ammunition, supplies, and men overseas in convoys of lightly armed ships, if they were even armed at all.

According to his Merchant Marine record, which took several weeks to track down and obtain from the government for this book, Coffey was the chief cook on the cargo ship SS Maine and died of a heart inflammation as his ship was rounding Cape Good Hope at the southern end of Africa. In March of 1940, shipping in the Mediterranean was getting more difficult because of the growing presence of Italian and German forces, and the Allies were beginning to route more traffic around the tip of Africa in order to deliver war supplies to Egypt via the Suez Canal, and so this is what his ship was likely doing.

Coffey was first buried at Port Elizabeth, South Africa, according to his record, and the American Battle Monuments Commission says his body was later moved to Algeria, and then to the North Africa American Cemetery in Carthage, Tunisia, after the war. The Merchant Marine's official Web site lists its first death from enemy activity as coming several months later in 1940.

Coffey is not a combat death, but he was transporting war cargo and was in the Merchant Marines, so it was a wartime death, one of the very first American deaths of the entire war.

The story behind the last Wisconsin entry in the database remains very uncertain: Army Pfc. Jerry Imramovsky has a date of death of July 21, 1948, nearly two years after the next-to-last death listed, and a status of missing in action. The database lists him as only "field artillery," with no specific unit. His name is on the Tablets of the Missing at the Honolulu Memorial in Hawaii. So his death was in the Pacific – somewhere. He is not on any POW list on the Web, so it is not likely he was a captive.

Charles J. Coffey

Coffey's death came less than seven months after Germany invaded Poland and a few months before battles in the Egyptian desert between Britain and Italy, which began in September and December 1940.

Other events of that period were the German invasion of the Netherlands, Belgium, and Luxembourg (May 10, 1940); the surrender of Belgium (May 27); the debacle of the British evacuation from Dunkirk (May 26 to June 4); the armistice/ surrender of France that sent Hitler into a happy jig (June 22); the aerial blitz of London (fall 1940 and early 1941); and the hungry packs of German U-boats in the Atlantic (they started in the fall of 1940). Germany had occupied Denmark and invaded Norway in February 1940.

The book "The Crucial Years 1939-1941: The World at War – From the Beginning Through Pearl Harbor," by Hanson W. Baldwin, says fascist Italy had a strongpoint between Sicily and Tunisia, prompting Britain and the United States to send some ships around the tip of Africa in order to supply British forces in Egypt. "Occasional convoys through the Mediterranean and from Gibraltar to the key British base at Malta ran the gauntlet of air-sea attack, usually with some – and sometimes heavy – loss" (Baldwin, 1976, p. 170). The British base became less and less usable due to Italian air strikes, Mussolini's fleet of 105 submarines, and its ships, Baldwin adds.

There was a major attack in Algeria on July 3, 1940, and it has to rate as one of the most bizarre of the war. A task force from the British Royal Navy targeted the French fleet, which had been docked at the port of Mers-el-Kebir after the French surrender to Germany, fearing that Germany might eventually try to use the ships. British forces also seized French ships that had taken refuge in British ports and in some French ports.

At Mers-el-Kebir near Oman in western Algeria, which was a French colony, British planes and ships attacked French battleships and destroyers. The attack killed 1,297 French sailors and wounded about 350 and stirred considerable discord between Britain and France.

The United States and Britain finally invaded North Africa in November 1942, landing at Morocco and Algeria. Vichy French forces fought back but surrendered within days. So in the first few years of the war, French forces surrendered to both Germany and the Allies.

A search by each letter of the alphabet of the Merchant Marine's list of dead found only two seamen who died earlier than Coffey – one from Feb. 8, 1940 (a man from Pennsylvania buried in the North Africa Cemetery, the same as the Wisconsinite), and another from March 2, 1940 (a man from Washington state buried in the Lorraine Cemetery in France). There were only 13 Merchant Marine men were killed in 1940, with 313 in 1941 and 4,363 in 1942, the highest number in the war (www.usmm.org).

Thus, Coffey was only the third of 8,421 men of the Merchant Marine dead in the entire war, as measured by that organization itself. A total of 243 American Merchant Marines were killed before Pearl Harbor as President Franklin D. Roosevelt sent hundreds of ships overseas in the Lend-Lease program to Britain and other European nations, plus supplies to the Soviet Union beginning in August 1941 on the dreaded Murmansk run, above the Arctic Circle on the Barents Sea (www.usmm.org).

The Wisconsin Veterans Museum in Madison has nothing on Coffey. Searching of the Web found that inquiries, using his service number Z-07487, could be sent to the US Coast Guard National Maritime Center in Martinsburg, W. Va., and a snail-mail letter was sent on May 22. Seven weeks later, a reply was received via snail mail, telling the author to write to someplace else – the Civil Reference Branch at the National Archives and Records Administration in Washington, D.C. That was quickly done, and on Aug. 15, the author received a letter saying the file was found and that it would take $15 to copy it. Things moved much quicker at that point, and Coffey's mystery was solved.

The record includes a letter from the American consulate in Port Elizabeth, South Africa, dated Oct. 12, 1944. It was responding to an order by the U.S. secretary of state, at the request of the War Shipping Administration, to submit the names of any American merchant seaman buried in other countries since Sept. 1, 1939, the date that Germany invaded Poland and began the war.

The letter says Coffey was one of only two burials of seamen in Port Elizabeth. It says he died between 11 p.m. March 28 and 8:30 a.m. March 29, 1940, "at sea aboard the American SS Maine, between Cape Town and Port Elizabeth." He was buried in South End Cemetery, Port Elizabeth, in the Roman Catholic section of the graveyard.

The record – complete with prints from all his fingers and thumbs – shows that Coffey had a certificate of service from the Port of New York as chief steward, No. E-154663. This form was dated Feb. 14, 1938. Charles James Coffey was born in Milwaukee on Nov. 26, 1889, the record says, so he was age 48 when he entered the Merchant Marine.

He died at age 50, and was far older than the vast majority of Wisconsin men who died in World War II. But he was not exceptional in his organization – an examination of all Merchant Marine men who were killed and whose last names started with the letter "C" showed that ages ranged from 17 to 66, although the vast majority were listed as an unknown age. As a comparison, similar numbers were found for men whose last names started with the letter "T."

He reported his address as 101-40 110th St. in Richmond Hill, Long Island, New York. His wife was Anna Coffey.

As a food handler, Coffey was "examined physically and found free from communicable disease," the record says. It was signed by a doctor, who, as usual, did not have a legible signature. The title of the signature line says "surgeon United States Public Health Service or registered physician of the state of New York."

Coffey also had to submit an affidavit of citizenship to the Bureau of Marine Inspection and Navigation of the U.S. Commerce Department, and it came from a friend, Joseph M. Behrman, an accountant and credit manager in Brooklyn. The form was notarized on Feb. 10, 1938, by Bessie Nathau. Another affidavit on behalf of Coffey's citizenship was submitted by Fenimore Kawaler, a retail store manager who lived in Richmond Hill, like Coffey.

Coffey also had to submit a statement saying "I have not received a Continuous Discharge Book, or Certificate of Identification, other than the one I am now making application for ..." This statement was signed by Coffey and Victor J. Ague, deputy U.S. shipping commissioner.

None of this gives any clue as to how long Coffey lived in Wisconsin, where else he may have lived before he got to New York, whether he had ever worked at sea before, or whether he had spent his entire life as a cook.

Men buried in one military cemetery often had been placed in a temporary setting earlier, and the facilities were consolidated after the war. The ABMC said that "Prior to interment at the North Africa American Cemetery, Merchant Seaman Charles J. Coffey, (service number) Z-074873 was interred at the temporary El Alia US Military Cemetery, Algiers, Algeria."

There is still a British Commonwealth cemetery in El Alia, and the Commonwealth War Graves Commission says it is 13 kilometers "southeast of Algiers on the road to El Harrash and is situated within a large civilian cemetery. The Commonwealth plot is 400 meters from the main gate, and is reached by turning left at the end of the central avenue" (www.cwgc.org).

It continues: "The cemetery was originally an Allied war cemetery, but was taken over as a civilian cemetery by the municipal authorities when most of the non-Commonwealth war graves were moved to other burial places. El Alia Cemetery now contains 368 Commonwealth burials of the Second World War. Eight war graves of other nationalities remain in the Commonwealth plot and there are also 15 non-war graves, mostly of merchant seamen whose deaths were not due to war service."

The Commonwealth commission has searchable databases for World Wars I and II. A search for deaths in 1940 in the British Merchant Navy yielded 7,616 names. Further refining the search showed there were seven Australians in the Merchant Navy who all were killed on Dec. 5, 1940 (the European way of listing these days is to say 5-12-1940).

It also lists 132 Canadian deaths, including that of Roy Hamilton Thomas Avery, with the rank of Able Seaman, from March 15, 1940, the closest date to Coffey's death that could be found. The commission also lists 1,237 deaths from India; three from New Zealand and 6,237 from the United Kingdom. The larger figures of the countries could not be searched further; and the Commonwealth site does not allow searches for specific days or months.

Coffey's final cemetery, the American facility, is in Tunisia, on a plateau one mile from the Mediterranean and one mile from the Bay of Tunis. He is buried in Plot D, Row 6, Grave 6.

The cemetery is near the site of an ancient Carthaginian city destroyed in 146 BC by the Romans – the same legions who salted the earth of Carthage. There are 2,841 graves in the cemetery, and "a high proportion of these gave their lives in the landings in, and occupation of Morocco and Algeria, and in subsequent fighting which culminated in the liberation of Tunisia," according to the cemetery's informational booklet. "Others died as a result of accident or sickness in these and other parts of North Africa, or while serving in the Persian Gulf Command in Iran."

The Persian Gulf Command was set up in 1942. Iran was occupied by the Soviets and the British, and was a reliable pipeline of supplies to Josef Stalin after Germany invaded the Soviet Union in 1941 (Schubert, 1992). The Merchant Marine got the supplies to Iran via the ports of Ahwaz, Khorramshahr, and Bandar Shapur (plus Basra, Iraq, the same place that often was in the news in recent years); the U.S. Army Corps of engineers built roads to get them into the Soviet Union. But again, all of that is long after Coffey.

When Coffey died in March 1940, the big news in the war was that Finland had surrendered to the Soviet Union, which had invaded it on Nov. 30, 1939. In April 1940, the news was that

Denmark had surrendered to Germany and Germany had invaded Norway (www.worldwariihistory.info/1940.htm).

There was a good amount of sea combat in March 1940, but it was off the coasts of Britain, not in the Mediterranean. And on March 11, two French ships sailed from Toulon, France, to Canada with a cargo of gold bars to keep them from Axis hands (Argyle, 1980, p. 21). And for the week ending March 17, little more than a week before Coffey died, "Atlantic shipping losses ... are three British, one French, four neutrals, [and] three Germans..." (p. 22).

For the day of Coffey's death, a Friday, Argyle says only this about the sea war: "Atlantic – French cruiser Algerie escorts two U.S. ships from Halifax (Nova Scotia) with cargoes of American-built warplanes" (p. 22). There is no listing for the Mediterranean war, either for the entire week before or after this date.

Coffey's ship, the Maine, cannot be found on the comprehensive list of American flag ships since 1939 that is on the Merchant Marine Web site (www.usmm.org/ships1939.html). There are 492 ships that conducted trade on the list, which notes that if a vessel "is not on this list, but was an oceangoing ship, it was probably engaged only in coastwise voyages, for example, New York to New Orleans, or Seattle to Los Angeles." The Maine, going around the Cape of Good Hope, is a long way from a U.S. coastal voyage. Ships that are on the list have owners such as United States Lines, Matson Line, Bull Insular Line Inc. and American-West African Line.

However, the Merchant Marine lists the Maine as a commercial freighter that was somehow damaged on Oct. 13, 1943, but says the location was "region unknown" (www.usmm.org/sunk43.html#anchor406099), the cause was unknown, the result was unknown, and there were no deaths, but at least one member of the Navy Armed Guard was wounded. The Armed Guard was a small cadre of regular Navy men assigned to guns on the cargo ship.

Coffey's ship was commercial, not part of the U.S. Navy. The most famous USS Maine, the one of "Remember the Maine," was an armored cruiser launched in 1889, whose sinking in Havana, Cuba, by an explosion, either internal or by foreign forces, on Feb. 15, 1898, precipitated the Spanish-American War.

The Merchant Marine Web site notes that 35 percent of the sinkings/ damage to ships and 52 percent of the mariner deaths occurred in 1942, two years after Coffey's death. "Late in the war, a typical Armed Guard crew comprised 27 men, but in 1942, there were few guns and few Armed Guard aboard. It took time to train and assign Armed Guard, and to arm the ships," the site says.

The first attack on a Merchant Marine ship occurred on Oct. 10, 1939, when the freighter SS City of Flint was captured by a German ship in the North Atlantic (www.usmm.org). There were no deaths. Another attack came on June 12, 1940, when the freighter Exochorda was shelled in the Mediterranean/Black Sea region and suffered slight damage but no deaths.

The first combat death in the Merchant Marine, according to that organization, came more than seven months after Coffey died – on Nov. 9, 1940: one crewman was killed when the freighter SS City of Rayville hit a German mine off the cost of Australia and sank. Six weeks later, on Dec. 21, 1940, the tanker Charles Pratt was torpedoed in the South Atlantic and sank, and two crew members were killed, the Merchant Marine said.

The Merchant Marine says 595 of its members are in cemeteries run by the ABMC or commemorated on its MIA memorials.

The seamen faced the danger of submarines and air attacks every day, but got little credit for it, and even fewer medals – and, as of six decades later, no veterans' benefits. Their campaign for such recognition has been stepped up in recent years, laid out in the 2004 book "The Forgotten Heroes: The Heroic Story of the United States Merchant Marine," by Brian Herbert.

While the Merchant Marine has not gotten the recognition, President Franklin D. Roosevelt declared a National Maritime Day, but did not live to see it – he died on April 12, 1945. The date was set for May 2, 1945, and his proclamation said "our ships, sailing every ocean, have been manned by courageous officers and seamen, all of whom have left the security of their firesides and many of whom have given their lives for the land of their allegiance" (www.usmm.org).

Gen. Dwight Eisenhower said this: "Every man in the Allied command is quick to express his admiration for the loyalty, courage, and fortitude of the officers and men of the Merchant Marine. We count upon their efficiency and their utter devotion to duty as we do our own; they have never failed us yet, and in all the struggles to come, we know that they will never be deterred by any danger, hardship or privation. When final victory comes, there is no organization that will share its credit more deservedly than the Merchant Marine" (Herbert, 2004, p. 106).

Jerry Imramovsky

The archives of the Wisconsin Veterans Museum have nothing on Imramovsky. The Army/Air Force book of state-by-state and county-by-county casualties came out in June 1946, so it has nothing on him because he was not yet posted as dead. He is not on its list of missing at that time, either.

But the database of the American Battle Monuments Commission provides his serial number – 36264300 – and that led to some progress in searching his background. The National Archives has a searchable database, but only for Army personnel. Punching in Imramovsky's service number yielded the fact that he was from Milwaukee, and went into the Army on Sept. 9, 1942. His service number begins with "362," meaning he was drafted. The Archives says he was born in 1912, so at that time, he was 29 or 30. He had one year of college. He was single.

Because he entered the Army in 1942, the 1948 date is likely to be merely a time where the records were closed. One man in this book, a Navy submariner, has a listed death date of 1946 even though his vessel disappeared in 1943.

The current Milwaukee phone book does not have anyone with the name Imramovsky. But the 1940 Polk City Directory showed that Imramovsky and family members lived at 2012-14 S. 5th St., between West Becher Street and West Rogers Street south of the downtown. This is not far from Mitchell Street, Goldman's department store, St. Stanislaus Church, St. Josaphat's Basilica, the Modjeska Theatre on Mitchell, the Avalon Theatre over on South Kinnickinnic Avenue, and Kosciuszko Park, named for a Polish hero of the American Revolutionary War. So they lived in the very heart of ethnic South Side Milwaukee.

The site of his home is now a parking lot and community garden along the entrance ramp to the Milwaukee freeway, so it was torn down in the 1950s or 1960s when the freeway was built. The houses on South 5th Place, right behind the Imramovsky block, still stand – many tiny homes on lots the size of a postage stamp or not even that, and several Polish Flats – the Milwaukee phenomenon in which immigrants got a tiny house, and when more family came from the old country the house was jacked up and another story or half-story was built underneath it.

The Imramovsky house was also was several blocks away from the Allen Bradley Co., a major factory whose roots extend back to 1903. It had thousands of workers, and millions of dollars in sales. In 1942, the year that Imramovsky entered the Army, its co-founder Lynde Bradley died, and in 1944, 80 percent of its orders were related to the war – mostly industrial controls and electrical components. Its famous 280-foot-high clock tower, the American version of London's Big Ben, was not built until 1962.

St. Josaphat was a few blocks to the south on West Lincoln Avenue, and St. Stanislaus a few blocks to the north on West Mitchell Street. Those Catholic churches were built in 1901 and 1873, respectively.

The name Imramovsky is found via Google in the modern-day Czech Republic, and immigrants from Czechoslovakia, particularly Bohemia, already had been in Milwaukee for nearly 100 years as of Imramovsky's era, according to the book "The Making of Milwaukee," by John Gurda. Bohemia is in the western Czech Republic and was independent until the 15th century, when it passed to Hungary and then to the Hapsburg dynasty of Austria. Bohemia became the core of the newly formed state of Czechoslovakia in 1918.

In the 1935 Wright's Milwaukee City Directory, Jerry's name is listed as "Jaroslav," but before and after that it appeared as Jerry.

The 1926 directory was the earliest one checked for this book, and his mother Anna was already listed as a widow and living at 794

Grove. In 1930, Alois was listed as a shoemaker, living with Anna, who already was the widow of Joseph and whose occupation was reported as a baker, and Jerry, listed as a "helper."

By the time the 1935 directory came out, all the Imramovskys were at 2012 S. 5th.

The 1940 Polk City Directory says Alois lived at 2014 S. 5th, and that his job was a stockman – so he possibly worked at the Milwaukee Stockyards, a mile or two to the north in the Menomonee River Valley, or in a warehouse. The directory also says Anna J. Imramovsky lived at 2012-2014 S. 5th, and that her trade still was a baker. It says Jerry, the future soldier, lived with her and also was a baker.

In the 1961 directory, Alois had opened Imramovsky's Bakery at 2014 S. 5th, right in his own home. Anna was not listed anymore.

The Pentagon has a unit named the Prisoner of War/Missing Personnel Office, and its Web site is www.dtic.mil/dpmo/WWII_MIA/MIA_MAIN.HTM. It has separate spots for MIAs and service people formally buried at sea in World War II, and Imramovsky is in the MIA area along with 17,095 other Army personnel, 20,683 from the Air Force, 3,119 Marines, 32,636 Navy, and 850 others.

Nationally, Imramovsky and his posted death date of 1948 is the last Army person of the names that begin with "I" on the list. A brief comparative check found no one with an "F" name from that late, nor of "P" names, nor of "R" names.

Another "hit" on the Imramovsky name via Google was from the Death Master File of the Social Security Administration (www.ssdmf.com). It shows that Alois was born June 2, 1910, so he was about two years older than Jerry. When Jerry went into the Army in 1942, Alois was 31 or 32.

Alois died in April 1985 in New Berlin, a Milwaukee suburb that is in Waukesha County. So at least one family member remained in the area.

Where was Imramovsky killed? That is like an Army needle in an ocean haystack when it comes to action by field artillery in the Pacific theater. He probably was in the U.S. Sixth or Eighth Armies, each with tens of thousands of men. Because Imramovsky was drafted in September 1942, he probably began seeing action in the spring of 1943.

Army actions starting in 1943 included the invasions of Rendova and New Georgia in the northern Solomon islands (June 1943 and later), the invasion of the island of Vella Lavella, reinforcing Marines in the invasion of Bougainville (Nov. 1, 1943), seizing the islands of Kiriwina and Woodlark (June 1943), seizing New Guinea's Salamaua and Lae (fall of 1943), landing on the island of New Britain (December 1943), landing at Saidor on the New Guinea coast (Jan. 2, 1944), and landing on the island of Los Negros (Feb. 29, 1944), Manus (March and April 1944), Hollandia and Aitape (April 1944), Wake Island and Biak (May 1944), Saipan (June 1944), Guam (July 1944), and many Philippine Islands starting in October 1944. In 1945 came Okinawa in April.

Imramovsky could have been part of those actions, but there were many more that are not listed here. And nothing says he actually fought on the ground – many ships transporting troops saw action and took casualties.

Field artillery battalions were attached to infantry regiments in order to provide fire for their attacks. A full infantry division had three or four field artillery battalions.

Typical jobs for a private in the field artillery included the forward observer, who dangerously crept ahead of the front line in order to determine where and how to fire to enable the infantry to advance; loaders; ammunition handlers and drivers, signalers, and antiaircraft men who set up and manned weapons to protect the bigger guns.

Bibliography

Argyle, Christopher (1980). Chronology of World War II: The day by day illustrated record 1939-45. London: Marshall Cavendish Bools Ltd.

Baldwin, Hanson W. (1976). The crucial years 1939-1941: The World at war – from the beginning through Pearl Harbor. New York: Harper & Row.

Commonwealth War Graves Commission, www.cwgc.org

Gurda, John (1999). The making of Milwaukee. Milwaukee: Milwaukee County Historical Society.

Herbert, Brian (2004). The forgotten heroes: The heroic story of the United States Merchant Marine. New York: Tom Doherty Associates.

Merchant Marine official Website, www.usmm.org

Schubert, Frank N. (1992). The Persian Gulf Command: Lifeline to the Soviet Union. In Builders and Fighters. U.S. Army Corps of Engineers in World War II, Barry W. Fowle (ed.). Fort Belvoir, Va. Office of History, U.S. Army Corps of Engineers. Chapter found at www.usace.army.mil/publications/ eng-pamphlets/ep870-1-42/c-5-1.pdf

Social Security Administration Death Master File, www.ssdmf.com

www.worldwariihistory.info

Other reading

Atkinson, Rick (2002). An army at dawn: the war in North Africa, 1942-1943. New York: Henry Hold and Co.

Kettle, Michael (1993). De Gaulle and Algeria: 1940 – 1960). London: Quarter Books Limited.

Klitgaard, Kaj (1945). Oil and deep water. Chapel Hill, NC: University of North Carolina Press. This is the story of one man's journey in the Merchant merchant Marine.

Chapter 3:

The bloodiest day – Oct. 24, 1944

One of the goals of this research project and book was to determine the worst day of losses for Wisconsin in the war. By a wide margin, it turned out NOT to be a widely known famous date in history, such as Pearl Harbor or D-Day or the Iwo Jima invasion. It also turned out NOT to be a day in which there were major land battles, bombing raids and sea warfare all over the globe at the same time.

Instead, the worst day for deaths of Wisconsin servicemen, as measured in the database of the American Battle Monuments Commission of men and women buried overseas or MIA, is this: Oct. 24, 1944.

It is not at all a famous day that schoolchildren learn about, but perhaps they should. On that day, a total of 49 men from the state were lost – 47 of them likely on one ship in the Pacific, and two elsewhere.

The answer may be different if someone could magically create a database of every single Wisconsin death in the war, no matter whether the body remained overseas or was returned home for a burial. But no such database exists, and the sheer size of it – there were about 8,400 Wisconsin deaths overall – make it unlikely to be created. One limitation of the ABMC database is that a large number of deaths at sea will skew the data, because when a ship sinks or a plane crashes at sea, families do not have the option later of returning a body home, as they do for a land battle. Nevertheless, the ABMC database is the finest one out there.

So what happened on Oct. 24, 1944?

What made the day the worst for Wisconsin in the war was that an American submarine torpedoed a Japanese freighter in the South China Sea, but the cargo ship was full of prisoners of war from the Bataan Death March of 1942 and from two years of brutal captivity and starvation in the Philippines. The ship had no markings about POWs, but this had been going on ever since the war started

– POWs were being transported on ships that also had cargoes of raw goods such as bauxite to be made into war products. The convoy that the Japanese freighter was in “stumbled into one of the largest concentrations of submarines assembled in the Pacific to date” (Michno, 2001, p. 250). One ship after another was picked off, starting on Oct. 23.

In other words, what became the worst day for Wisconsin deaths in the war was an action taken by American forces. These men had already endured multiple forms of hell, including being abandoned on Bataan and Corregidor by U.S. military leaders; they were headed toward an uncertain destination in Japan and still more hell, and on the way they received their final dose of hell.

There were 1,782 POWs on board the Arisan Maru when it was torpedoed by the submarine USS Shark II on Oct. 24, and only eight survived, according to John Glusman’s 2005 book “Conduct Under Fire: Four American Doctors and Their Fight for Life as Prisoners of the Japanese 1941-1945.” The book has an entire chapter (p. 354-367) devoted to the Arisan Maru. Another good source of information is “Death on the Hellships: Prisoners at Sea in the Pacific War,” a 2001 book by Gregory Michno.

The men on the accompanying list of those killed on the date involved were not necessarily all on that ship, but it is safe to assume that they were, or on a similar one, because many were in units that had heavy numbers of POWs.

The number of MIAs on the wall at Manila is 36,285, and this one ship represents nearly 5 percent of the total.

Hours later, the Shark itself was sunk by Japanese depth charges, but none of the men on the sub’s crew list was from Wisconsin.

The Japanese ship was sunk in the area between the northernmost Philippine island and Formosa, which is known as Taiwan today. The same day, Oct. 24, was the third day of the Battle of Leyte Gulf, but by far the worst day of that battle for the United States was Oct. 25, not the day the Arisan Maru went down. And Leyte Gulf was hundreds of miles away.

Many, and possibly all, of the men on the Oct. 24 list were from units that had been in the Philippines at the start of the war, so they were POWs, and definitely were not in the Battle of the Leyte Gulf. These units (Army records give only the home counties of the men involved) included:

• The Army's 192nd Tank Battalion, which consisted of 99 men from Janesville; plus others from Clinton, Iowa, Maywood, Ill., and Harrisburg, Ky. The Wisconsin men from the 192nd who died on Oct. 24 were Sgt. Leroy Anderson of Racine County, Pvt. Fay Baldon of Walworth County, and these others, all from Rock County: Pfc. Melvin Buggs, Pvt. John Burke, Sgt. Leslie Krause, Pfc. Clarence Lustig, Staff Sgt. Henry Luther, Staff Sgt. John Luther (the Luthers were twins, according to "The Janesville 99: A story of the Bataan Death March" by Dale R. Dopkins), and Pfc. Kenneth Schoeberle.

• 194th Tank Battalion: Cpl. Marvel Peterson of Rock County.

• The Army's 60th Coast Artillery Regiment: Pvt. Edmund Cornelius of Brown County, Cpl. Herbert Joas of Forest County, Pvt. Lawrence Palkovic of Milwaukee County, Pfc. Stephen Paquin of Polk County, and Pvt. Jerome Slavik of Milwaukee County.

• 59th Coast Artillery Regiment: Pfc. Phillip Aubol of Shawano County, and Pvt. James Straus of Dane County.

• 200th Coast Artillery Regiment: Pfc. Walter Brinkerhoff of Fond du Lac County, and Pfc. John Lemke of Outagamie County.

• The Army's 31st Infantry Regiment: Pvt. Clinton Buyatt of Taylor County, Cpl. Edward Whalen of Marathon County, and Pvt. Charles Zenchenko of Price County.

Another of those killed on the Arisan Maru was Navy Lt. George Ferguson of Missouri, a doctor whose wife, Lucille, was from Wausau, Wis. He is one of the four doctors who is the focus of John Glusman's book "Conduct under Fire" (2005). Glusman's father, Murray, was another of the doctor POWs, but Ferguson was the only one of the four on the ship.

As the forces of Gen. Douglas MacArthur drew ever closer to the Philippines and his fabled return, the Japanese began shipping more and more Allied prisoners to Japan to use as slave labor. They had been doing this throughout the war, packing into ships Filipinos, Singaporeans, Dutch, British, Australians, Indians, Sumatrans and those of many other nationalities and sending them to Japan, China, or, more often, places like Burma to be worked to death. Also throughout the war, Allied submarines had been conducting unrestricted warfare, which meant shooting at any enemy vessel, period.

Worst days of war for Wisconsin as measured in database of foreign burials and MIAs		
1.	49	Oct. 24, 1944
2.	39	Dec. 7, 1941
3.	28	Dec. 15, 1945 (actually March 1, 1942)
4.	27	July 30, 1945
5.	25	Dec. 18, 1944
6.	24	Nov. 25, 1944
7.	21	Nov. 27, 1943
8.	19	June 6, 1944
9.	18	Feb. 19, 1945 July 11, 1944 June 15, 1944 June 13, 1943
10.	17	Nov. 20, 1943
11.	16	March 24, 1945 Feb. 21, 1945 Dec. 25, 1944
12.	15	July 26, 1944

Michno (2001) estimates that 21,000 POWs died at sea, of which 19,000 were from these submarine attacks (p. viii). He itemizes each one (p. 309-317), and lists the worst loss of life on a hellship as 5,620 in September 1944, on a ship going from Java to Sumatra, the Junyo Maru. The ship was carrying mostly Dutch and Javanese prisoners, and was torpedoed by a British submarine (p. 235-241). One survivor was Stanley Gorski, a Merchant Marine seaman from Wisconsin, whose experience swimming in the Great Lakes paid off (p. 239).

The hellships usually were ancient commercial vessels and were unmarked. This even happened in the Mediterranean, and the International Red Cross tried but failed to convince all parties to protect prisoners being shipped at sea. "Axis and Allied powers had the same cynical suspicions of each other. Distrust and the fear of losing some sort of strategic advantage combined to leave the Red Cross suggestion in limbo" (Michno, 2001, p. 88). The suspicions were that if the vessels were clearly marked, they might become a bigger target for enemies, and warring parties also did not want to reveal the routes of convoys. The worst month for POW ships in the war was September 1944, when more than 9,300 prisoners were killed in sinkings (p. 244).

The ship in question on Oct. 24, 1944, was a 6,886-ton cargo vessel that had been part of a convoy of prisoner ships. On Oct. 11, the nearly 1,800 Allied POWs had been crammed into the upper compartment of the No. 2 hold on the Arisan Maru, an area that could hold only 200 to 300 people (Glusman, 2005, p. 354). The ship also was carrying coal, nickel ingots and boxes of airplane parts. The voyage originated in Manila Bay, and nine submarines were lying in wait for the convoy in the area between the Philippine island of Luzon and Formosa (Michno, 2001, p. 250), along with U.S planes. The voyage started and stopped, and even returned to Manila for rice, bananas and the like. None for the POWs, though.

On Oct. 23, U.S submarines attacked the convoy, sinking several ships and causing the group to split up, leaving the Arisan Maru, one of the slowest ships, on its own. "In less than 24 hours, the U.S. Navy had sunk eight of the 12 ships in convoy MATA-30" (Glusman, 2005, p. 358). One of the many subs in the wolfpack was the USS Cobia, which has been a tourist mainstay in Manitowoc, WIs., for years. But the Cobia had no sinkings in this period. The Cobia was built in Groton, Conn., but it was the same generation – the Gato class – as the 28 subs built in Manitowoc during the war. It sank 13 Japanese ships, including two headed for Iwo Jima, before the U.S. invasion. One of those ships was carrying a Japanese battalion and 28 tanks.

On Oct. 24, Cmdr. E.N. Blakely of the USS Shark spotted the Arisan Maru through his periscope and fired two torpedoes, both connecting. "The usual conditions were present in the bowels of the hellship, and many prayed that a bomb or torpedo would end their miserable existence. They got their wish" (Michno, 2001, p. 252).

Avery E. Wilber, one of the nine survivors, described the situation for the United Press wire service, which was reprinted in the Wheeling (W.Va.) News-Register on Feb. 16, 1945: "Each prisoner was fed about one teacup of cooked rice twice daily and given a canteen full of dirty water once a day. Sanitary facilities consisted of four five-gallon buckets which were grossly inadequate. Scores of men were afflicted with dysentery and other sickness. The heat was stifling, the stench unbearable. ... Hundreds went out of their minds. There was room to lie down for only a few. Most of the prisoners stood or squatted on the floor, hour after hour, for 14 days" (www.wvculture.org/history/wvmemory/vets/hellships.htmldetails).

Another survivor, Robert S. Overbeck, told his story to the Associated Press, which was printed in the Logan (W.Va.) Banner on Feb. 17, 1945: "The men were crammed into an area nine feet high, 50 feet wide and 90 feet long, divided into three tiers each three feet high. They couldn't even sit erect. ..." The heat was almost unbearable with the sides of the ship "so hot nobody could touch them as they lay naked...' Jap machine guns were trained on a tiny entrance to the hold so small only one man could pass through at a time .... Only 10 men who cooked rice for them were allowed on deck (www.wvculture.org/history/wvmemory/vets/hellships.htmldetails).

As the ship broke apart from the torpedo, Overbeck and Wilber made it to an overturned lifeboat and eventually were rescued by a Chinese fishing junk. They had many perils remaining and had to be disguised as Chinese peasants while traveling to safety, but astonishingly, by Dec. 1 the two were in New York City, having been flown home (Glusman, 2005, p. 363). The few other survivors spent days on floating wreckage and somehow were picked up by the Japanese, who had been taking care only of their own.

The Shark was in turn sunk by a depth charge hours later, and all of its 87 men were killed. The Shark was the second submarine by that name lost in the war. The first was in 1942; the second was built in Groton, Conn., and was commissioned in 1944, so it did not last more than a few months. The list of the Shark's crew is at www.oldsubsplace.com/USS%20Shark%20II.htm.

For Oct. 24, the Wisconsin death toll included one man in Europe. Of those in Asia, there is only one who is buried; the other 47 are MIA and thus it can be assumed that all or most were on the POW ship, because the worst U.S. losses in the Battle of Leyte Gulf did not come until the next day.

Sgt. Forrest Knox of Janesville and the 192nd Tank Battalion was on another hellship in October, and said in Michno's book that men were passing out and dying from the heat inside the hold, which was turning soldiers "into zombies." Because of their screaming, the Japanese were going to cover up the hatch that was providing at least some air, which would have doomed the entire group. "Knox wore a small towel wrapped around his head and a man who had worked in a mental institution showed him how to use it to strangle a screaming man. 'As a guy goes crazy he starts to scream,' said Knox, 'not like a woman, more like the howl of a dog.' The crazy ones howled because they were afraid to die. But, said Knox, now the ground rules changed. If they howled, they died.' Some were strangled, others were beaten to death with canteens" (Michno, 2001, p. 246).

The Janesville unit had been activated by the Army in November 1940 and arrived in the Philippines just before Pearl Harbor. After fighting in the Philippines, under siege by the Japanese on Bataan, being in the Death March, being in prison camps, being shipped to other prison camps under severe conditions, and being worked under even worse conditions, by the end of the war, only 35 of the original 99 men from Janesville were still alive, according to Dopkins (1981).

The hellship issue makes for a moral debate long after the war. Michno (2001) notes that the Allies had broken Japanese code, and thus the intercepts often showed prisoners were on the ships, yet they were torpedoed anyway, with multiple submarines frequently in any one area. "In the grand scheme of things, 2,218 Allied lives were worth less than several ships carrying gasoline, oil and tons of bauxite ore to be used in making aluminum for airplanes" (p. 211), he says of the case of another ship. On the other hand, "hospital records later indicated that the survivors were 16 pounds underweight, 95 percent had malaria, 67 had recurrent dysentery, and 61 percent had tropical ulcers. ... Regardless of the loss of life, almost every prisoner was glad the hellships they had been on were destroyed and they were free again" (p. 221).

Moving on to Oct. 25, the day after the sinking of the prisoner ship, the Wisconsin death toll was 15, of whom 12 were in Asia, all on the MIA wall at Manila, and all from the Navy.

The Battle of Leyte Gulf took place in the central Philippines, in places like the Suriago Strait and the San Bernardino Strait. This was several hundred miles away from the sinking of the Arisan Maru prisoner ship at Takao, which is on the southwestern coast of Formosa. But because the Oct. 25 battles killed so many Wisconsin men, they are being included in this chapter, and on the list of names – a two-day total of 64 is notably huge and is the biggest of the war for the database of foreign burials and MIAs, with Dec. 7 and 8, 1941 being the next highest at 43.

The Leyte Gulf battle featured 300 ships and an estimated 200,000 men, and covered an area of 100,000 square miles, Evan Thomas writes in "Sea of Thunder: Four Commanders and the Last Great Naval Campaign 1941-1945" (2006). And, like many other Asian battles that are discussed in this book, people who have researched them call them "largely forgotten" (Thomas, p. 4). A total of 13,000 men died in the Leyte Gulf, of whom 472 were Americans (p. 322).

The U.S. sank four Japanese aircraft carriers, three battleships, 10 cruisers and nine destroyers. But the Japanese fleet and/or kamikaze pilots sunk three small aircraft carriers (the USS Princeton, St. Lo, and Gambier Bay), two destroyers (the Johnston and the Hoel) and one destroyer escort (the Samuel B. Roberts). The Johnston daringly positioned itself broadside to protect a line of American carriers, and its captain posthumously received the Medal of Honor.

All in all, “the Japanese navy was effectively finished as a fighting force” (Thomas, 2006, p. 322).

Here is a listing of the other worst days for Wisconsin deaths in the war – the result of a hand count of the 3,800 individual ABMC listings by the author of this book, and a brief discussion of the main events involved. Some of the bloodiest dates are the subjects of other chapters in this book.

No. 2:
39 dead on Dec. 7, 1941,
plus 4 on Dec. 8 in the Philippines
(Dec. 7 Hawaii time)

This obviously is one of the best-known days in world history, with an estimated 2,000 people killed on Battleship Row and on the ground at Hickam Field and elsewhere around Pearl Harbor. As for everything else in this book, the figures here are only for those buried overseas or MIA – if a serviceman’s body was brought back to Wisconsin, it is not in the database of the American Battle Monuments Commission, which is the basis of this book.

This book chooses to emphasize the Philippine action. The Japanese struck there several hours after Pearl Harbor, but it already was Dec. 8 in Manila, which is on the other side of the International Date Line.

The story is told in “The Crucial Years 1939-1941: The World at War – From the Beginning Through Pearl Harbor,” by Hanson Baldwin. Two Navy Hellcat F-6 fighter planes were moored “in a quiet bay in the Gulf of Davao (on the island of) Mindanao, along with their seaplane tender (boat), the Preston, as the dawn light brightened the sea that Monday. Japanese bombers, followed quickly by destroyers, attacked the ‘Cats’ and destroyed them. ... Ensign Robert G. Tills of PatWing (Patrol Wing 10) was the first American killed in the Philippines ... ” (Baldwin, 1976, p. 407).

Tills was a Navy man from Manitowoc and is on the MIA wall at Manila, although his fragmentary remains were identified in 2008, as discussed in the final chapter of this book.

On Luzon, the main island, and at Clark Field there, a total of 192 long-range Japanese bombers attacked from Formosa. The news at Pearl was known, but not much had been done to prepare for a Japanese attack. "There was, apparently, a shadow of hope in the minds of some in the Commonwealth government that a Japanese attack against Pearl Harbor did not necessarily mean an attack against the Philippines" (Baldwin, 1976, p. 407). The Clark base of B-17 bombers and other pursuit planes had been out on missions in the morning and then were back on the ground, refueling, "a sitting target" when Japanese bombers and zeroes hit. (p. 408-409).

"The virtually complete destruction of American airpower in the Philippines, a full nine to 10 hours after first news of the Pearl Harbor attack, has been termed, quite correctly, less excusable than Pearl Harbor" (Baldwin, 1976, p. 408).

Besides Tills, the three other Wisconsin men killed in the Philippines were:

• Air Force Staff Sgt. William Hainer of Iowa County, who is on the Manila MIA wall. He was a member of the 20th Pursuit Squadron, 24th Pursuit Group. Among other things, this group had P-40 Interceptor planes.

• Air Force Sgt. William Jones of Milwaukee County, buried in Manila. He was in the Headquarters Squadron, 19th Bomber Group, Heavy. This group flew B-17s.

• Air Force Sgt. George Loritz, home county not available, buried in Manila. He was a member of the 7th Material Squadron, 5th Air Base Group.

Here is how the veterans of the 43rd Bomb Group, another unit in the Philippines, discuss the day:

"The first word of the Japanese attack on Pearl Harbor is received on Luzon ... by commercial radio between 0300-0330 hours local. Within 30 minutes radar at Iba Field, Luzon, plots a formation of airplanes 75 miles offshore, heading for Corregidor Island. P-40s are sent out to intercept but make no contact. Shortly before 0930 hours, after Japanese aircraft are detected over Lingayen Gulf heading toward Manila, B-17s at Clark Field, Luzon, are ordered airborne to prevent being caught on the ground.

"Fighters from Clark and Nichols Fields are sent to intercept the enemy but do not make contact. The Japanese airplanes swing east and bomb military installations at Baguio, Tarlac, Tuguegarao, and airfields at Cabanatuan are also attacked. By 1130 hours, the B-17s and fighters sent into the air earlier have landed at Clark and Iba Fields for refueling, and radar has disclosed another flight of Japanese aircraft 70 miles west of Lingayen Gulf, headed south.

"Fighters from Iba Field make a fruitless search over the South China Sea. Fighters from Nichols Field are dispatched to patrol over Bataan and Manila. Around 1145 hours a formation is reported headed south over Lingayen Gulf. Fighters are ordered from Del Carmen Field to cover Clark Field but fail to arrive before the Japanese hit Clark shortly after 1200 hours. B-17s and many fighters at Clark Field are caught on the ground, but a few P-4Os manage to get airborne. Second Lt. Randall B. Keator of the 20th Pursuit Squadron (Interceptor), 24th Pursuit Group (Interceptor), shoots down the first Japanese aircraft over the Philippines. The P-40s earlier sent on patrol of the South China Sea return to Iba Field with fuel running low at the beginning of a Japanese attack on that airfield. The P-40s fail to prevent bombing but manage to prevent low-level strafing of the sort which proved so destructive at Clark Field.

"At the end of the day's action it is apparent that the Japanese have won a major victory. The effective striking power of [the] Far East Air Force has been destroyed, the fighter strength has been seriously reduced, most B-17 maintenance facilities have been demolished, and about 90 men have been killed." (www.kensmen.com/dec41.html)

As for Hawaii, 25 of the Wisconsin men killed Dec. 7 in the database of those killed overseas or MIA or buried at sea that is being used for this book are MIA, and 14 are buried, all in Honolulu. The 39 dead consist of 32 Navy men, six from the Air Force and one Marine.

No. 3: 28 dead on Dec. 15, 1945 (actually March 1, 1942 for nearly all of them)

All but one of these men were from the Navy and were actually killed on March 1, 1942, in the Battle of the Sunda Strait between the Java Sea and the Indian Ocean, according to the Pentagon's Prisoner of War/Missing Personnel Office (www.dtic.mil/dpmo/WWII_MIA/MIA_MAIN.HTM).

Because large numbers of seamen in this battle were taken prisoner by Japanese ships, these Wisconsin men and others were not logged as dead until Dec. 15, 1945, four months after the war ended. Presumably, the men did not return when POWs were freed, and hence were declared as dead.

The one exception on the list was Air Force Pvt. Roger Feind of Lincoln County, who was in the 65th Bomber Squadron. But he also was MIA and is on the same wall in Manila as the other 27 Wisconsin men are.

One of the 27 Navy men was Arthur Gerke of Eau Claire. Thanks to an excellent Web project at Eau Claire Memorial High School based on material from World War II veteran Diz Kronenberg, information about dozens of men from the Chippewa Valley has been compiled for future generations. The site is at www.memorial.ecasd.k12.wi.us. Similar information no doubt appeared in other papers across the state about the other men.

The site reprints a 1942 Eau Claire newspaper story that said (the original wording is changed slightly here): "Arthur Vernon Gerke, 22, Hospital Apprentice, First Class, U.S. Navy, is reported 'missing following action in the performance of his duty and in service of his country,' according to a telegram received last night by his parents, Mr. and Mrs. Arthur E. Gerke, 649 Summer St.

"The text of the telegram, signed by Rear Adm. Randall Jacobs, chief of the Bureau of Navigation, follows:

"'Washington, D.C., March 19, 1942. The Navy Department deeply regrets to inform you that your son, Arthur Vernon Gerke, Hospital Apprentice, Second Class, United States Navy, is missing following action in the performance of his duty and in the service of his country. The Department appreciates your great anxiety and will furnish you further information promptly when received. Rear Admiral Randall Jacobs.'

"Young Gerke enlisted in the Naval Service in November 1940 and attended the Naval Hospital School in San Diego for six months and then six months more at Mare Island. A graduate of the Eau Claire Senior High School, he had attended St. Patrick's Parochial Grade School previous to that.

"The last letter received from young Gerke by his parents was sent by airmail. It was dated Pearl Harbor, Nov. 24, 1941, and was received by his parents a few days before the Japanese attack on Pearl Harbor. In it, he said he was aboard a transport (the name of which was given but which it is not permitted to mention) and was to leave Nov. 28 for the island of Guam. No word had been received from him since."

Here is what happened to make this day so bad for Wisconsin:

The Battle of the Sunda Strait came two days after the Battle of the Java Sea (Feb. 27), in which a Dutch-American-British-Australian fleet of heavy cruisers, light cruisers, and destroyers under the command of a Dutch admiral (the area was the Dutch East Indies) attacked a powerful Japanese convoy carrying out the invasion of the island of Java. It lost – something that jars the reader today — but this was very early in the war; a time when the U.S. was not yet winning very often.

Two cruisers of the Dutch navy were sunk, along with two British destroyers and a Dutch destroyer. The American cruiser Houston was heavily damaged by fire. The task force commander, Dutch Adm. Karel Doorman, was killed. All of this information is from the U.S. Naval Chronology of World War II (www.navsource.org/Naval/1942).

On Feb. 28, in the Sunda Strait between the Indonesian islands of Java and the island of Sumatra connecting the Java Sea to the Indian Ocean, the remaining Allied vessels ran into the main Japanese invasion force, and in a fierce nighttime battle that lasted into March 1, the crippled Houston was sunk along with an Australian cruiser and another destroyer from the Netherlands. The Houston was hit by torpedoes and gunfire. The destroyer USS Pope was sunk by a dive bomber and surface gunfire. The Wisconsin dead were likely on these two ships, although elsewhere in the Pacific on that day, the destroyers Edsall and Pillsbury were sunk by naval gunfire south of Christmas Island, also known as Kiritimati, along with the oiler Pecos. Christmas Island is a few hundred miles from Java.

The U.S. Navy would not begin its string of winning massive sea battles until the fabled Battle of Midway four months later.

No. 4:
27 dead on July 30, 1945

This date may at first appear to be the same kind of technicality of some earlier day, because it came only two weeks before VJ Day. However, it is correct, and it is one of the saddest and shocking tales of the war.

On this day, the heavy cruiser USS Indianapolis was torpedoed and sunk by a Japanese submarine as it inexplicably sailed in a straight line without any standard defensive measures for a combat zone. It also did not have the protection of a destroyer escort, a precaution that previously had been standard for such a big ship.

The Indianapolis had just delivered to the island of Tinian the major parts for the first atomic bombs – the ones that would vaporize Hiroshima on Aug. 6 and Nagasaki on Aug. 9 and end the war. After delivering the bomb parts on July 26, the Indianapolis sailed for Guam, where it was directed to go to the Leyte Gulf in the Philippines to prepare for the invasion of Japan, which was then being planned.

In the first minutes of July 30, a Japanese submarine, the I-58, fired six torpedoes at it, and two hit – in the bow and in a fuel tank and powder magazine — creating an explosion that sunk the cruiser in only minutes.

Of the 1,196 aboard, about 900 made it into the water, although most were in life jackets and not life rafts because of the speed the ship was sinking.

But it would be four days – repeat, four days – before any rescue came. And that was only when a pilot on routine antisubmarine patrol noticed groups of men in the water. Only 317 remained alive. The rest had succumbed to their wounds, thirst, exposure, hunger and sharks. Thus, many more died from the delayed rescue than from the actual torpedoing.

The 27 Wisconsin men from this date consist of 24 Navy men, two Marines who were on the ship and one Army man. The Army man is buried at Honolulu. All the others are commemorated on the MIA wall at Manila.

Because the ship was operating on a secret mission, no notification had been sent to Leyte that the Indianapolis was en route. As a result, it was not reported as overdue. Three SOS messages were sent before the ship sank, but the Navy's cumbersome message system resulted in them being lost (http://militaryhistory.about.com/od/shipprofiles/p/ussindianapolis.htm).

The ship's captain, Charles Butler McVay III, was court-martialed for failing to be zig-zagging. But because of evidence that the Navy had put the ship in danger and because of the testimony of Mochitsura Hashimoto, the I-58 's captain, which stated that an evasive course would not have mattered, Fleet Adm. Chester Nimitz remitted McVay's conviction and restored him to active duty, according to the military history site.

However, crewmen and others, including Dan Kurzman, author of the 1990 book "Fatal Voyage: The Sinking of the USS Indianapolis," have worked for years to try to overturn the verdict entirely.

They say vital information pertinent to the case was not made public until long after the court-martial: that U.S. intelligence had broken the Japanese code and was aware that two Japanese submarines were operating in the path of the Indianapolis.

It did not become known until the early 1990s that – despite knowledge of the danger in its path – naval authorities had sent the cruiser into harm's way without any warning, refusing McVay's request for a destroyer escort, and leading him to believe his route was safe. Critics also note that no big ship lacking anti-submarine detection equipment, such as the Indianapolis, had made this transit across the Philippine Sea without an escort during the entire war.

No. 5: 25 dead on Dec. 18, 1944

This day was a high toll, and the main reason was not war but rather a typhoon so big and so strong that it sunk three Navy destroyers east of the Philippines and damaged several others.

A total of 14 Wisconsin Navy men died on this day, presumably aboard the ships. They are on the MIA wall at Manila.

The sunken destroyers were the USS Hull, the Spence, and the Monaghan. The storm also damaged the light aircraft carriers Monterey, Cowpens, Cabot and San Jacinto; the escort carriers Altamaha, Nehenta Bay, Cape Esperance and Kwajalein, the light cruiser Miami, the destroyers Dewey, Aylwin, Buchanan, Dyson, Hickox, Maddox, and Benham, plus the destroyer escorts Melvin R. Nawman, Tabberer and Waterman, plus others. (www.ibiblio.org/pha/chr/chr44-12.html)

A 31-year-old crewman on the Monterey went on to become president of the United States 30 years later. This is how Gerald R. Ford described the ordeal in "A Time to Heal," his 1979 presidential memoir: "On Dec. 18, we ran into a vicious typhoon in the Philippine Sea. Rain and hundred-knot winds (about 115 m.p.h.) whipped the ocean into a mountainous fury. That night was pure hell. I had the deck watch from midnight to 4 a.m. In the pounding seas, three destroyers simply rolled over and capsized, with an enormous loss of life" (p. 59).

Ford is referring to the Hull, the Spence and the Monaghan.

His carrier suddenly listed about 25 degrees amid the chaos. "I lost my footing, fell to the deck flat on my face, and started sliding toward the port side as if I were on a toboggan slide. Around the deck of every carrier is a steel ridge about two inches high. It's designed to keep the flight crews' tools from slipping overboard. Somehow, the ridge was enough to slow me. ... I was lucky; I could easily have gone overboard. ... Fifteen or 20 fighters and torpedo bombers were tied down on the hangar deck below. At the height of the storm, one of the planes broke loose from its cables. Every time the ship rolled, it crashed into other planes. Soon, a number of planes were darting around there like trapped, terrified birds. Gas tanks were punctured, the friction produced sparks, and a fire broke out" (p. 59).

Adm. William Halsey, commander of the 3rd Fleet, authorized the Monterey's captain, Stuart Ingersoll, to abandon ship, but Ingersoll persisted, and after seven hours of work, the fire was out, the storm abated, and the carrier was safe. Ford said one crewman was killed, and 33 injured.

On the San Jacinto, the 20-year-old pilot of a torpedo bomber was George Herbert Walker Bush. The future president had been shot down on Sept. 2, 1944, with the loss of his two crewmen. He was rescued by a U.S. submarine and was back on the San Jacinto two months later when it encountered the typhoon. All told, Bush flew 58 combat missions in the war.

On this day in Europe, the Battle of the Bulge was in its third day. Army men are buried at four cemeteries – six at Henri-Chapelle in Belgium, one at Ardennes in Belgium, one at Lorraine in France, and one at Luxembourg. There also was one Army MIA on the wall at Lorraine. Of the men, three were from the 9th Armored Division and two were from the 28th Infantry Division.

The Battle of the Bulge had begun with a German attack on the morning of Dec. 16. Under cover of heavy fog, 38 divisions struck along a 50-mile front and managed to push American forces back nearly to the Meuse River and surround the town of Bastogne in Belgium.

No. 6:
24 dead on Nov. 25, 1944

This day consisted of 16 Navy men honored on the MIA wall in Honolulu and one on the MIA memorial in Manila. In Europe there are five from the Army – each from a different infantry division – and two from the Air Force. So this day is the first on this list to reflect fighting in a world war taking place on multiple continents and multiple seas.

The Navy's comprehensive list of ships and submarines lost shows one small vessel lost on this day – PT boat 363, destroyed by Japanese shore batteries in Knoe Bay, Halmahera, in the Netherlands East Indies. A patrol vessel, YP-383, also was sunk by collision. However, neither one would have had enough numbers to make for 17 Wisconsin deaths (www.history.navy.mil/faqs/faq82-1.htm#anchor327957).

In Europe, there are four buried at Lorraine in France, one at Epinal in France, one at Henri-Chapelle in Belgium, and one in the Netherlands. There are no MIAs. The toll reflects fighting in southeastern France, but it is not particularly massive, as would be happening in a month with the Battle of the Bulge.

No 7:
21 dead on Nov. 27, 1943

This was a particularly bad day for the Air Force, which suffered 20 of the 21 Wisconsin deaths. Most of them, however, were not in the air or at a ground base – they were on a ship at sea.

Thirteen members of the 853rd Engineer Battalion were killed when about 30 German bombers attacked a convoy and sunk a British ship bound from Algeria to Bombay, India, according to the U.S. Army Corps of Engineers (Logue, 2000, "Sinking of the Rohna – a virtually unknown WWII tragedy").

They are MIA and are honored on the monument at the North Africa Cemetery in Tunisia. The sinking killed 1,105 Americans overall.

The British ship was an old transport and was carrying Americans plus crewmen from India and British officers. Its convoy was attacked on Nov. 26 by Luftwaffe long-range bombers carrying "remote-controlled glider bombs. … The Hs293 was, in effect, the first air-launched cruise missile. A rocket engine launched the bomb away from the bomber, then it glided toward its target under remote (radio) control," said the article by Logue, a member of the Corps of Engineers in the district of Vicksburg, Miss.

The Rohna sank in less than an hour. There were 90 American survivors and about 60 of the crew.

One of the survivors in the 853rd Battalion was Raymond Cecil Taylor, who said everything suddenly went dark. "Off to the port side of the ship I could see some light and the dining table had fallen on my leg. I pulled myself from under the table and walked in the direction of the light. There was a large opening in the side of the ship where just a few minutes before had been a solid wall. The dining area that had been filled with soldiers was now only dead bodies and debris. I felt as though God was leading me to the opening in the side of the ship. The hole was large enough to drive several trucks through at the same time."

Taylor made it out and onto a raft, and was rescued by the USS Pioneer, a minesweeper, the next morning (www.rohna.org).

Lt. Charles Beard of the 853rd Battalion grabbed "all the life vests that I could that were floating near me. I had one around my waist and one under each arm. I had that much sense about me" (Logue, 2000).

It was all hushed-up by the military for security reasons because of the use of the missile, according to a program on The History Channel, "The Rohna Disaster: WWII's Secret Tragedy" (http://shop.history.com) and the Rohna Survivors Memorial Association. Like many other World War II disasters, this did not come fully to light for a few decades. But it is not clear why, if the Germans had this weapon in 1943, it was not reported in other attacks in the last two years of the war.

Sea Waves magazine discusses the incident in its day-by-day history of sea incidents, and gives somewhat different numbers than Logue does: "Attempts to abandon ship were disastrous. Many of the lifeboats and rafts were frozen by rust or paint to their moorings. Instead of life vests, which would hold heads out of the water if the wearer was unconscious, soldiers had inflatable life rings. Many drowned while wearing them. Seas were rough enough to inhibit visibility, and night fell shortly after the attack. Five ships crisscrossed the water searching for survivors, who bobbed in and out of sight of the searchlights. The 853rd had 30 officers and 793 enlisted men when the Rohna left port. Now, 495 were gone, and 147 of the survivors were injured. In addition, 134 British and Australian officers and Indian crew members died. The total death toll was 1,149 (www.seawaves.com/newsletters/TDIH/november/26nov.txt).

The 13 Wisconsin men in the 853rd Air Force Engineer Battalion – a group whose main job was building airport runways – were:

- Technician 5th Class Frank Benderling, of Winnebago County

- Technician 5th Class Clarence Beyer, Forest County

- Pvt. Raymond Boos, Sauk County

- Pfc. Charlie Cochran, Outagamie County

- Pvt. Richard Coleman, Milwaukee County

- Pvt. Stanley Kutasiewicz, Kenosha County

- Pvt. Everett Loos, Clark County

- Pvt. Archie Nelson, Sawyer County

- Pvt. Elwyn Nelson, Sawyer County

- Technician 5th Class Walter Smith, Outagamie County

- Pvt. Herbert Thiel, Ozaukee County (He was 21 and from Saukville, and family members memorialize him at http://marsss0.tripod.com/rohna.html.)

- Sgt. Lester Urban, Ozaukee County

- Technician 5th Class John Zagar, Milwaukee County (Army enlistment records show he was born in Michigan in 1912 and entered the military via Marquette, Mich., on Jan. 13, 1943.)

The others from Wisconsin who were killed on this day are honored on the MIA wall in Tunisia, which means they may have been on the same ship. They were two men from the Air Force, with no unit given in the ABMC database, and three members of the 322nd Fighter Squadron.

Another Air Force man was killed on this day and is on the MIA wall at the East Coast Memorial in New York City. Two men died in the Pacific – an Air Force man honored on the MIA wall at Honolulu, and a Marine buried in Honolulu.

No 8: 19 dead on June 6, 1944

D-Day is a story detailed elsewhere in this book, along with a list of the dead buried at the ABMC's cemetery at Omaha Beach. No serviceman was killed in Asia on June 6, according to the ABMC database, but as can been seen in the chapter on June 1944, there would be plenty in the following days and weeks.

No. 9 (tie): 18 dead on Feb. 19, 1945; July 11, 1944; June 15, 1944; and June 13, 1943

There were nine deaths in Asia and nine in Europe on the 1945 day, and the spread across military services also was large – 10 from the Army, four from the Air Force, three Marines and one from the Navy.

Fifteen of the men are buried; three are MIA. Six are in Honolulu (three MIA and three buried), three in Manila, three at Epinal in France, two at Ardennes in Belgium, two in Luxembourg, one in the Netherlands and one at Florence, Italy.

In Asia, this was the day of the invasion of Iwo Jima, and the Marines who are buried overseas from this historic day are Pfc. Robert Deya of West Allis, Pfc. Desmond Kurth of Chippewa Falls and Cpl. Harry Ours of Kenosha. All are buried in Honolulu.

In Europe, the war was in its final two months and millions of Allied servicemen were pounding away all along the front via land,

and deep into Germany via air. The Wisconsin deaths in the Army on this day were from the 94th Infantry Division (three men), the 70th Infantry Division (two men), and others from the 503rd Parachute Infantry Regiment, 37th Infantry Division, 5th Infantry Division, 69th Infantry Division, and 63rd Infantry Division.

The Air Force also was attacking in the Pacific and in Europe. Its deaths came in the 871st Bomb Squadron (two men buried in Honolulu), the 9th Fighter Squadron (one man buried in Manila) and the 717th Bomb Squadron (one buried at Florence, Italy).

For July 11, 1944, the deaths are heavily from Europe – seven are buried in Normandy and five are on the MIA wall at Sicily-Rome – as the battles in France and Italy roared along. Two men are buried or on the MIA wall at Honolulu, two at Manila, one at Cambridge, England, and one MIA is on the East Coast Memorial in New York City.

Eleven of the men are Army, five from the Navy and two from the Air Force. There are 11 bodies and seven are MIA.

The Army deaths in Normandy are two from the 121st Infantry Regiment, and single ones from the 47th Regiment, 8th Regiment, 120th Regiment and the 12th Regiment. The number of units reflects the massive scope of the battle between D-Day and the Breakout Breakout at the end of July and in early August.

The men at Sicily-Rome are all MIA – four Navy men and a member of the Army's 108th Infantry Regiment.

June 15, 1944, was the invasion of Saipan by the Marines and the Army, along with continued fighting in Normandy, little more than a week after D-Day. A list of the men killed on this date is in another chapter of this book, but 12 died in Asia and four in Normandy, with two elsewhere in Europe.

All but one of the 1943 deaths on this date are from the sinking of the Coast Guard cutter Escanaba in the North Atlantic, a story also detailed in another chapter of this book, along with a list of the dead.

No. 10:
17 dead on Nov. 20, 1943

The deaths are from the Marine invasion at Tarawa and Betio, the second beach invasion of the war in the Pacific – Guadalcanal in August 1942 being the first. Betio is a small island on the western side of the Tarawa atoll.

The invasion began Nov. 20, with pulverizing fire from a U.S. invasion force of 17 aircraft carriers of all sizes, 12 battleships, eight heavy cruisers, and four light cruisers, plus 66 destroyers (www.nationmaster.com/encyclopedia/Battle-of-Tarawa).

But the 2nd Marine Division met with hideous fire going to the beach, and then it got worse. Some units found their amphibious carriers got stuck on a reef 500 yards off shore because of a miscalculation of the tide level during planning, and became sitting ducks. Those that made it over the reef were hammered. "The first wave was able to land only a few men, who were pinned down against the log wall on the beach" (www.nationmaster.com/encyclopedia/Battle-of-Tarawa).

The landing craft of John Laughlin, a Protestant chaplain, got stranded on the coral reef for 24 hours. Laughlin worked to help wounded Marines all around him, and eventually took medical supplies to the men on shore. (Crosby, 1994).

The Wisconsin dead from this day consist of 16 Marines and one Navy man. There are 12 MIAs honored in Honolulu, and five men buried there.

One has to wonder why so many Wisconsin dead were from Tarawa, when the Marine losses on Iwo Jima a year and a half later are written about much more often, but have much fewer Wisconsinites in the ABMC database of overseas burials and MIAs.

And of particular note is that six of the 17 dead were from Milwaukee, according to the Navy's 1946 book of dead and wounded – Pfc. Clarence Belter, Cpl. Thomas Berg, 2nd Lt. Willis Carpenter, Pfc. Gregory Fedorski, Pvt. Louis Mrkvica and Pvt. Henry Verhaalen.

In addition, two were from the suburbs – Pfc. Walter Miller of Menomonee Falls and Pfc. Patrick Gresk of Cudahy. And two more were from Racine – Pfc. Henry Thielen and Pvt. David Harcus.

The bulk of the battle ended on Nov. 23, and on other small islands it was over a week later. But 990 Marines were killed and 2,296 wounded. These heavy losses "sparked a storm of protest in the United States, where the high losses could not be understood for such a tiny and seemingly unimportant island in the middle of nowhere (www.nationmaster.com/encyclopedia/Battle-of-Tarawa).

No. 11 (tie):
16 dead on March 24, 1945; Feb. 21, 1945; and Dec. 25, 1944

These tolls came, respectively, from the final massive drop of paratroopers in Europe, the third day of the Marine invasion of Iwo Jima, and from the Battle of the Bulge, including the Christmas Eve torpedoing of a troop ship in the English Channel that is told in another chapter of this book.

In March 1945, American forces were crossing the mighty Rhine River and penetrating into the heart of Germany. The end of the war was only a few weeks away, but the fighting still was intense in many places.

This raised an important fact: American dead were not going to be buried in the country of the enemy Nazis – they would be buried in neighboring countries.

Eleven of the dead from March 24,1945, are buried in the Netherlands Cemetery at Margraten, two in France at the Lorraine Cemetery at St. Avold, one at Henri-Chapelle in Belgium and one at Cambridge, England. And the only Pacific loss on this day is a Marine buried in Honolulu. There are no MIAs from this day.

The dead in Europe numbered nine from the Army and six from the Air Force. The airborne assault was dubbed Operation Varsity, and was planned in conjunction with a land assault by the 2nd British Army.

The 17th Airborne Division jumped at the southern edge of the Diersfordter Forest, three miles northwest of the city of Wesel. Nearly 4,000 aircraft from the British 6th Airborne Division and the 17th US Airborne dropped behind enemy lines via parachute and gliders (www.ww2-airborne.us/18corps/17abn/17_overview.html).

As for Feb. 21, 1945, a total of 11 of the 16 dead are Navy men who are on the MIA wall at Honolulu, and probably died in kamikaze attacks including those that sunk the escort aircraft carrier Bismarck Sea off of Iwo Jima.

According to a Navy history, on the evening of Feb. 21, "a swarm of Japanese planes appeared. The escort carrier splashed one bomber, but another one crashed into the ship abeam of the after-elevator. The crash knocked four torpedoes onto the hangar deck, parted the elevator cables, and damaged the after fire-main. The fire appeared controllable until its glow attracted a second Japanese plane, which also crashed her just forward of the elevator well, killing or mortally wounding the entire fire-fighting party. This explosion buckled bulkheads and collapsed the decks in the ammunition clipping rooms, adding fuel to the fire. The planes on the hangar deck added gasoline to the holocaust. Soon, the flames raged out of control and a variety of ordnance began to explode, so the captain ordered Bismarck Sea abandoned. In less than 30 minutes, her entire crew made it into the water. After many explosions and two hours of burning, the ship rolled over and sank.

"Rough seas, cold water and Japanese strafing cost the lives of many members of the escort carrier's crew. Three destroyers and three destroyer escorts spent 12 hours picking up survivors, but 318 gallant sailors were lost" (www.history.navy.mil/danfs/b6/bismarck-sea-i.htm).

Besides the Bismarck Sea, several other ships – including the carrier Saratoga, the heavy cruiser Pensacola, and some tank landing ships — were damaged in kamikaze attacks, Japanese shelling, or bombings.

The high toll of this day came only two days after the No. 9-worst day, Feb. 19, 1945.

Besides the 11 Navy men, there are two Marines – Pfc. Donald Wishowski of Johnson Creek and Sgt. Robert Gahlman of Beaver Dam – buried at Manila and one Army man buried at Manila, and two Army men killed in Europe; buried at Lorraine in France and Henri-Chapelle in Belgium.

The 16 Christmas deaths are detailed in another chapter of this book – these came from the sinking of the Leopoldville in the English Channel and in the Battle of the Bulge.

No. 12: 15 on July 26, 1944

This day was the heart of the Breakout from Normandy, and 11 of the 15 are Army men. The others are two from the Air Force and two Marines.

Eight of the men from this day are buried in Normandy, one in Florence, Italy, and one at Lorraine, France. Two are MIA – one each at the Sicily-Rome cemetery and Cambridge.

Of the Army men buried in Normandy, two are from the 9th Infantry Division, two from the 90th Division, two from the 5th Division, and one each from the 83rd and 1st Divisions.

Bibliography

Army 17th Airborne veterans: www.ww2-airborne.us/18corps/17abn/17_overview.html

Baldwin, Hanson W. (1976). The crucial years 1939-1941: The world at war – from the beginning through Pearl Harbor. New York: Harper & Row.

Crosby, Donald F., S.J. (1994). Battlefield chaplains: Catholic priests in World War II. Lawrence, Kan.: University Press of Kansas.

Day-by-day losses of Navy reference site: www.ibiblio.org/pha/chr/chr44-12.html

Defense Department Prisoner of War / Missing Personnel Office: www.dtic.mil/dpmo/WWII_MIA/MIA_MAIN.HTM

Dopkins, Dale R. (1981). The Janesville 99: A story of the Bataan Death March. Janesville, Wis.: Published by the author.

Eau Claire (Wis.) Memorial High School World War II history project: www.memorial.ecasd.k12.wi.us.

Ford, Gerald R. (1979). A time to heal: The autobiography of Gerald R. Ford. Harper & Row, Publishers, and the Reader's Digest Association Inc.

Glusman, John A. (2005). Conduct under fire: Four American doctors and their fight for life as prisoners of the Japanese 1941-1945. Viking. New York: The Penguin Group.

Kurzman, Dan (1990). Fatal Voyage: The sinking of the USS Indianapolis. New York : Atheneum.

Michno, Gregory (2001). Death on the hellships: Prisoners at sea in the Pacific war. Annapolis, Md.: Naval Institute Press.

Navy Historical Center information on aircraft carrier Bismarck Sea: www.history.navy.mil/danfs/b6/bismarck-sea-i.htm

Navy Historical Center list of ships sunk in World War II www.history.navy.mil/faqs/faq82-1.htm#anchor327957.

Navy photographs at private site: www.navsource.org

On Eternal Patrol – USS Shark (SS-314): www.oneternalpatrol.com/uss-shark-314.htm. Site is privately run and dedicated to men lost while serving in the U.S. submarine Force.

Logue, Michael, of U.S. Army Corps of Engineers (2000). Sinking of the Rohna: A virtually unknown WWII tragedy. At Corps of Engineers Web site, www.hq.usace.army.mil

Military History.com: http://militaryhistory.about.com/od/shipprofiles/p/ussindianapolis.htm

Rohna Survivors Memorial Association: www.rohna.org

Sea Waves magazine: www.seawaves.com/newsletters/TDIH/november/26nov.txt

Submarine loss information: www.oldsubsplace.com/USS%20Shark%20II.htm

Tarawa battle: www.nationmaster.com/encyclopedia/Battle-of-Tarawa

Thomas, Evan (2006). Sea of Thunder: Four commanders and the last great naval campaign 1941-1945. New York: Simon & Schuster.

West Virginia survivors of Arisan Maru: www.wvculture.org/history/wvmemory/vets/hellships.htmldetails

1944 typhoon information: www.patriotwatch.com/va/tribute.htm

43rd Bomb Group, veterans' Web site: www.kensmen.com/dec41.html

Oct. 24 and 25, 1944

This list is compiled from the database of the American Battle Monuments Commission and cross-referenced with the 1946 official booklets of Navy / Marine losses (including hometown) and of Army/ Air Force casualties (which lists only counties), and with Army enlistment records. This list gives a hometown for Army/ Air Force men if it was found via other processes. If a serviceman is on an MIA monument, it is noted; otherwise he is buried.

Oct. 24, 1944

Army Sgt. Leroy Anderson, Racine County, Manila MIA wall

Army Pfc. Phillip Aubol, Shawano County, Manila MIA wall

Army Pvt. Fay Baldon, Walworth County, Manila MIA wall

Army Pfc. Walter Brinkerhoff, Fond du Lac County, Manila MIA wall

Army Pfc. Melvin Buggs, Rock County, Manila MIA wall

Army Pvt. John Burke, Rock County, Manila MIA wall

Army Pvt. Clinton Buyatt, Taylor County, Manila MIA wall

Navy Pharmacist's Mate 2nd Class Jerry Carey, not listed in booklet, Manila MIA wall

Army Pvt. Edmund Cornelius, Brown County, Manila MIA wall

Air Force Cpl. Robert Damon, Dane County, Manila MIA wall

Navy Seaman 2nd Class Francis Elsinger, Hartland, Manila MIA wall

Navy Lt. Thomas Evert, not listed in booklet, Cambridge, England, MIA wall

Navy Water Tender 3rd Class Paul Gerson, Racine, Manila MIA wall

Army Capt. Leslie Gilbert, Dane County, Manila MIA wall

Navy Hospitalman's Apprentice 1st Class Wayne Hempelman, not listed in booklet, Manila MIA wall

Army Maj. Harry Hull, Dodge County, Manila MIA wall

Army Cpl. Herbert Joas, Forest County, Manila MIA wall

Army Pvt. Jesse Jones, Rock County, Manila MIA wall

Navy Seaman 1st Class Harry Karwoski, not listed in booklet, Manila MIA wall

Army Pfc. Donald Knipshield, Rock County, Manila MIA wall

Army Sgt. Leslie Krause, Rock County, Manila MIA wall

Army 1st Lt. William Leisenring, Dane County, Manila MIA wall

Army Pfc. John Lemke, Outagamie County, Manila MIA wall

Army Pfc. Maurice Lustig, Rock County, Manila MIA wall

Army Staff Sgt. Henry Luther, Rock County, Manila MIA wall

Army Staff Sgt. John Luther, Rock County, Manila MIA wall

Navy Chief Electrician's Mate Oscar Marriott, not listed in booklet, Manila MIA wall

Army Pvt. Robert McGrath, Crawford County, Manila MIA wall

Navy Seaman 1st Class Walworth Mensenkamp, Racine, Manila MIA wall

Army Pvt. Lawrence Palkovic, Milwaukee County, Manila MIA wall

Army Pfc. Stephen Paquin, Polk County, Manila MIA wall

Navy Aerographer's Mate 3rd Class Harold Payne, not listed in booklet, Manila MIA wall

Army Cpl. Marvel Peterson, Rock County, Manila MIA wall

Navy Seaman 1st Class Eugene Richie, Hudson, Manila MIA wall

Army Cpl. Emanuel Rada, Dane County, Manila MIA wall

Air Force 1st Lt. Harry Rusch, Fond du Lac County, buried in Manila

Air Force Cpl. Wesley Salzmann, Shawano County, Manila MIA wall

Air Force Staff Sgt. Kenneth Schenning, Kenosha County, Manila MIA wall

Army Capt. Marvin Schmidt, Fond du Lac County, Manila MIA wall

Army Pfc. Kenneth Schoeberle, Rock County, Manila MIA wall

Army Pvt. Henry Schraml, Milwaukee County, Manila MIA wall

Army Pvt. Jerome Slavik, Milwaukee County, Manila MIA wall

Army Pvt. James Straus, Dane County, Manila MIA wall

Navy Machinist's Mate 3rd Class Arthur Studden, Hurley, Manila MIA wall

Navy Painter 1st Class Peter Swinconos, not listed in booklet, Manila MIA wall

Navy Seaman 1st Class Edward Toporski, South Milwaukee, Manila MIA wall

Army Maj. Albert Tousignant, Oconto County, Manila MIA wall

Army Cpl. Edward Whalen, Marathon County, Manila MIA wall

Army Pvt. Charles Zenchenko, Price County, Manila MIA wall

Oct. 25, 1944

Navy Coxswain Samuel Akey, Spooner, Manila MIA wall

Air Force 2nd Lt. John Green, Jefferson County, buried at Ardennes, Belgium

Navy Electrician's Mate 3rd Class Leigh Gillette, Wauwatosa, Manila MIA wall

Navy Seaman 1st Class Ernest Hill, Viola, Manila MIA wall

Navy Coxswain Carson Hooks, Platteville, Manila MIA wall

Navy Machinist's Mate 3rd Class Otto Huebscher, Milwaukee, Manila MIA wall

Navy Fireman 1st Class Harry Jaeger, Milwaukee, Manila MIA wall

Navy Machinist's Mate Chief Walter Kalbe, Milwaukee, Manila MIA wall

Air Force Sgt. Carl Kintz, Fond du Lac County, buried at Ardennes

Navy Lt. John Palmer, Milwaukee, Manila MIA wall

Navy Fireman 1st Class George Pickett, Milwaukee, Manila MIA wall

Navy Electrician's Mate 3rd Class Arthur Rozmarynowski, Milwaukee, Manila MIA wall

Army Sgt. John Schmitt, Milwaukee County, buried at Florence, Italy

Navy Seaman 1st Class Frank Skotzke, Milwaukee, Manila MIA wall

Navy Machinist's Mate 2nd Class Leslie Tellier, Milwaukee, Manila MIA wall

Chapter 4:

The colonel's tragedies

The MIA memorial in Manila lists 36,285 names, more than twice the number of bodies that are in the immense American cemetery there. Both are the largest, by far, of the facilities of the American Battle Monuments Commission.

Manila is so huge because it honors those who gave their lives in the region from Australia all the way to Japan, and from the Palau Islands westward to China, India and Burma. The MIA memorial lists the land and sea battles of the region: Makassar Strait, Java Sea, Coral Sea, Eastern Solomons, Cape Esperance, Santa Cruz, Tassafaronga, Kula Gulf, Vella Gulf, Empress Augusta Bay, Leyte Gulf, Guadalcanal and Peleliu. And that is just the western half of the wall. The eastern half lists Bataan, Corregidor, Papua, Bismarck Sea, Huon Gulf, Admiralties, Aitape, Hollandia, Wake Island, Biak, Noemfoor, Burma, Angaur, Leyte, Manila, New Britain, Bougainville and New Georgia.

Somewhere on one of the many MIA walls at Manila, formed in a semicircle around a chapel, is Col. William Starr Van Nostrand of Merrill. He was a 1934 West Point grad who was in the horse cavalry in the Philippines and was training the Filipino infantry before having to surrender on the island of Mindanao in 1942.

Van Nostrand, 34 when he died three years later, was with the 26th Cavalry Regiment of the Philippine Scouts. His experience was the stuff of a long, long horror movie: lightly armed forces versus the Japanese invasion, surrenders by the tens of thousands, POW in multiple facilities that were marked by illness, starvation and malnutrition, crammed onto a POW ship that was bombed by American planes, evacuated from the ship, and finally killed in Taiwan on a second POW ship which was bombed by more American planes.

Van Nostrand was doing all of this as a new father: his son William III was born June 14, 1941, at Sternberg General Hospital on Arroceros Street in Manila, and was evacuated only a few weeks

William Van Nostrand, Merrill, 1928 high school yearbook

William Van Nostrand, as athlete in 1928 yearbook

William Van Nostrand, at U.S. Military Academy at West Point

later, at the end of June or in early July, because of the impending war. The colonel did not ever see his son again.

Van Nostrand was killed on Jan. 9, 1945, and received the Silver Star, Bronze Star with Oak Leaf Cluster, and of course the Purple Heart.

The research for this book determined that Van Nostrand and the men in Chapter 11 had the highest rank among the dead. The entire list of 3,800 names in the database of the American Battle Monuments Commission was printed out and cut into individual names, then sorted by year and month. Then each month was sorted into individual days, and the days were cataloged along with anything significant about them – such as numbers, heavy concentration in one cemetery, ranks, clusters of Navy or Army men or Marines or aviators, or the units the Army men belonged to.

Next, a computer word search of the entire list was done for high ranks such as general, colonel, admiral, and commander, in the case of the Navy, for example. A spot check also was made of one month per year of the war, looking specifically for rank in order to bear out the conclusions.

The Philippine Scouts had been created in 1901. They were Filipinos serving in U.S. Army units and commanded by Americans, such as Van Nostrand. In his case, they fought the Japanese invaders of the Philippines in December 1941 and the early months of 1942, holding off their advance until Gen. Douglas MacArthur could fall back to the Bataan Peninsula, Corregidor, and then finally be spirited out of the country on a PT boat in March 1942, leaving thousands to keep trying to fight amid starvation, losses, disease and then surrender.

A month later, the Scouts surrendered along with other American and Filipino forces amid starvation, widespread diseases, and overwhelming Japanese power. Van Nostrand was not on the Bataan Peninsula at this time and thus was not in the legendary Death March there; he was a leader in Philippine Army forces on the island of Mindanao, under Gen. William Sharp, who surrendered shortly after the forces on Bataan and Corregidor capitulated. Van Nostrand was held in prison at Davao on Mindanao, but he and hundreds of others were sent to the main island of Luzon in 1944.

Tens of thousands of the prisoners were shipped to other islands and countries on the hellships described in the previous chapter of this book, and died there or en route, sometimes when their ships were torpedoed by American submarines, or attacked by American planes, and sometimes from heat and starvation on the ships themselves.

Van Nostrand and about 300 others were killed when Americans bombed a prisoner ship in the port of Takao on Taiwan, which was called Formosa in that era. Takao was a major Japanese naval base. The POWs were being taken to Japan for use as slave labor and were being evacuated from the Philippines as the U.S. invasion neared. The bombing date is coincidentally when the Americans began invading Luzon, several hundred miles away.

Finding Van Nostrand's story

There is no one with the last name of Van Nostrand in Merrill any more, nor in Lincoln County, nor in Wausau, the closest larger city. The Army book of casualties lists people only by county. The Tomahawk American Legion post reported it had a newspaper or tourist booklet that said briefly that Van Nostrand was from Merrill. However, the Merrill VFW Post had no information on him.

There was another Van Nostrand on the Lincoln County list of Army dead – Peter, a corporal, who died of non-battle injuries. The Army database of 9 million enlistees showed Peter was born in 1909, and had gone to college and entered the Army on Nov. 27, 1940, via Wausau. William Van Nostrand is not in this enlistment database, because his serial number is that of an officer.

So the author of this book plugged Peter's name into the ABMC database of overseas burials – he was not there. If he is not buried overseas, he likely is buried in Merrill, the reasoning went. The author called the local cemetery, Merrill Memorial Park, and asked whether Peter was buried there. That call was answered by Dan Caylor, cemetery superintendent, who frequently writes items about soldiers for the local newspaper, and frequently uses the Merrill Historical Society's assistance.

Here, then, is the Van Nostrand story, pieced together with the aid of Caylor and Beverly King of the Historical Society.

Peter and William were the sons of a local dentist, William, and his wife, Marie. King said "it was a real nice family," a pillar of the community.

William was born on July 28, 1910, a year after Peter.

King's records showed that the colonel's son now lived in Brownsville, Texas, and a listing for that last name was called. It was for Margaret Van Nostrand, who said the colonel's son, her husband, had died of cancer in 1994.

But Margaret knew several of the essentials, including how the mother and the infant had to leave the Philippines as war neared. "I think he was on the last ship that left Manilla," leaving with his mother, Jane, who went by the nickname of Pidge, for Pigeon, because "she was a very tiny thing, like four feet high," Margaret said. The nickname dated back to her college days.

Lt. Edwin Ramsey, who was in the 26th Cavalry like Van Nostrand, said President Franklin D. Roosevelt had ordered in late 1940 that families of diplomats and soldiers based in the Philippines should leave for their own safety, as the winds of war were becoming closer and closer (Ramsey & Rivele, 1990, p. 27). This was a full year after Germany invaded Poland, and Japan was on the march, seizing China and pressuring Indochina. But Pearl Harbor was still a year away.

What happened

The Merrill Daily Herald newspaper reported on the front page on July 30, 1945: "Word was received here Saturday from the War Department that Lt. Col. William S. Van Nostrand Jr., husband of Mrs. William S. Van Nostrand Jr., New Orleans, and son of Dr. and Mrs. William S. Van Nostrand Sr., of this city, was killed in action in the Pacific area on Dec. 15, 1944, while being transported aboard a Japanese vessel."

The story continued: "Recent press dispatches revealed that the Japanese government had notified the U.S. government that 942 American prisoners of war had been killed when a Japanese prison ship was torpedoed and sunk in Subic Bay. Two prisoners escaped, 59 died following the sinking and 618 survived and were presumably taken to the Japanese mainland.

"This ship left Manila on Dec. 13, 1944, and was torpedoed two days later. This was believed to have been the ship which was disclosed last February to have been sunk by American aerial torpedoes." That would have been a reference to torpedo bombers, a staple of the Navy.

That was one story about Van Nostrand's death at the time, and it matches up well, but not totally, with two more.

There indeed was a prisoner ship, the Oryoku Maru, that left Manila on Dec. 14, 1944, bound for Formosa. It had been loaded one day earlier. It carried 1,620 POWs, and was the last group of prisoners to be evacuated from the Philippines. "Thin, ragged, and weakened by nearly three years of confinement, they were the last survivors of the Bataan Death March, defenders of Corregidor and

Mindanao. Two-thirds of them were senior officers – combat unit commanders as well as doctors from Bilibid and Cabanatuan" (Glusman, 2005, p. 454-455). Bilibid was the prison in Manila and Cabanatuan was another prison on the main island of Luzon.

These numbers are confirmed in a table on page 316 of "Death on the Hellships: Prisoners at Sea in the Pacific War," a 2001 book by Gregory Michno.

Men suffocated from the lack of air in the hold where they were packed tightly. The ship was bombed by planes from the American aircraft carriers Hornet and Hancock. "That night was 'the most horrible of my life,' said Col. (Curtis Thurston) Beecher of the 4th Marines. The hatches were closed, and men went insane from dehydration and lack of oxygen. They stripped off their clothes to let the pores of their skin breathe. They slit their own veins to drink blood" (Glusman, 2005, p. 455). And it got a lot worse than that.

Glusman says the attacks disabled the ship, and the 1,333 prisoners who still were alive eventually swam to the nearby shore while Navy bombers returned for a second attack, which destroyed the ship. The POWs endured more hell in the hot sun and cold night, without food, having been herded onto a fenced tennis court. They were trucked to a new site, then put on a train. Then they were marched to Lingayen Gulf and 1,070 were put on another ship, the Enoura Maru, and 250 on a different ship. The ships went to Takao, Formosa, where the Navy bombed the Enoura Maru.

More than 300 men died in that bombing, including Van Nostrand. "'The carnage,' said Maj. John M. Wright Jr. of the Coast Guard Artillery Corps, 'was beyond description'" (Glusman, 2005, p. 456).

A third, more detailed story about Van Nostrand's fate is contained in a 2001 book by Hampton Sides about a raid by U.S. Army Rangers to free men from the Cabanatuan prison camp several months after the colonel's group was removed for shipment to Japan. Sides' book is "Ghost Soldiers: The Forgotten Story of World War II's Most Dramatic Mission." First, however, one must note that, unlike many war books involving research by the author (as opposed to personal memoirs by a veteran), the book does not list specific information about where a particular fact was obtained, nor does it contain a formal bibliography. But it does include a section of acknowledgments that briefly lists various general sources and its many interviews with veterans, including some who were on the ships involved.

That final story in the war service of hundreds of men – one that already had included the Bataan surrender and Death March, then nearly three years in prisons – had three hellish pieces (Sides (2001, p. 204-215)), and even more for those who survived past Jan. 9, 1945.

First, about 1,600 men were crammed aboard the Oryoku Maru on Dec. 13, after being shipped out of Cabanatuan and spending two months at the Bilibid prison in Manila. Conditions were foul indeed – packed far beyond the way that sardines are packed: stifling tropical heat, little if any ventilation, no food, little water, and high panic. About 50 men died from that.

Then, the ship was bombed in a large raid on Dec. 14, with some of the POWs cheering on the attackers. The bombs disabled the ship and it ran aground. The POWs were told the next day to swim the 500 yards to shore. The ship was bombed again during this process. The swimmers were reorganized on a tennis court, while the ship was bombed yet again and this time was sunk. The men were on the baking tennis court for six days. Things then got only a little better – they were crammed onto trucks and then train cars to elsewhere on Luzon, to the Lingayen Gulf.

Second, on Dec. 28, 1944, the surviving 1,300 prisoners then were herded aboard an old ship named the Enoura Maru, a freighter, and packed into holds that previously held large numbers of horses: substantial manure and urine, and especially billions of flies, remained. The ship sailed for four days, pursued by American submarines. A few men each day were dying. On New Year's Day 1945, it reached Takao on Formosa, where it unloaded wounded Japanese troops while the POWs were kept in their holds.

Third, on Jan. 9, American dive bombers found the Enoura Maru. "Hot shrapnel shot through the hold. As the Enoura Maru shuddered and rolled in the harbor, a black rain of splintered decking sifted down upon the men. An immense steel girder fell through the hold, pinning a hundred prisoners to the floor, instantly killing scores of men" (Sides, 2001, p. 214). The ship did not sink, but was a disabled hulk. It took three days for the Japanese to come aboard to provide assistance of any kind.

A total of 295 Americans – including Van Nostrand – were dead. A total of 1,600 had left Manila aboard the Oryoku Maru; now nearly half – 700 – were dead (Sides, 2001, p. 214). Michno (2001) has similar figures – on the Oryoku Maru, 330 died, and on the Enoura Maru, 316 were dead (p. 316-317). Glusman (2005, p. 456) says the dead totaled 621 to that point.

There was a fourth chapter for some: the 925 survivors soon were put on a third ship that sailed for Japan; 450 died because of horrid conditions on that voyage (Michno, 2001, p. 317; Sides, 2001, p. 215).

According to the database of the American Battle Monuments Commission that is being used for this book, 11 other Wisconsin men were killed in Asia on Jan. 9, and 10 of them are on the MIA wall at Manila, and thus likely were with Van Nostrand on the ill-fated ship. The Army men who were killed on Jan. 9 were:

• 2nd Lt. Andrew Grignon of Winnebago County, of the 201st Philippine Engineer Battalion.

• Cpl. Walter Ronowski of Milwaukee County, of the 60th Coast Guard Artillery Regiment.

• Capt. Russell Thorman of Rock County, of the 192nd Tank Battalion, the battalion from Janesville whose story in the Bataan Death March and the torpedoing of a different POW ship is told elsewhere in this book.

• 1st Lt. Henry Wiora, home county not found, of the Quartermaster Corps.

• Capt. Mathias Zerfas of Fond du Lac County, of the 2nd General Hospital.

Beyond these, other Wisconsinites killed on Jan. 9 in the Pacific and on the MIA wall in Manila were two Navy MIA men and three MIAs from the Air Force.

Back at Cabanatuan, the approximately 500 remaining prisoners, all in such poor health that they were not moved to Japan like the others – they were the feeblest of the feeble – could hear the American invasion in Lingayen Gulf, featuring immense fire from an armada of ships and aerial attacks.

They did not know that a special expedition of American Army Rangers was on the way to spring them from the prison. Sides' book details the planning, execution and exciting aftermath of the raid the night of Jan. 30-31, which rescued all the men. Many of the Japanese guards had pulled out, but their troop strength in the area was still high, because it was on a route to the main defenses being set up against the U.S. invasion. Pulling off the raid was no easy task, and the aftermath was hairy, too – water buffalo slowly pulled about 70 oxcarts full of emaciated men on a 25-mile journey to freedom. But all of that was a few months after Van Nostrand's group was removed.

The American commanders at Cabanatuan at the time of raid were Col. James Duckworth, a doctor, and his assistant, Capt. Ralph Hibbs. The previous commander, Col. Curtis Beecher, had been shipped out in the group whose two ships were bombed.

Merrill, West Point and beyond

The July 30, 1945, Merrill newspaper story said Van Nostrand graduated in 1928 from Merrill High School. "He attended Carleton College, Northfield, Minn., before entering West Point in 1930," it added. West Point records say he was appointed from the 11th Congressional District of Wisconsin, so his congressman was Republican Hubert H. Peavey of Washburn. Wisconsin's senators in 1930 were Republicans Robert M. La Follette Jr. and John J. Blaine.

Page 30 of the 1928 yearbook of Merrill High School had "Billy Van" as his nickname and "Stan" as his middle name, even though it really was "Starr." It selected this quotation to list with Van Nostrand: "He oft has burned the midnight oil/but never, ever, was it in toil."

He certainly was a busy guy – class treasurer his freshman year, basketball all four years, football as a junior, orchestra as a junior, in the Science Cub his last two years, in the Dramatic Club as a junior, in Glee Club all four years, in debate as a senior, and in the class play as a senior.

Besides Van Nostrand, the hoops squad consisted of eight boys, identified in their team photo only by first initials – W. Bacher, L. Fleischfresser, T. Elbe, A. Hitzke, C. Leskey, M. Podeweitz, L. Nott (the captain) and A. Bucholtz. The coach was listed as a Coach Field.

When Van Nostrand was in the Science Club, he served as president in the second semester, following Virginia Walker. The vice president in both semesters was Ted Elbe (of the basketball team). The passage for the club said: "The Protons and Hot Molecules were in constant combat in the entertainment contest waged by the Science Club of 1927-1928. These were two teams headed by the vice presidents. Dorothy Emerich had charge of the Protons and Ted Elbe, the Hot Molecules. The team planning the best program of the year was given a party by the defeated. By employing scientific methods at the two initiations held, interest was aroused in research work of today and resulted in the material increase in membership."

The club's photo shows it had about 50 members, which must have been a healthy percentage of the school.

The yearbook was intricately designed, placing oval photos of six students over a drawing; on Van Nostrand's page the drawing was one of a bridge in a pasture.

The essentials of Van Nostrand's record at the U.S. Military Academy are on-line, in the form of the once-a-decade summaries of the careers of its graduates. The site is at the West Point Library, www.library.usma.edu/archives/special.asp.

The 1940 book shows he attended West Point from July 1, 1930, to June 12, 1934, when he graduated and was made a second lieutenant in the cavalry. His class rank was No. 173 out of 250; his West Point ID number – known as the Cullum number – was 10105.

Starting in September 1934, Van Nostrand was stationed at Fort Bliss, Texas, in the 7th Cavalry. In the summer of 1936, he was in the A.C. Primary Flying School at Randolph Field, Texas, then was back at Fort Bliss in the 1st Armored Car Squadron, and became a first lieutenant on June 12, 1937. He held several positions at Forts Buliss and Bliss in Texas, then in May 1938 was sent to Fort Riley, Kan., as a student officer in the Cavalry School, Special Advanced Equitation Class, (the word means the art of riding on horseback) until February 1940, when he was sent to Fort Knox, Ky.

The 1950 West Point record book continues Van Nostrand's abbreviated story. He was promoted to captain on Sept. 9, 1940, while at Fort Knox, and to major on Dec. 19, 1941, while on Luzon, the main island in the Philippines. This was right after the attacks at Pearl Harbor in Hawaii and those at various air bases in the Philippines, and just as the Japanese were invading. On April 16, 1942, he was promoted to lieutenant colonel. This was a week after the surrender on the Bataan peninsula.

Then the record notes that he was a "POW. KIA – POW ship, 9 Jan. 45, a-34. (SS PH)." It cannot be readily found what those last numbers mean.

There is nothing in the West Point record book about Van Nostrand becoming a full colonel, before or after his death, and the Army list of war deaths from Lincoln County has him as a lieutenant colonel. The database of the American Battle Monuments Commission ranks him as a full colonel, as does the list of the Defense Prisoner of War/Missing Personnel Office.

The Merrill newspaper story said he was married on Oct. 3, 1936, in El Paso, Texas, while stationed at Fort Worth. His son was born in Manila, Philippine Islands, on June 14, 1941.

The birth certificate showed the soldier was a captain at the time, and lived at No. 36 Fort Stotsenberg. His wife was age 25 at the time; the captain was 30. Helen Jane Burke was from Gary, Ind., it said. The certificate was signed by Capt. Clinton S. Laupin.

The Merrill newspaper story also said: "Before the war he was detached to the infantry by Gen. MacArthur and was in charge of induction for the Philippine Army on the island of Mindanao. He served as executive officer on the staff of Gen. Sharp."

Sharp, a brigadier general, was the leader of American and Filipino forces on the island of Mindanao in the southern Philippines as of late January (Young, p. 143). His "tongue was known at times to match his name" (p. 144). He was commander of the Visayan-Mindanao Force, composed of the 61st, 81st, and 101st Infantry Divisions of the Philippine Army. Gen. Jonathan Wainwright, who took over command after MacArthur was evacuated, ordered these forces to surrender on May 8, a month after the Bataan surrender and a day or two after Corregidor.

Sharp then ordered his scattered forces, preparing to fight on as guerrillas, to surrender. Some units refused at first to comply, but one by one they followed orders. Many individuals, however, escaped to carry on the fight as guerrillas. By 9 June, almost all commands had surrendered (www.ibiblio.org/hyperwar/USA/USA-C-Philippines).

26th Cavalry

When the war began, Edwin P. Ramsey was a 24-year-old lieutenant in the 26th Cavalry Scouts and went on to become a guerrilla leader after the Bataan siege and surrender. He wrote about it all in his 1990 book "Lieutenant Ramsey's War."

Ramsey told the author of this book via e-mail in 2008: "I knew Van Nostrand, but only casually. I vaguely remember him as being a major, but the only records I have of the Regiment were one of notes from Col. Clinton A. Pierce, who was the C.O. of the regiment before and during the early stages of the war, until being promoted to brigadier general, and Van Nostrand was shown as a captain. That list, which probably referred to the period around January 1942, also showed that he was killed by a bomb in B #3 on Jan. 9, 1945. A second list, undated, showed him as a lieutenant colonel."

The B #3 refers to a POW ship or a hold on a particular ship, Ramsey said.

Like Van Nostrand, Ramsey trained as a devotee of the Army cavalry manual "Horsemanship and Horsemastership." His loyal steed was named Bryn Awryn and was with Ramsey in all forms of training and in polo games. Ramsey was trained at the Oklahoma Military Academy, enlisted in the Army in 1941, and volunteered to serve with the 26th and the Philippine Scouts. He was stationed at Fort Stotsenberg near Clark Field at Manila, and was a troop leader in Troop G of the 2nd Squadron of the 26th, under Maj. Jim Blanning. A colleague, in Troop B, was Capt. Joe Barker.

Names of the 26th Cav's leaders are being used as often as possible here, because they would have been familiar to Van Nostrand, even though he was in some other part of the 26th. So are places like Fort Stotsenberg and Bongabonga, 120 miles away, and another place where Ramsey was stationed.

A troop in the cavalry consisted of a sergeant, a corporal and 25 Filipino privates (Ramsey & Rivele, 1990, p. 34). The horses had to be loaded into trailers in order to be trucked long distances. More and more, they were becoming moot, because the cavalry dated from long before there were airplanes, mobile guns, tanks and the like.

The 26th Cav was "by far the best-trained and most professional combat unit among the Philippine defense forces, yet that a mounted unit should be the backbone was an index of the impoverishment of our strategy," Ramsey said. "Cavalry might be useful in the rugged foothills that flanked Luzon's central plain, but its flat, open expanses were an invitation to tanks and artillery. It was a lesson that had been carved from the flesh of men and mounts in France in World War I. Yet in the Philippines, cavalry remained the elite, held in place by tradition and untested by modern war" (Ramsey & Rivele, 1990, p.37).

For example, on Dec. 17, 1941, the cavalry and civilians near Bongabonga were strafed by Japanese Zeroes, and on Jan. 7, 1942, horses were killed by Japanese artillery fire near Layac, as Ramsey recounts. Horses obviously did not have much of a chance against either.

In the futile defense of Bataan, Ramsey and the horses were sent into battle at Morong along with Capt. John Wheeler to try to hold off Japanese forces.

“Now I could see scores of Japanese infantry in brown fatigues firing from the village center, and behind them hundreds more wading the river and crowding toward the Batolan bridge. In a few minutes more the main body would be flooding across to seize Morong.

“Over the rattling gunfire I ordered my troopers to deploy … and I raised my pistol. A charge would be our only hope to break up the body of Japanese troops and to survive against their superior numbers. For centuries the shock of a mounted charge had proved irresistible; now the circumstances and all my training made it instinctual.

“I brought my arm down and yelled to my men to charge. Bent nearly prone across the horses’ necks, we flung ourselves at the Japanese advance, pistols firing full into their startled faces. A few returned our fire, but most fled in confusion, some wading back into the river, others running madly for the swamps. To them we must have seemed like a vision from another century, wild-eyed horses pounding headlong; cheering, whooping men firing from the saddles” (Ramsey & Rivele, 1990, p. 66).

This was regarded as the last cavalry charge in U.S. military history, and it came on Jan. 16, 1942 (Ramsey & Rivele, 1990, p. 66). The Japanese soon were firing mortars into the ranks, but the 26th Cav held the town until being replaced that afternoon.

As Bataan became more and more squeezed, food became scarcer and scarcer, both for men and equines. All became weakened – “we staggered into the village of San Isidro. There we found the remnants of the 26th main body streaming in. It was literally a skeleton of the regiment I had joined six months before. The men were haggard and showed signs of malnutrition. The horses that were left could scarcely walk, and the few remaining vehicles limped along behind them, riddled with bullet holes” (Ramsey & Rivele, 1990, p. 53).

Finally the Army Quartermaster Corps ordered that the remaining starving horses, including Ramsey's Bryn Awryn, be slaughtered in order to feed the starving troops. Ramsey was not there because he was hospitalized with jaundice. "In the midst of such tragedy one horse more or less made no difference, I told myself. I dared not mourn an animal when wounded men lay all around me. Besides, the cavalry was finished long ago. The Army knew it; only we resisted in our pointless pride" (Ramsey & Rivele, 1990, p. 74).

After the surrender on Bataan, Ramsey and some others melted into the jungle in order to form guerrilla units under Col. Claude Thope, a cavalryman. Ramsey wound up being one of the regional commanders, and by the end of the war was in charge of nearly 40,000 guerrillas who gathered intelligence about the Japanese, about conditions on the ground, communicated several times a day with MacArthur's headquarters before the general's return to the Philippines, and staged some guerrilla attacks. Those who were captured were imprisoned, tortured and beheaded.

Margaret Van Nostrand provided a two-page biography that goes through the various stages of the colonel's career and imprisonment. It is not clear when this was written, or by whom.

It says that at West Point, he was in D Company and "was active in athletics, winning letters in soccer, hockey and la crosse." Van Nostrand was stationed at Fort Bliss and Randolph Field, and met his future wife, who lived in El Paso. They were married on Oct. 3, 1936.

"In September 1941, he was sent, with other American officers, to assist in the mobilization of the Philippine Army. His first assignment was with the 2nd Battalion, 61st Regiment, 81st Division, stationed at Dingle, Iloilo, on the island of Panay. Later, when war became imminent, the American officers were relieved as instructors and given command assignments in the Philippine Army. Van became regimental executive and was promoted to major. Soon after this, the 61st Infantry (Regiment) was sent to the island of Negros, where it remained until after the attack on Pearl Harbor, when it was moved to Mindanao, arriving on New Year's Day 1942."

Philippine Scouts

The Philippine Scouts Heritage Society is dedicated to preserving the history of the units, and its Web site and periodic newsletter honors the history of the group: those who died and those who survived. Although the Heritage Society has published many articles, newsletters, and history articles, those who run it had nothing about Van Nostrand, even though his rank was so high.

Three members of the Philippine Scouts received the Medal of Honor for heroism because of the fighting before the April 1942 surrender. None of them were from Van Nostrand's 26th Cavalry, nor the 61st Infantry that he was training, but one – Capt. Willibald Bianchi of the 45th Infantry Regiment – wound up being a POW and being killed on the same day as Van Nostrand, and is on the Manila MIA wall, just like the Wisconsinite.

Bianchi was from New Ulm, Minn., and was 29 when he was killed.

Bianchi received the Medal of Honor for fighting on Feb. 3, 1942, near the town Bagac on the Bataan peninsula. The citation said:

"When the rifle platoon of another company was ordered to wipe out two strong enemy machine-gun nests, 1st Lt. Bianchi voluntarily and of his own initiative, advanced with the platoon leading part of the men. When wounded early in the action by two bullets through the left hand, he did not stop for first aid but discarded his rifle and began firing a pistol. He located a machine-gun nest and personally silenced it with grenades.

"When wounded the second time by two machine-gun bullets through the chest muscles, 1st Lt. Bianchi climbed to the top of an American tank, manned its antiaircraft machine-gun, and fired into strongly held enemy position until knocked completely off the tank by a third severe wound" (http://www.medalofhonor.com/WillibaldBianchi.htm).

Of 25,000 American servicemen – this includes the many units beyond the Philippine Scouts – who surrendered, more than 10,000 died from any or all of the above, according to Gregory J.W. Urwin, a history professor who wrote the foreword to the 2004 book "Bataan: A Survivor's Story," by Lt. Gene Boyt (p xviii). Boyt received equestrian training at Fort Riley in Kansas – the same place Van Nostrand was based – while he was an ROTC student in college. He wound up as an Army project engineer at Clark Field, overseeing all construction work at the giant airbase.

The 26th Cav was "one of the most exposed units in the early stages of the war, (and) by the time it reached Bataan, the 26th had lost nearly one-fourth of its original complement of 800 in the early battles and during the painful withdrawal into the peninsula (Young, 1992, p. 6). The 26th Cav was an 'integral part' of the important withdraw-delay tactics implemented on Dec. 23" (p. 8), and members of C Troop were being cut off by the rapidly advancing Japanese, so they "took to the hills where they became seeds for the soon-to-be, highly organized and effective Philippine guerrilla army" (p. 9).

Other Scouts found dead horses, partially eaten by the Japanese, nearly a month after the attack at Morong and figured they were from the 26th Cav, as well as 25 horses and mules in an emaciated condition, so they put them out of their misery. Philippine Army men were "eating the uncooked flesh of the dead horses" (Young, 1992, p. 181).

In 2003, twin plaques honoring the Scouts and the three Medal of Honor recipients were dedicated at the Admiral Nimitz Museum in Fredericksburg, Texas, and at the Fort Sam Houston Museum in San Antonio, Texas. The Fort Sam Houston Museum has artifacts donated by the Scouts, but no records per se, such as tables of organizations or citations for Silver Star recipients, including Van Nostrand, so it cannot be found out what he did to earn it.

The plaques say: "In grateful memory of the more than 12,000 gallant officers and men of the U.S. Army's Philippine Scouts, half of whom died in combat or during the Bataan Death March or in Japanese prison camps. Scouts were awarded 3 Congressional Medals of Honor, 34 Distinguished Service Crosses, 134 Silver Stars and 31 Bronze Stars for combat bravery from December 1941 to May 1942."

Those numbers include Van Nostrand's Silver Star and Bronze Star with Oak Leaf Cluster.

Bibliography

Army Campaigns of World War II, www.ibiblio.org/hyperwar/USA/USA-C-Philippines.

Boyt, Lt. Gene, with Burch, David L. (2004). Bataan: A survivor's story. Norman, Okla.: University of Oklahoma Press.

Glusman, John A. (2005). Conduct under fire: Four American doctors and their fight for life as prisoners of the Japanese 1941-1945. Viking. New York: The Penguin Group.

Houlahan, J. Michael (undated) The Philippine Scouts on Bataan: Their Finest Hour www.philippine-scouts.org/history/bataan-their-finest-hour.html

Medal of Honor official Web site, www.medalofhonor.com

Ramsey, Edwin Price, and Rivele, Stephen J. (1990). Lieutenant Ramsey's war. New York: Knightsbridge Publishing Co.

Sides, Hampton (2001). Ghost soldiers: The forgotten epic story of World War II's most dramatic mission. New York, N.Y.: Doubleday.

U.S. Military Academy Library, www.library.usma.edu/archives/special.asp

Young, Donald J. (1992). The battle of Bataan: A history of the 90-day siege and eventual surrender of 75,000 Filipino and United States troops to the Japanese in World War II. Jefferson, N.C.: McFarland & Co. Inc.

Chapter 5:

High losses in the dangerous North Atlantic

The sinkings of two ships in the icy, windy, stormy, foggy and otherwise perilous North Atlantic in 1943 took a large toll of Wisconsin men. Both of these tolls are the highest for the state on any single day in the first two years of World War II after the initial bloodshed at Pearl Harbor, as measured in the database of overseas burials and MIAs by the American Battle Monuments Commission.

One was a big ship that became famous amid tragedy because four heroic chaplains gave up their life vests so that others would have a chance of surviving; the other was a Coast Guard ice cutter based on Lake Michigan that had been pressed into service escorting troop ships to American bases in Greenland.

The first ship was the USS Dorchester, an old liner that was transporting hundreds of men from the East Coast to Greenland. The ship was full of people who had been in the military for only a few months, and a total of 11 men from Wisconsin were killed when it was torpedoed by a German U-boat in the early hours of Feb. 3, 1943; the overall death toll was 672. The Dorchester went under in only 25 minutes; the four chaplains were memorialized forever on a 3-cent postage stamp in 1948.

The second vessel was the USS Escanaba, carrying a crew mainly from Michigan and Wisconsin. A total of 16 Wisconsin men died when the Escanaba exploded around dawn on June 13, 1943, while in a convoy from Greenland to Newfoundland; the overall death toll was 101. The Escanaba went down in only three minutes, and there were only two survivors. It had been conducting sweeps for submarines, but none had been located and so it is more likely that it hit a drifting mine, even if it was far out in the ocean.

The deaths on the Escanaba rank as the No. 2 worst day for the Coast Guard in the entire war; the worst was 193 when a cargo ship exploded while being unloaded at Guadalcanal one month before the Escanaba was lost.

Virgil De Munck,
Plymouth,
USS Dorchester

William Hartzheim,
Juneau,
USS Dorchester

Ray Buddenhagen,
Kewaskum,
USS Escanaba

Victor Salm,
Appleton,
USS Escanaba

The North Atlantic was no place for the faint-hearted. The 34-degree water would kill a man in less than 20 minutes; if he made it onto a lifeboat, he would not last a whole lot longer because of winds, waves and exposure. There were Titanic-style icebergs. Ships regularly became coated with heavy layers of ice from the waves and winds, and that ice had to be chopped off as soon as possible or else the weight would pose many problems. And, oh yes – there were packs of U-boats feasting on lightly guarded troop ships and cargo vessels.

In a sad coincidence, the Escanaba was one of the escort ships for the Dorchester, although it was lightly armed and poorly equipped for wartime service. The Escanaba rescued 132 panicked and almost-frozen men from the Dorchester, only to join its fellow American ship at the bottom of the Atlantic a few months later.

There was another sad coincidence in that more than few men on each ship had the same background: Boys from small Wisconsin farms and towns like Appleton, Kewaskum, Plymouth and Juneau who wound up in the Coast Guard, the Army and the Air Force, all meeting death in the middle of the ocean.

Their names are enshrined in New York City on the East Coast Memorial of the Battle Monuments Commission. The memorial is in Battery Park, at the southern end of Manhattan, and overlooks the Statue of Liberty. The memorial commemorates the 4,609 soldiers, sailors, Marines, Coast Guardsmen, Merchant Marines and airmen who died in the West and North Atlantic during the war. A total of 94 from Wisconsin are on the memorial.

Among them are Victor Salm of Appleton, Ray Buddenhagen of Kewaskum, Virgil De Munck of Plymouth and William Hartzheim of Juneau.

The Coast Guard men

Salm, 29, was a carpenter's mate on the Escanaba. He was No. 4 of the nine children of Nick and Frances Salm; there were six boys and three girls, according to Clara Sprangers of Little Chute, the youngest kid, born nine years after Vic. Growing up on the family's 120-acre farm on the north edge of Appleton, which is now in the city and is near Erb Park, Vic needed to be very handy. That meant running equipment, repairing fences, planting and harvesting corn and cabbage and raising their 20 Holstein and Guernsey cattle, hitching up the big workhorses Maude and Ted to haul grain and plow fields – and anything in between.

He graduated from Appleton High School, which is now Appleton West, and was a bruising and fast 6-foot-4 football player who suffered a broken jaw in one game, loved baseball, loved hunting, loved fishing. He attended the hometown Lawrence University for a time and wanted to be a dentist, even bringing a package of oral tools home to show the family.

"I can still see him unrolling the cloths and all the instruments in there – picks and mirrors," says Sprangers, whose other brothers and sisters all have died over the decades.

But then came the war. One of their brothers already was in the Wisconsin National Guard and was sent with the 32nd Division to New Guinea. They were on the attack in the fall of 1942. "We always expected my brother John to get it, not Vic," Clara says. John made it through all the fighting.

Vic went to an Army recruiter right after Pearl Harbor, but was advised that he would be a better candidate for the Coast Guard, because he would be much older than Army enlistees and draftees. "The guys on the farm know how to fix and build stuff, and he had worked in the Appleton Concrete Block factory making cement blocks," Sprangers says. Combining his age, his muscularity, his handy nature and his outdoors passions, the Coast Guard was a better fit. The service was established in 1915, but its roots extend back to 1790, and its motto of Semper Paratus, (Always Ready), put it in plenty of action both foreign and domestic.

So Salm left Appleton in the first few months of 1942.

"He came home around Christmas 1942. He told us he rescued some guys in the ocean and that it was very dangerous. He also told my Dad, 'I don't want to come home a cripple'," Sprangers says.

A few months later, he was hospitalized in Boston with pneumonia, she continues, but his sense of duty impelled him to leave it in time join his ship on what became his fateful voyage in June.

Another Appleton native, Seaman George Gmeiner, 24, also was on the Escanaba's crew. The two survivors shared the floating wreckage with him, one other man and the captain, Carl Peterson, for a few minutes, according to an official history by Robert Browning Jr. that is on the Coast Guard Web site of www.uscg.mil.

Browning says the two survivors passed out but were saved because their clothing froze to the wreckage, while the others slipped into the water to their deaths.

Ray Herbert Buddenhagen, 18, of rural Kewaskum, was another Wisconsin farm boy on the Escanaba. He was a twin (his brother Ralph was in the Navy), and he had twin cousins plus his mother, Lillian, also had twin cousins.

Buddenhagen was from a 140-acre farm, and he, his twin, and the three other siblings all did typical chores of milking more than a dozen cows, raising corn and grain and potatoes, said Beulah Kurtz of Menomonee Falls, the eldest child, born in 1916. Ray and Ralph were a decade younger. Although Ray and Ralph were identical twins, the Coast Guardsman did not have glasses and the sailor did, along with being slightly heavier. Beulah describes Ray as "a little quiet and reserved and guarded."

Kewaskum was a town of only 2,618 at the time, and the family attended Peace Heaven Evangelical Church in Kewaskum and Elm Grove Country School, a one-room school.

Ray did not go on to high school, instead working on the farm full-time. His father, Arthur, and mother had to sign Ray's enlistment papers in the Coast Guard because he was still 17. Ray never came home in the few months between his enlistment and death, Beulah says – "We never saw him in his uniform." Twin Ralph did not go into the Navy until a bit later.

Ray was a machinist's mate second class, helping run the DeLaval double-reduction geared turbine and the two Babcock and Wilcox boilers on the Escanaba.

The Buddenhagen family has several newspaper clippings from the sinking, including an undated Associated Press story from the Milwaukee Journal that quoted the two survivors after they were brought back to Boston.

Seaman First Class Raymond O'Malley of Chicago had been down below and got up to the main deck, but the ship was quickly sinking. Boatswain's Mate 2nd Class Melvin Baldin of Staples, Minn., was at the wheel and was "blown upward and hit the overhead of the wheelhouse," then staggered out the door and was washed overboard. Both clung to a strongback, described as a 38-foot log that is used to keep lifeboats from bumping against the ship's side. They lost consciousness and were revived after being pulled from the waves by the Coast Guard cutter Raritan, the story said.

The Coast Guard Web site carries the transcript of a wide-ranging interview with O'Malley, who says the ocean in the area was like "a frozen Daiquiri ... shaved ice."

Despite what the AP story reported at the time, O'Malley said he also was at the wheel of the ship when the Escanaba was hit, and he had been conducting a starboard turn in its zig-zag anti-submarine pattern. "The ship was split in half because the bow came up and the stern came down. ... As I started to go I got pulled down with the ship and I don't know how far down I went but I was swimming very hard to get back to the surface and now there is another explosion (from either depth charges or the boilers) ... but I was pawing up to the surface."

While the Escanaba was assigned to escort troop and cargo ships, it was not a warship in any sense other than that it was a Great Lakes cutter that was assigned to war duty. It originally was built for icebreaking, law enforcement and rescue work. It was all of 165 feet long. The Navy was trying to use it as a destroyer. And the 2004 book ""No Greater Glory," by Dan Kurzman, which is about the sinking of the Dorchester, says the Escanaba did not even have radar, meaning it was rather ineffective hunting for U-boats.

The Coast Guard says 241,093 of its men served in World War II and that 574 were killed in action. So the Escanaba's loss, in only a couple minutes, was nearly one-sixth of its fatalities for the entire war. Coast Guard ships were credited for sinking several German and Japanese submarines. The Escanaba and other cutters dropped depth charges, but otherwise they were there to provide screening for the bigger ships.

The Escanaba was built in 1932 and began its ocean work in the summer of 1942, participating in several rescues. For example, in June of that year, it retrieved 22 men from a torpedoed passenger ship, the Cherokee, according to the Coast Guard's official history of the ship. This is likely what Salm told his family about. Then came its biggest action, in February 1943, when it was one of three cutters escorting the troop ship USS Dorchester.

Troops on the Dorchester

Virgil De Munck of Plymouth and William Hartzheim of Juneau were two of the 900 men on the Dorchester, which was headed from its home base of Boston to bases in Greenland. De Munck was a private in the Army Air Corps and Hartzheim was an Army corporal in the field artillery – hardly seafaring, iron-stomach types like the Coast Guard.

The book "No Greater Glory" says all the ships were essentially sitting ducks – the Dorchester averaged only 8 knots, and the cutters were slower yet. Newer ocean liners that were taking 15,000 or more men to Europe on a single trip usually made 14 knots. Kurzman calls the cutters "a few Chihuahuas trying to fend off a pack of wolves" (p. 96) in an area long known as Torpedo Junction, between Newfoundland and Greenland.

Nine hours before the actual attack, it became known that the Dorchester was being trailed by U-boats, and all hands were told at 6:30 p.m. to don life jackets and parkas and be sure to wear shoes when going to bed, in order to ensure a faster evacuation. Tension grew and grew, and rumors grew even faster, and the torpedoing finally came at 12:55 a.m., only a few hours before the ship would have reached safety in Greenland.

The Dorchester sank in 25 minutes.

Throughout the voyage, the chaplains – the Rev. Clark Poling (Dutch Reformed and son of prominent radio evangelist Daniel A. Poling), Rabbi Alexander Goode (Jewish), Father John Washington (Catholic) and Rev. George Fox (Methodist) – had been aiming to keep up morale on the ship, including organizing events to take the troops' minds away from chronic seasickness. They also of course conducted religious services and provided counseling. They had worked for hours to see that the men were outfitted for evacuation if and when the U-boats found it.

And when that happened, they helped troops get into lifeboats and rafts and pushed men over the railing to have a better chance of survival than staying on a sinking ship, even giving up their own life vests amid the chaos so that others could have a chance of surviving the sinking, the waves and the icy, icy water.

"The ship started sinking ... and as I left the ship, I looked back and saw the chaplains ... with their hands clasped, praying for the boys. They never made any attempt to save themselves, but they did try to save the others. I think their names should be on the list of the greatest heroes of this war," soldier Grady L. Clark said in an affidavit sent to the Army. And trooper Thomas W. Myers Jr. attested, "I saw all four chaplains take off their life belts and give them to soldiers who had none. ... The last I saw of them they were still praying, talking and preaching to the soldiers" (Kurzman, 2004, p. 221).

Capt. Joseph Greenspun, commander of the three cutters (he was aboard the USS Tampa), ordered the Escanaba to find the submarine and to refrain from immediately trying to pick up survivors, Kurzman says. This made for quite a controversy afterwards.

"Their humanitarian instincts clashed with Greenspun's view that the potential danger to a second ship deserved priority over saving the lives of those who were doomed to die if not reached immediately" (p. 134). A total of 48 minutes after the torpedoing, the commander finally ordered the Escanaba to aid the evacuees, but that was well beyond the 20 minutes that anyone could survive in the water. The Escanaba eventually was able to rescue 132 men, and the Coast Guard cutter Commanche saved 94.

Virgil De Munck of Plymouth, which has a population of 8,200 today, was quite typical of the troops being transported – age 22, an Army Air Corps private, never been to sea before.

De Munck attended St. John's Lutheran Church in Plymouth, so technically his chaplain would have been one of the two Protestants, although none of the four clerics was known for dealing only with his own faith – all hands were welcome.

He was the oldest of five kids of farmers Al and Claudia De Munck, but they divorced and so Claudia brought them to the city to live. Virgil left high school after his sophomore year in order to do farm work and odd jobs, helping his single mother support the family amid the Depression, said his sister, Jean Rasmussen, No. 3 in the family.

In the fall of 1942, De Munck enlisted in the Air Corps, and "I never saw him again," said Rasmussen, of Sheboygan Falls. He did not come home on leave during training or just before embarking on the ocean voyage, and in fact was killed only about five months after going into the military.

De Munck's training was in New Mexico and Maine, then he was sent on the fatal voyage to Greenland. His fiancee, from the Plymouth area, traveled to the East Coast along with her mother and his own mother for a brief visit before the voyage, Rasmussen said.

William Hartzheim of Juneau in Dodge County also was an Army newbie, a 27-year-old corporal in the field artillery. He was working at the post office in Beaver Dam, delivering mail, when he enlisted on Sept. 6, 1942. Like De Munck, he was dead only a few months later.

Hartzheim was born July 26, 1915, to Bill and Margaret Hartzheim of Juneau. The father was the well-known proprietor of The Hub tavern in the Dodge County town, built by his own father, Mike Hartzheim, 50 years earlier. Mike "came out of Milwaukee to Juneau and sang tenor at St. Mary's Roman Catholic Church in Juneau, says Joe Hartzheim of Horicon, cousin of the soldier.

Joe's father, Elmer, tended bar with his brother Bill. All the boys of the brothers did various chores, such as sweeping and straightening things out after a long night of conviviality in order to get ready for the next night of fun and imbibing. Juneau was the county seat of Dodge County, but its population was only 1,301 at the time.

Joe says the bar was typical of the day, equipped with ample spittoons and well-known in the Wisconsin winter for its Tom and Jerrys, the rich and warming holiday mix of brandy, rum, cream and spices.

William Hartzheim graduated from Pio Nono High School in Milwaukee, and attended college for a time in Winona, Minn., and in Milwaukee.

The Dorchester sank at 1:20 a.m. There was a massive oil slick and the night was moonless so visibility was poor, and the nearby ships could not use illumination because of the danger that they too would be seen by the U-boats.

The Coast Guard's history on its Web site says that when the Escanaba finally was allowed to begin rescuing Dorchester men, the cutter – including the Wisconsinites Salm and Buddenhagen – found "the majority of the men were suffering from severe shock and could not climb up the sea ladders or the cargo net. In fact, they could not even hang on to the lines with running bowlines on them long enough to secure the lines under their arms so they could be hauled on board."

So Escanaba men jumped into the icy waters to try to grab them. "They would get hold of the men or of the rafts and the men tending the retrievers' lines could pull the group close to the ship. The retrievers could then quickly put lines around the survivors and they were hauled aboard in short order. This system saved much valuable time and many lives."

Bibliography

Associated Press story in Milwaukee Journal, undated, 1943. Escanaba survivors tell about explosion.

Browning, Robert Jr. (undated). The sinking of the US Coast Guard cutter Escanaba. At www.uscg.mil

Coast Guard Oral History Program (undated). Interviewee: Raymond O'Malley World War II Coast Guard veteran and survivor of the sinking of the cutter Escanaba. At www.uscg.mil

Coast Guard (undated). Escanaba, 1932. At www.uscg.mil

Kurzman, Dan (2004). No greater glory: The four immortal chaplains and the sinking of the Dorchester in World War II. New York: Random House.

Wisconsin men killed on USS Dorchester – Feb. 3, 1943

Air Force Pvt. Harold F. Beckman, Outagamie County

Air Force Pvt. Virgil J. De Munck, Sheboygan County

Air Force Pvt. Frederick J. Gennrich, Milwaukee County

Army Pvt. Robert P. Giltner, Milwaukee County

Army Pvt. Robert L. Goodwin, Waukesha County

Army Cpl. William M. Hartzheim, Dodge County

Pvt. Donald H. Jacobson, Rock County

Army Pvt. John L. Jones, Milwaukee County

Army Pvt. Harold L. Nau, Marathon County

Air Force Pvt. Stanley V. Palm, Polk County

Army Pvt. Ervin R. Sack, Milwaukee County

List compiled from database of American Battle Monuments Commission and book of Army / Air Corps casualties, which lists counties but not hometowns. Confirmed against lists reported in "No Greater Glory," by Dan Kurzman.

Wisconsin men killed on USS Escanaba – June 13, 1943

Coast Guard Machinist's Mate 2nd Class Ray H. Buddenhagen, Kewaskum

Coast Guard Coxswain Raymond J. Bykowski, Milwaukee

Coast Guard Seaman First Class Eugene G. Chapleau, Menasha

Coast Guard Boatswain's Mate 2nd Class Clarence E. Christenson, Sturgeon Bay

Coast Guard Yeoman 3rd Class Sam Chudacoff, Milwaukee

Coast Guard Radioman First Class Leonard Delsart, Sawyer

Coast Guard Seaman First Class George W. Gmeiner, Appleton.

Coast Guard Seaman First Class Quiren Hostak, Oconto Falls

Coast Guard Soundman 2nd Class Kenneth A. Kletzien, Sheboygan

Coast Guard Boatswain's Mate Chief George W. Larson, Two Rivers

Coast Guard Seaman First Class Ralph F. Lietz, home unknown

Coast Guard Water Tender First Class Victor J. Londo Jr., Kaukauna

Coast Guard Coxswain Leo R. Peterson, Neenah

Coast Guard Carpenter's Mate 3rd Class Victor N. Salm, Appleton

Coast Guard Radioman First Class Kenneth E. Sattler, Fond du Lac

Coast Guard Seaman First Class Clayton R. Smith, Waupaca

List compiled from database of American Battle Monuments Commission and 1946 book of Navy dead and wounded, which lists hometowns. Confirmed against list of Coast Guard crew for Escanaba. Newspaper stories of the time were including a few other names and saying they were from Wisconsin, but the ABMC goes by the official Navy state-by-state list. Those men in the newspaper stories were, variously, from Michigan, Iowa and Ohio on that official Navy list.

* Navy Machinist's Mate Second Class Jack H. Wachsmuth Jr., no hometown available, is not on the official list of Escanaba crew, but he died on this day and his name is on the commission's East Coast monument.

Chapter 6:

The toll jumps amid huge invasions on both sides of the world

Wisconsin had gradually gotten used to a few dozen servicemen being killed in each month since Pearl Harbor – 1942 tolls like 28 in July and 57 in December, 1943 tolls like 40 in June and 89 in November, and 1944 tolls like 40 in January, 61 in February and 83 in May.

But that was just the beginning. It got far worse.

In June 1944, the long-expected invasion of Normandy was added to the months of fighting in Italy and bombing raids over Germany, and the bloody invasion of Saipan was added to the months of sea and island battles in the Pacific. So the death toll took a staggering jump – from June 6 to 17, a total of 96 Wisconsinites were killed, according to a count by the author of this book.

That figure, in less than two weeks, exceeded any monthly total to date in the war.

All of this is from the database of the American Battle Monuments Commission, which runs overseas cemeteries and MIA monuments. The ABMC says its names are only about 45 percent of the full figure, given that many families wanted their serviceman's body brought home after the war. So while this book is talking about a toll of 96 from Wisconsin, the actual number for that period of only 12 days would mirror that percentage and be well over 200.

The total for the full month of June in the ABMC database is 176. It was nearly twice as much as the top total so far in the war – 89 in November 1943. And the monthly tally would keep going up until peaking in December 1944 at 247, according to unofficial hand counts of individual listings made for this book. That one would be the highest toll of the war. Again, that is just the ABMC database, so the total Wisconsin toll is far higher.

Merlin Mosey,
La Crosse,
Saipan

Willis Oftedahl,
Viroqua,
Saipan

Gerald Rehfeldt,
Appleton,
D-Day Utah Beach

Norton Feierday
Milwaukee,
D-Day

Two Marines killed in their first day on Saipan were Cpl. Merlin Mosey of La Crosse and Pfc. Willis Oftedahl of Viroqua. Somehow, 6,000 miles from home, the invaders included two Marines who grew up only about 30 miles apart. Mosey already had received a Bronze Star for heroism for saving a buddy in the invasion of Roi-Namur, twin islands in the Kwajalein Atoll, in the first days of February 1944.

Their life stories are not much different from two of the invaders killed on D-Day in Normandy: Army combat engineer Pfc. Gerald Rehfeldt of Appleton and Army paratrooper Pfc. Norton Feierday of Milwaukee. Mosey was 23, Oftedahl 22, Rehfeldt 20 or 21 and Feierday 32. Oftedahl is honored on the MIA wall at Honolulu and Mosey is buried in Honolulu; Feierday and Rehfeldt are buried in Normandy.

Saipan

The invasion of Saipan was huge – a force of 71,000 Marines and Army men, plus sea support (Goldberg, 2007, p. 50) – but not nearly the grand scale of the American-British-Canadian invasion by 175,000 men at five separate beaches and two huge landing zones for paratroopers in Normandy (Ambrose, 1994, p. 576).

Saipan also is not as well-remembered in movies and books and presidential visits to the battlefield as is D-Day. But 11 Wisconsin men are buried in Honolulu or honored on the MIA wall there from that day, June 15, 1944, compared with 19 buried in Normandy from D-Day. Do the math and, technically, you will find that a greater percentage of Wisconsin men were killed on Saipan than on D-Day.

Saipan veterans gathered on the island in 2004 to commemorate the 60th anniversary of the battle, and the New York Times reported that they believed "the American popular mind relegates the Pacific theater to second-class status" because Normandy gets much more fanfare. "It is just like the 50th; we were overshadowed by Normandy. We are so remote, people just forget," said Jerry Facey, co-chairman of the Saipan event (www.signonsandiego.com).

This book will emphasize the Saipan action, perhaps helping to finally give those men their deserved coverage. It is helped along by the 2007 book "D-Day in the Pacific: The battle of Saipan" by Harold J. Goldberg, which serves well for anyone seeking far more information. Goldberg interviewed 36 veterans directly and corresponded via e-mail with more, plus utilized original documents and memoirs, among other things.

Saipan is one of 15 islands in the Marianas. Tinian and Guam, also in the chain, became battle sites a month after Saipan. The Navy's 5th Fleet, under Adm. Raymond Spruance, transported an expeditionary force of hundreds of ships and three Marine divisions, a Marine brigade and two Army infantry divisions to the Marianas. The force and its 18 aircraft carriers were split into two, with half aiming at Saipan and Tinian and the rest aiming at Guam five weeks later.

The Saipan force consisted of the 2nd and 4th Marine Divisions; Mosey was in the 4th and Oftedahl in the 2nd Division's Armored Amphibious Battalion. The commander of the 4th was Maj. Gen. Harry Schmidt, and the leader of the 2nd was Maj. Gen. Thomas Watson. The overall commander was the legendary Lt. Gen. Holland Smith, known as "Howlin' Mad" for his everyday temperament, which got even worse when he became really steamed, which was often, especially when dealing with other branches of the military.

The leader of Mosey's 24th Marine Infantry Regiment of the 4th Division was Col. Franklin Hart; and his 3rd Battalion was run by Lt . Col. Alex Vandegrift Jr. The 1st Battalion was run by Lt. Col. Maynard Schultz, who was hit in the head by shrapnel and died of wounds the next day, June 16 (Goldberg, 2007, p. 240). Like Mosey, Schultz is buried in Honolulu.

The Marines landed on the west side of the island, south of the capital city of Garapan, in a cacophony of fire from gunboats, battleships and destroyers, accompanied by Navy and Marine air support. The Japanese had zeroed in the landing beaches, and out of the 68 armored amphibian craft to come in with the 6th and 8th Marine regiments, 31 were destroyed or disabled (www.ibiblio.org/hyperwar/USMC/USMC-M-Saipan/USMC-M-Saipan-2.html).

Two LVTs (landing vehicle tanks) carrying Mosey's 3d Battalion overturned in the heavy surf, and when the men reached the beach, they faced artillery fire. Vandegrift "deployed his battalion and moved it on foot to an assembly area some 700 yards inland from Yellow 1, near a fork in the railroad tracks. The men had no more than taken entrenching tools in hand when a barrage of well-directed Japanese artillery fire engulfed them. After the day's casualties were totaled, it was discovered that the unit had suffered heavily, though it had yet to enter the front-line fighting: 25 killed, 72 wounded, 39 missing (mostly those lost on board the overturned LVTs). Other battalions had suffered more heavily, but the real significance of these figures lies in the fact that the 3d Battalion did not arrive on the beach until 17:27 (5:27 p.m.)" (www.ibiblio.org/hyperwar/USMC/USMC-M-Saipan/USMC-M-Saipan-2.html).

Oftedahl's 2nd Division had 238 dead and 1,022 wounded on the first day, while the 4th Division fared slightly better, with a total of 800 KIA and wounded.

Pfc. Richard Hertensteiner of Sheboygan found out quickly what Saipan would be like. He was in an artillery battery and was with two other Marines on the beach, when "we heard incoming rounds and we dived into a shell crater. I was the last person to fall into the hole when the first round hit. After the shelling, I got up off the other two men and began talking to them. It was at this time that I learned that both of them were killed while I never got so much as a small scratch. That was my first experience in combat" (Goldberg, 2007, p. 82).

Another Wisconsin Marine on Saipan made it past the first day and even the first weeks, but then met his fate. Pfc. Harold Christ Agerholm, 19, of Racine was in the 10th Artillery Regiment of the 2nd Marine Division. He received the Medal of Honor for his actions on July 7, and the citation said:

> "When the enemy launched a fierce, determined counterattack against our positions and overran a neighboring artillery battalion, Pfc. Agerholm immediately volunteered to assist in the efforts to check the hostile attack and evacuate our wounded. Locating and appropriating an abandoned ambulance jeep, he repeatedly made extremely perilous trips under heavy rifle and mortar fire and single-handedly loaded and evacuated approximately 45 casualties, working tirelessly and with utter disregard for his own safety during a grueling period of more than three hours.
>
> "Despite intense, persistent enemy fire, he ran out to aid two men whom he believed to be wounded Marines but was himself mortally wounded by a

Japanese sniper while carrying out his hazardous mission" (www.history.army.mil/html/moh/wwII-a-f.html).

Agerholm first was buried in the 2nd Marine Division cemetery on Saipan, but his body was brought home to Racine in 1947. A school in Racine is named after him and Air Force Maj. John Jerstad, and is discussed in a later chapter of this book.

The main places in the Saipan bloodbath were the town of Charan Kanoa, Agingan and Afetna Points, plus Mounts Fine Susu, Tapotchau and Tipo Pale. Huge naval battles followed a few days after the invasion. In what became known as the Great Marianas Turkey Shoot, U.S. carrier-based planes wiped out hundreds of attacking Japanese planes.

The battle finally ended in early July, but not before a banzai charge by an estimated 2,500 Japanese against the Army's 105th Infantry Regiment. Marine artillery who were with the infantry fired their 105mm guns directly into the charging Japanese. And hundreds of soldiers and civilians – some carrying babies – jumped off cliffs into the ocean rather than surrender. One, dubbed Suicide Cliff, was 800 feet high, and another, named Banzai Cliff, was 265 feet.

The final Saipan toll was more than 14,000 Americans killed, wounded or MIA, 10,000 of them Marines. For KIA, there were 1,100 in Mosey's 4th Division, 1,250 in Oftedahl's 2nd Marine Division and 1,030 in the Army's 27th Infantry Division (Goldberg, 2007, p. 210).

The result of the victory in Saipan and elsewhere in the Marianas was getting a place for bases for the B-29 superbombers to begin attacking Japan. The Enola Gay, which dropped the atomic bomb on Hiroshima on Aug. 6, 1945, took off from Tinian, as did Boxcar, which destroyed Nagasaki on Aug. 9.

But that was more than a year after Saipan. Mosey and Oftedahl did not make it past their first day there.

Mosey and Oftedahl

Merlin Joseph Mosey was born March 19, 1921, in Oshkosh, the son of Anton and Anna Mosey, and was the third of four children;

two girls and two boys. When he was 3, the family moved to La Crosse, and he attended parochial schools, and went to Thomas Aquinas High School for one year, followed by three years of vocational school training to be an auto mechanic. He enlisted in the Marines in 1940.

His brother, Ray Mosey of La Crosse, was eight years younger. Ray says Anton was a farm hand, and met Anna Hoffman because he was working on her father's farm at Knowlton, south of Wausau. After their parents died, Anton and Anna "headed to California but never got farther than La Crosse," he laughs. Ray was born in La Crosse and Anna died when he was only 7.

"Merlin was a wiry guy, muscular, and loved fishing on the Mississippi River more than anything. We loved all kinds except catfish. We smoked carp, sunfish, bluegills and walleyes. We didn't have money for rods and reels. You simply bought the biggest cane pole you could get, a line and a Daredevil" lure. One time, Merlin "made his own rod. He found a piece of bamboo and taped a used reel onto it, and put screw eyes into it to run the line. It could cast three times farther out than mine."

The boys also made their own kites from newspapers, "and used Ma's flour for paste, and made a crossbar from slats used for plaster in houses. I don't remember stores having kites to sell until I was a teenager."

Ray Mosey was only 12 when the news about his brother arrived via telegram. That did not keep him from enlisting in the Marines himself, in 1946. He worked 32 years in the La Crosse Fire Department. He visited his brother's grave in Honolulu in June 2008, when he was 79.

When he was still a private first class, Merlin Mosey visited La Crosse on a 15-day leave and was interviewed by the La Crosse Tribune. The story noted that during the attack on Pearl Harbor, he was about 60 miles out to sea returning from a mission to the Philippines and Wake Island aboard the heavy cruiser USS Chester, and that in the battle of the Coral Sea on May 10, 1942, the cruiser picked up 400 to 500 men evacuating the sinking carrier USS Lexington.

"We were about two blocks away from the Lexington," Mosey told the newspaper. "... For a while they thought they had the fire under control and could get back, but then another fire started. We stood up on top with some of the Lexington's men and watched it go down. The tears were rolling down their cheeks as they looked at it."

Mosey also told how during battles in the Marshall and Gilbert Islands in late 1943, concussions from 500-pound Japanese bombs split the seams of the ship. At that time, he was a Marine antiaircraft gunner. "We saw the (Japanese) planes coming, and when those eight bombers flew over, they just spelled death – you could see it as clearly as day."

The story ended by saying Mosey expected to be transferred into amphibious forces (which he was in for the Saipan invasion) and "after the fighting is over, he would like to train ... for a position as customs officer."

In February 1944, and by then a corporal, he earned the Bronze Star in action on Namur Island on Kwajalein Atoll. This is what the citation said he did: "Cooly and with complete disregard for his own life, Cpl. Mosey voluntarily exposed himself to intense hostile fire in order to reach the side of a wounded Marine and, in the face of continuous fire from the enemy, removed his injured comrade to a place of comparative safety. By his quick initiative, courageous performance of duty and gallant spirit of self-sacrifice, Cpl. Mosey upheld the highest traditions of the United States Naval Service."

However, he was dead by the time the medal could be presented, so it was given to his parents in a La Crosse ceremony. The La Crosse paper reported the family received a letter from Maj. Gen. D. Pick, acting commandant of the Marine Corps, that said: "I wish to assure you of my deep appreciation of the meritorious achievement of your son, the late Corp. Merlin J. Mosey ... The Marine Corps shares you pride in the gallant action of your son."

Oftedahl was in the 2nd Armored Amphibious Battalion. This meant he was in the first wave, a vehicle that would swim ashore and start moving when it hit the beach, providing fire for Marine landing craft that were more lightly armed. Using 2nd Division records, Marine Maj. Carl Hoffman wrote in a historical review of Saipan:

"Farther out, hundreds of landing vehicles circled dizzily as boat waves organized. The first wave, comprised of the 2d Armored Amphibian Battalion and the Army's 708th Amphibian Tank Battalion, began firing their weapons about 300 yards from the beach. Some troop-carrying tractors, because of their superior speed, crossed in front of the armored amphibians between the reef and the beach, masking their fire.

Of the 68 armored amphibians which preceded the 2d Division, three were disabled before reaching the beach, and 28 more were disabled between the beach and the tractor control line, 200-500 yards inland" (www.ibiblio.org/hyperwar/USMC/USMC-M-Saipan/USMC-M-Saipan-2.html). "Extremely heavy fire, registering on the southern approaches to the Green Beaches, caused landing vehicles to veer to the north to escape it."

Because Oftedahl was MIA, one can assume his amphibious vehicle likely was hit in the water, not on land.

Then again, there is another view: "In general, although most of the tanks and tractors made it to the beaches unharmed, the combination of their thin armor and slow movement made them easy targets for the Japanese artillery once ashore. The amphibious vehicles were under-powered and were easily stopped by obstacles (loose sand, trenches, holes, and trees) that normal tanks would not have had a problem with" (www.leatherneck.com/forums/archive/index.php/t-15272.html).

Oftedahl was born in the Town of Jefferson near Westby April 4, 1922, according to the family's Bible, so he was 22 when he was killed, a year younger than Mosey. His parents were Hans and Tillie, and there were three older siblings. The family was Norwegian, with Hans coming to America from that country when he was 10.

His family attended Bethel Lutheran Church between Westby and Viroqua, on County Road B. His cousin, Norman Oftedahl, of rural Viroqua, about eight years younger, was able to find some notes saying Willis was confirmed on Oct. 11, 1936, with four sponsors – Chris and Elizabeth Larson, Esther Gronning and a Mr. Eitland, all of whom were the family's neighbors. He also says Willis attended North Springville School for eight years.

Hans Oftedahl died in 1933, the heart of the Depression, and the family lost its 38-acre farm and moved three miles to a vacant house in the unincorporated burg of Esofea, "which had two grocery stores, a park and a cheese factory," Norman says.

"He and his brother (Harold, who fought World War II in the Air Force) were gun nuts," Norman says. "Harold could drop a bullet from chin-high and draw a revolver and fire it before the bullet hit the ground." That was quite impressive to the younger cousin. Willis was "quite athletic and strong, blond with a touch of red hair, and worked in the cheese factory in Esofea. He got tired of that and so he joined the service," Norman says.

Willis enlisted in the Marines in October 1943, and boot camp was in San Diego. His letters home discussed all the attractive women, and he requested a camera in order to take their pictures, says Kay Burke of Viroqua, his niece.

"He was cute – a good-looking guy," Burke adds.

After training, he went overseas in April 1944, and was dead two months later. His last letters talked about how nice the Pacific islands were, not anything about his fears going into war, a sense of duty, or even small things such as what exactly his job was in an amphibious vehicle.

A monument to Mosey, Oftedahl, Agerholm and the other Marines and the Army stands on Saipan, near the beach overlooking Tanapag Harbor. It is a part of the American Memorial Park and honors the battles on Saipan, Tinian and Guam, in which 24,000 Marines, Navy men and soldiers were killed, according to the American Battle Monuments Commission.

Normandy

On the other side of the world, more Wisconsin men were dying in large numbers between June 6 and 17 of 1944. Many of them were in Normandy, but as the lists and burial sites at the end of this chapter show, there also was substantial fighting in Italy, bombing missions over Germany, and sea combat.

The story of D-Day is very familiar from the epic Cornelius Ryan book "The Longest Day," the movie of the same name plus "Saving Private Ryan," television specials and the dozens of other books it spawned: the daring nighttime American parachute drops, the massive American and British attacks via glider, the H-Hour landings at the beaches code-named Omaha, Utah, Gold, Sword and Juno, the incredible climb of the cliffs at Pointe du Hoc by U.S. Army Rangers and so on.

One of the glidermen was Pfc. Norton Feierday, 32, of Milwaukee, a member of the 319th Field Artillery Battalion of the 82nd Airborne Division. That meant he was in one of the hundreds of gliders, towed by a C-47 from Britain to Normandy and then let loose in order to land silently with its load of men and weapons. It was not much, but it was far more than the parachutists of the 82nd and 101st Airborne Divisions were carrying – when they landed safely, the first thing they needed was bigger weaponry, to hold off the Germans. Another member of the same glider unit was Pvt. Lloyd Olson of La Crosse County (he was born in 1906 and so, like Feierday, he also was in his 30s), who died one day after Feierday. Both are buried at Omaha Beach.

Many gliders broke apart on landing (especially amid fields of iron spikes known as "Rommel's asparagus" put up the Germans), were destroyed by German guns or crashed into the sea. Brig. Gen. Donald Pratt, assistant commander of the 101st Airborne Division, was killed when his glider slammed into a hedgerow.

The gliders – some made of plywood and some of canvas – were carrying things like 75mm artillery guns, small jeeps to pull the howitzer, antitank guns, etc. A glider crew carrying artillery usually consisted of a pilot, sometimes a co-pilot, plus two crewmen.

There were two glider missions for the 82nd Airborne on D-Day, and one the next morning. Books about D-Day say the 319th Glider Field Artillery Battalion of Feierday and Olson was on a mission code-named Elmira, which came at dusk.

Elmira consisted of 418 men plus engineers and medical personnel, and the equipment was 12 howitzers of 75mm, 31 jeeps, 26 tons of ammunition and 25 tons of other combat equipment (Mrazek, 1975; Masters, 1995).

The gliders encountered German fire en route and after landing. Only 13 of the British Horsa gliders arrived intact and 56 were destroyed. None of the 14 American-made Waco gliders were intact, and eight were destroyed (Mrazek, 1975, p. 152). "Twenty-eight glidermen died, and 106 were wounded or injured."

It had not been much better for the 82nd Airborne's gliders in the early hours of D-Day, either. That mission, code-named Detroit, saw 22 of the 52 gliders destroyed, with many others badly smashed. "Several jeeps broke loose during the landings, making a shambles of the interiors. Eleven of the 22 jeeps were inoperable on arrival. The howitzers proved more durable" and soon were put into action (Mrazek, 1997, p. 146).

Feierday and Rehfeldt

Feierday was "a neat guy. Everybody liked him," his sister-in-law, Muriel Mondl of Fort Atkinson, said in 1989 when he was part of a Memorial Day story in the Milwaukee Sentinel. His wife was Grace, Mondl's sister, who died in 1988.

Mondl said he appeared to be a quiet type but was "full of mischief like nobody's business," such as when he made a surprise visit to his in-laws' home at 2321 N. 15th St., Milwaukee, on Christmas 1942 while on leave from training in Illinois.

"That was the first Christmas that the guys had all been gone," Mondl said. "We had a tree of just blue lights and tinsel. That was supposed to be a blue Christmas, without those boys."

It instead was a fine, fine holiday, but that also was the last time the family saw him.

As for Olson, the name is so common that it is impractical to search for relatives in La Crosse County. His record at the National Archives shows he was a farmhand, was single, had a grammar-school education and went into the service in March 1942 via Eau Claire.

So sons of La Crosse County were fighting on both sides of the world in June 1944, and no doubt at many points in between and no doubt quite close together, too. A total of 125 men from that county who were in the Army or Air Force were killed in the war, according to the official 1946 booklet that is used many times in this book. Plus many more from the Navy and Marines, whose booklet listed people alphabetically, not by county.

Another D-Day sacrifice was by Pfc. Gerald Rehfeldt of Appleton, a member of the Army's 298th Combat Engineer Battalion. Combat engineers did things like blow up obstacles on the invasion beaches and along roads before the Allies came along, made new roads, cleared minefields, built footbridges and / or heavier bridges across marshes, ditches, streams, gullies, rivers, etc. – all while being shot at. Army units always had combat engineer elements attached to them; combat engineers built bridges across the Rhine River later in the war and across other obstacles almost every day. Baseball great Warren Spahn and comedy giant Mel Brooks were very young combat engineers in the war. (Mueller, 1985; www.hq.usace.army.mil/history/Vignettes/Vignette_109.htm)

Rehfeldt graduated from Appleton High School (now Appleton West) in 1942, so he would have been age 20 or 21 two years later when he was killed, according to a "shirttail relative," Don Rehfeldt of Fallbrook, Calif. The Rehfeldts probably were second cousins, but were roughly the same age. Gerald was president of the nature club as a junior, and was a member as a sophomore and senior.

Gerald graduated in the same class as Robert Rehfeldt, who was Don's brother. Don says the exact lineage of the families no longer is clear to him, but that both his grandmother and grandfather had that last name before they got married.

Don was in the Navy, serving as a motor machinist's mate third class on destroyers, and made 13 round trips across the Atlantic Ocean escorting troop ships and cargo to the Mediterranean (such as Casablanca and Algiers) or northern Europe (including England and Londonderry, Northern Ireland). He says "all the ships looked like they were painted brown" because of the thousands of soldiers like Gerald Rehfeldt on the deck.

"After one of my trips, I came home. My Dad and I met Gerald's Dad somewhere, and he was interested in talking to me because he wasn't getting letters," Don says.

Gerald's family attended Mount Olive Lutheran Church. Don was two years younger than Gerald and also attended Appleton High School, but left it in 1943 to go into the military. Don not only lost his relative in the war; he also lost a neighbor, Jack Williamson, who was killed on Sept. 22, 1944, in the invasion of Holland.

On D-Day, engineers like Gerald Rehfeldt played vital roles, landing before the waves of infantry attackers in order to blast holes through the many forms of defenses on Omaha and Utah Beaches. More than a dozen battalions of engineers were in the historic assault (Office of History, Corps of Engineers).

Cornelius Ryan's book discusses the 112th, 146th and 299th Combat Engineer Battalions, along with three special brigades – the 1st, 5th and 6th. Rehfeldt was part of a special 12-man group from the 298th Battalion that was put into service for D-Day; the rest of his unit did not arrive in Normandy until July 9; so one can assume Rehfeldt was a very good soldier and had some special skill that caused him to be put in a special group.

Rehfeldt was the only one of that particular group that died on D-Day, according to the 298th Battalion's Web site. (freepages.genealogy.rootsweb.ancestry.com/~kipke/298army/298th1.htm). The leader of that special unit was 1st Lt. Bernard Stafford, and 10 of the men were privates first class (like Rehfeldt) or privates.

Sgt. Eugene D. Shales, 19, was also at Utah Beach, but as a member of the 299th Engineer Battalion, which was not Rehfeldt's group. However, what he experienced was typical. "Our team consisted of six or seven combat engineers (my half-squad contingency), and about the same number of Navy underwater demolition specialists. ... The teams were called Naval Combat Demolition Units, and the assignment of each unit was to clear its designated 50-yard beach sector of all German beach obstacles as these would impede, and even damage, subsequent landing craft when the tide came in. That is why we had to land at an early morning hour, when the tide was low and the obstacles were readily visible.

"The time of our landing was about 06:30 a.m., which was planned to give us enough time to destroy all the obstacles before the tide came in. We had to place our demolition charges on the backside of the obstacles so that the explosions would hurl the fragments seaward. ... The job was finished around mid-morning, but there was pain associated with it, due to the loss of a member of my squad, Leo Indelicato, who was killed by artillery fire during that task" (www.6juin1944.com/veterans/shales.php).

Historian Stephen Ambrose said the 237th Combat Engineer Battalion, also under fire at Utah Beach, got explosives wired to obstacles, only to find that incoming infantrymen would hide behind the obstacles because of German fire. "A medic pulled several out of the way and yelled at the rest, and was 15 to 20 feet away when the blow came. Within less than an hour, the teams cleared eight 50-yard gaps in the obstacles and were still working on others. Next, the 237th went to work blasting holes in the seawall" (Ambrose, 1994, p. 281).

At much-bloodier Omaha Beach, "Sgt. Barton A. Davis of the 299th Engineer Combat Battalion saw an assault boat bearing down on him. It was filled with 1st Division men and was coming straight in through the obstacles. There was a tremendous explosion and the boat disintegrated. It seemed to Davis that everyone in it was thrown into the air all at once. Bodies and parts of bodies landed all around the flaming wreckage" (Ryan, 1959, 1984, p. 227-228).

It was even worse in Davis' own group, another Army-Navy Special Engineer Task Force. "The landing boats carrying their explosives had been shelled, and the hulks of these craft lay blazing at the edge of the beach. Engineers with small rubber boats loaded with plastic charges and detonators were blown apart in the water when enemy fire touched off the explosives. The Germans, seeing the engineers working among the obstacles, seemed to single them out for special attention. As the teams tied on their charges, snipers took careful aim at the mines on the obstacles. At other times they seemed to wait until the engineers had prepared whole lines of steel trestles and tetrahedra obstacles for blowing. Then the Germans themselves would detonate the obstacles with mortar fire – before the engineers could get out of the area. By the end of the day casualties (dead and wounded) would be almost 50 percent" (Ryan, 1959, 1984, p. 228).

Harold Agerholm,
Racine,
Saipan,
Medal of Honor

Bibliography

Ambrose, Stephen E. (1994). D-Day June 6, 1944: The climactic battle of World War II. New York: Touchstone.

Brooke, James (2004). Saipan lacks Europe's pomp, but vets remember. New York Times, June 16. Accessed at www.signonsandiego.com/uniontrib/20040616/news_1n16pacific.html

D-Day veterans, www.6juin1944.com/veterans/shales.php.

Office of History, Army Corps of Engineers (undated). Combat engineers in World War II. www.hq.usace.army.mil

Goldberg, Harold J. (2007). D-Day in the Pacific: The battle of Saipan. Bloomington, Ind: Indiana University Press.

Marine Corps Historical Monograph, Saipan: The beginning of the end, by Maj. Carl Hoffman, www.ibiblio.org/hyperwar/USMC/USMC-M-Saipan/USMC-M-Saipan-2.html.

Marine veterans, www.leatherneck.com/forums/archive/index.php/t-15272.html

Masters, Charles J. (1995). Glidermen of Neptune: the American D-Day glider attack. Carbondale and Edwardsville: Southern Illinois University Press.

Medal of Honor citation for Harold Agerholm, www.history.army.mil/html/moh/wwII-a-f.html

Mrazek, James E. (1975). The glider war. London: Robert Hale & Co.

Mueller, Tom (1989). Tale of 2 vets reflects change in eras. Milwaukee Sentinel, May 29, p. 1, 8. Used with permission of Milwaukee Journal Sentinel.

Mueller, Tom (1985). Famous names recall wartime. Milwaukee Sentinel, May 1, p. 1, 7. Used with permission of Milwaukee Journal Sentinel.

Ryan, Cornelius (1959, 1984). The longest day. New York, NY: Simon & Schuster.

www.worldatwar.net

Other reading

Butcher, Capt. Harry C. (1946). My three years with Eisenhower 1942-1945. New York: Simon & Schuster Inc.

Dank, Milton (1977). The Glider Gang: An eyewitness history of World War II glider combat. Philadelphia: Lippincott.

Marine veterans of the 2nd Division: www.2marine.com

Marine veterans of the 4th Division: www.fightingfourth.com

Sledge, E.B. (1981). With the old breed: At Peleliu and Okinawa. New York: Oxford University Press.

Deaths in the heavy period from June 6 to 17, 1944

This list is compiled from the database of the American Battle Monuments Commission and cross-referenced with the 1946 official booklets of Navy / Marine losses (including hometown) and of Army / Air Force casualties (which lists only counties), and with Army enlistment records. This list gives a hometown for Army / Air Force men if it was found via other processes. If a serviceman is on an MIA monument, it is noted; otherwise he is buried.

June 6

Army 2nd Lt. Gilbert Allis Jr., Dane County, buried in Normandy

Navy Lt. Jg. Norman Bensman, Milwaukee, Normandy MIA wall

Army Pfc. Norton Feierday, Milwaukee, Normandy

Army Cpl. Edmund Greenwood, Sauk County, Normandy

Army Technician 5th Class William Hengst, Racine County, Normandy

Army Pvt. Frank Karafotis, Winnebago County, Normandy

Air Force Tech Sgt. Dave Kramer, Milwaukee County, Normandy

Air Force Staff Sgt. Albert Margotto, Barron County, Normandy MIA wall

Air Force 2nd Lt. Jack Martell, Milwaukee County, Normandy

Army Pfc. Gerald Rehfeldt, Appleton, Normandy

Army Pvt. Rolland Revels, Vernon County, Normandy

Army Pvt. Raymond Skaleski, Brown County, Normandy

Army Pvt. Edward Siemion, Milwaukee County, Normandy

Army Technician 5th Class Bruno Sievert, La Crosse County, Normandy

Army Pfc. Joseph Trainor, Dane County, Normandy

Army Pvt. Raymond Vosen, Sauk County, Normandy MIA wall

Army Tech 5 Sgt. William G. Weber, Milwaukee County, Normandy

Army Pfc. William H. Weber, Vilas County, Normandy

Army Pvt. James Wellinghoff, Milwaukee County, Normandy

June 7

Army Pvt. Arthur Doebert, Sheboygan County, buried in Normandy

Air Force 2nd Lt. John Hustis, Milwaukee County, Normandy

Air Force Flight Officer Sylvester Kempen, Manitowoc County, Normandy

Air Force 2nd Lt. Edgar Lynch, Dodge County, Manila

Army 2nd Lt. Irvin Mager, Milwaukee County, Normandy

Army Pvt. Lloyd Olson, La Crosse County, Normandy

June 8

Army Pvt. John Daum, Wood County, buried in Normandy

Army 2nd Lt. Richard Hansen, Milwaukee County, Manila

Air Force Staff Sgt. Robert Harder, La Crosse County, Honolulu

Navy Soundman 2nd Class Clifford Kalupa, Milwaukee, Normandy MIA wall

Navy Electrician's Mate 1st Class Edward Klopotic, Pulaski, Normandy MIA wall

Navy Water Tender 1st Class Melvin Lambert, hometown not listed in booklet, Normandy MIA wall

Navy Machinst's Mate 1st Class Ralph Thompson, Milwaukee, Normandy MIA wall

Army Pfc. Raymond Tucker, Kenosha County, Normandy

Army Technician 4th Class Carl Zahn, Door County, Manila

June 9

Army Sgt. Salvador Flores, Milwaukee County, buried in Normandy

Army Pfc. Rudolph Knapp, Crawford County, Sicily-Rome

Army Staff Sgt. John Selmer, Eau Claire County, Normandy

June 10

Army Staff Sgt. Carl Becherer, Milwaukee County, buried in Normandy

Air Force Sgt. Warren Brunn, Milwaukee County, Manila MIA wall

Army Sgt. Ernest Hetzke, Chippewa County, Normandy

Army 2nd Lt. William Lechnir, Grant County, Normandy

June 11

Air Force 2nd Lt. Paul Cermak, Milwaukee County, MIA wall in Brittany

Navy Ammunition Machinist's Mate 3rd Class Lloyd Chouinard, hometown not listed in booklet, MIA on East Coast Memorial

Army Chaplain Capt. Raymond Hansen, Eau Claire County, buried in Normandy

Air Force Sgt. Lisle Hole, Richland County, Brittany

Army Pvt. Albert Jaeger, Milwaukee County, Normandy

Army Pfc. Allan Johnson, Oconto County, Normandy

Army Pvt. Samuel Meek, La Crosse County, Normandy

Army Staff Sgt. Raymond Pedley, Kenosha County, Cambridge, England

Air Force 1st Lt. Glenn Read, Milwaukee County, MIA wall in Brittany

June 12

Army Pvt. Fred Falkner, Milwaukee County, buried in Sicily-Rome

Army Pvt. Vernon La Page, Brown County, Manila

Air Force Staff Sgt. Melvin Masek, Richland County, Manila MIA wall

Army 1st Lt. David Neville, Milwaukee County, Normandy

Air Force Tech Sgt. Laurence Snifka, Milwaukee County, Ardennes in Belgium

June 13

Army Tech 4 Sgt. Leonard Simon, Winnebago County, buried in Cambridge

Army Tech 5 Sgt. Joseph Slosarczyk, Milwaukee County, Normandy

Army Sgt. Maurice Strutz, Outagamie County, Manila

June 14

Army Technician 5th Class Daniel Koziel, Milwaukee County, buried in Normandy

Air Force Capt. Joseph Marr, Lafayette County, Brittany

Air Force Pfc. Joseph Mauer, Fond du Lac County, Sicily-Rome

Air Force 2nd Lt. Russell Schroeder, Oconto County, Epinal, France

Army Pvt. William Shipley, Chippewa County, Normandy

June 15

Marine 1st Lt. Clifford Ahasay, De Pere, Honolulu MIA wall

Marine Cpl. Walter Brown, Madison, buried in Honolulu

Marine Pfc. Bertram Hoyer, Winnecone, Honolulu MIA wall

Marine 1st Lt. Morris Kessier, Montello, Honolulu

Marine Sgt. Eugene Kuehl, Milwaukee, Honolulu

Army Pfc. Ray Larson, Douglas County, Normandy

Army Pfc. Raymond Merchlevich, Racine County, Manila

Marine Cpl. Merlin Mosey, La Crosse, Honolulu

Air Force Cpl. Robert Nerby, Winnebago County, Sicily-Rome

Marine Pfc. Willis Oftedahl, Viroqua, Honolulu MIA wall

Army Tech Sgt. Matthew Petek, Milwaukee County, Cambridge

Army Pfc. Robert Poehling, home county not available, but enlisted via Milwaukee, Normandy

Air Force 1st Lt. William Roycraft, Douglas County, Normandy

Marine Cpl. Joseph Rutkowski, Racine, Honolulu

Navy Radio 3 Gordon Schirmer, Goodman, Normandy MIA wall

Marine Pfc. Theodore Schleicher, Kenosha, Honolulu MIA wall.

Marine Sgt. Maj. John Sollien, Wausaukee, Honolulu

Marine Pfc. Clayton Verhagen, Kimberly, Honolulu

June 16

Army Tech Sgt. Norman Anderson, Ashland County, buried in Normandy

Marine Pfc. Robert Birk, Milwaukee, Honolulu MIA wall

Navy Ens. William Brannon, Madison, Honolulu MIA wall

Marine Pfc. Lawrence Knop, Union Grove, Honolulu

Army Sgt. Jack Marinko, Florence, Italy

June 17

Marine Pfc. Robert Baldeshwiler, hometown not listed in booklet, buried in Honolulu

Army Technician 5th Class William Bratz, Manitowoc County, Manila MIA wall

Air Force Maj. Wayne Brown, Clark County, Cambridge

Navy Motor Machinist's Mate 3rd Class Joseph Keller, Hawkins (Rusk County), Honolulu MIA wall

Marine Pfc. William Larson, hometown not listed in booklet, Honolulu MIA wall

Marine Sgt. Herb Rieder, Madison, Honolulu

Army 1st Lt. Leo Sadler, Milwaukee County, Normandy

Marine Sgt. William Schneider, Merrill, Honolulu

Army Pfc. Edward Spikula, Milwaukee County, Normandy

Navy Seaman 2nd Class Robert Ulrich, Westfield, Manila MIA wall

Chapter 7:

One day in Hedgerow Hell

Author's note: Most of the quotes for this chapter were gathered in 2003 and 2004 in a separate project about four of the men. Some of those interviewed died in the next few years. The fifth man from Aug. 1, Harvey Hyllested of Rice Lake, is being added for this book.

On Aug. 1, 1944, fighting raged all across northwestern France as the long-overdue Allied breakout from Normandy finally was underway, with tens of thousands of American forces beginning to race ahead and soon encircle a massive German army. Action also was hot in Italy, where Rome had fallen on June 4 after months of fighting but Germans still had to be rousted to the north, which would take nearly a year. There also were bomber raids galore, as thousands of Allied planes flying from bases in Britain pummeled factories and other targets all over Germany. The invasion of southern France would begin in a couple weeks.

And in Asia, fighting was heavy in New Guinea. The United States had just invaded Guam and took Saipan amid heavy losses a month earlier, and ships battled air and sea attacks, too.

The newspaper headlines focused on war, war, war and more war. For 3 cents in Milwaukee County and a nickel outside the county, readers could explore the reports galore in the Milwaukee Sentinel. "New MacArthur Landing Traps 15,000 Guinea Japs," the black sans-serif font blared in two lines of all-capital letters across the top of the page, above the paper's name. Then came a deck that added, "200 Mile Jump Puts Yanks 600 Mi From Philippines." On the other side of the page was a headline that focused on France and Poland: "Yanks Capture Avranches; Reds At Gate of Warsaw." The deck headline on the story about the fighting in France said, "Drive On Toward Brittany; Capture Perils Nazi Defense." The first paragraph of the story called it "pivotal Avranches."

Ken Miller,
Appleton

Martin Miller,
Waunakee

Andy Popielarski,
Milwaukee

Billie Weiss,
Baileys Harbor

Harvey Hyllested,
Rice Lake

The war map on page 2 of the Sentinel had a caption that said there was a "sensational 12-mile dash to Avranches." This map included a major crossroads city named St. Lo to the northeast, where there had been heavy fighting over the weeks, and a town named Percy a few miles south of St. Lo.

Percy.

The name would be branded forever into the hearts and minds of five Wisconsin families. In one Army infantry division in one small part of this giant war, five state men – Pvt. Martin Miller of Waunakee, Sgt. Ken Miller of Appleton, Pfc. Billie Weiss of Baileys Harbor, Pfc. Andy Popielarski of Milwaukee and Pvt. Harvey Hyllested of Rice Lake – were just north of Percy, beginning their second day of combat amid the bloody and pulverized and dusty and smelly maelstrom of Normandy. It was their final day of combat, too.

On Aug. 1, 1944, there are six Wisconsin deaths recorded in the database of the American Battle Monuments Commission of soldiers buried overseas or MIA. Five of those six came on a single hill at Percy – Hill 210 – and they were members of the 28th Infantry Division (the sixth was Marine Pvt. Robert McVey of Beloit, probably on Guam, which had been invaded on July 21; he is buried at Honolulu).

In France, American tanks were roaring through a small hole in the German lines that had been blasted out a few days earlier in one of the heaviest bombing campaigns of the war, kicking off Operation Cobra. Death was coming on a scale of thousands or even tens of thousands. Dozens of the dead were Americans who were killed by Allied bombs a few days earlier, when more than a few pilots missed their narrow target. To the sides of that hole, hundreds of thousands of Allied forces also attacked and held off any possible German reinforcements. Within a few weeks, what began on D-Day and had proceeded slowly, sometimes agonizingly so, finally would end in the liberation of France. At the end of August, the 28th Division – minus Weiss, Miller, Miller, Hyllested and Popielarski – would be marching past the Arc d'Triomphe in Paris in a victory parade.

Martin Miller was a carrier of ammunition and Ken Miller was a leader of a squad of riflemen; both of them in Company A of the 112th Regiment. Popielarski was in D Company, a weapons group that included heavy machine guns and mortars, and Weiss was a rifleman in Company F. It is not known what Hyllested's duty was in the 110th Regiment, but the main duty of an infantryman is to shoot.

Popielarski and Hyllested were only 20. Weiss was 11 days shy of his 23rd birthday. Ken Miller had turned 24 less than a month earlier, and Martin Miller was almost 25.

Two views of Percy

Troops from the 28th Division enter Percy, France, on Aug. 1, 1944. The division's history book has this caption: "Alert soldiers examine Percy, first town captured by the 28th 'Keystoners.'" Five of the division's men from Wisconsin – Martin Miller, Ken Miller, Andy Popielarski, Billie Weiss and Harvey Hyllested – were killed that day on Hill 210 outside Percy or within the town itself.

The small town of Percy lies along Highway D-999, named the Liberty Highway. This photo is from 1984 and is on the northern edge of the town.

Ken Miller

Kenneth Charles Miller, the only child of Willis and Edith Miller of 216 N. Meade St. in Appleton, was a soldier of another kind, always signing letters to his parents with a salute to the highest authority: "A very Happy New Year in the Lord Jesus Christ," "Your loving son in God," "Your loving son in the Lord," "Your loving Christian son," "Your son in Christ."

Ken lived his Christian Missionary Alliance religion on a daily basis. The Millers originally had belonged to the First United Methodist Episcopal Church at Drew and Franklin Streets near their home, but later helped organize the new congregation that would become the focus of their lives.

In a letter on Christmas Day 1942 from Camp Livingston, La., the draftee who had been in the Army only three months said other men had defiled the true meaning of Christmas: "Last night we had a small Christmas party. You may call it anything you like. They had some singing. Only one song had a Christmas thought and they sure made awful light of that. They also cracked jokes which some do not bear repeating. After this they gave each of us a small gift for the sake of laughter. I sure was lost last night."

Ken listed each item in the big turkey dinner that was served, but added: "I sure had my chance but didn't use it. I believe I ate the least I have eaten at a meal. I sure didn't feel very hungry."

Ken wrote: "There isn't anyone around to give me any Christian encouragement. My encouragement comes from the Lord himself through his precious word. I sure have been digging in the scriptures daily for guidance each day. He sure is my close friend. ... I do enjoy reading. I sure do a lot of it now. That is about my only enjoyment around camp. There isn't much one can do and live up to his Christian teachings."

Ken was using a special envelope from a religious printer. The envelope had this New Testament verse printed in blue in what ordinarily is the return address area: "Follow peace with all men and holiness without which no man shall see the Lord. Hebrews 12:14"

In another letter on Feb. 6, 1943, while in training at Camp Gordon Johnston, Fla., Ken said he turns to the Bible after long days of Army maneuvers, duties, procedures and the like. "I find myself pretty much to myself. ... I have started reading the Bible through again. I find it much more interesting this way. You get the complete idea or thought this way."

Carol Parker of Neenah, one of Ken's three cousins and the only one old enough to remember him, says Ken's family lived their faith on a daily basis. "Uncle Will said the longest prayers in the world at every meal. We'd look around and ask if he is ever going to finish." But the family was fun to be with, and did not try to convert her family into their church. "Kenny was much more down to earth compared to his parents, and he was religious but not fanatical at all. He was always smiling and having fun."

Willis Miller sold Watkins products, such as cleaning goods and soaps, going door to door on a regular route. He also painted houses. Edith was a cleaning woman at nearby Lawrence University. "They worked hard but they never had very much," Parker says.

Ken had a plan for after the war: He would come back to Appleton and back to Heckert Shoes, the downtown store where he worked several years for his Uncle Earl (Parker's father) and the founder, Herman Heckert. He aimed to become Earl's partner after Mr. Heckert would retire. "I always felt real close to Kenny. He was like a brother to me," Earl said.

Heckert Shoes was located at 119 E. College Ave., although today it is next door at 123 E. College. It has been in business well over 100 years. The building is known for more than just shoes: A historical plaque on the store says that from 1874 to 1883, Rabbi Mayer Samuel Weiss conducted religious services and Torah studies and taught Hebrew upstairs above what at that time was Heckert's Saloon, precursor of the much-tamer business of shoes. Weiss is not a household name, but his son Ehrich became famous around the world: Houdini.

Ehrich was born in Budapest, Hungary, in 1874, the same year his father began using the Heckert building. Four years later, he arrived in Appleton with his mother, Cecelia, and four brothers. In 1887, the Weisses moved to New York.

"Kenny was a happy-go-lucky kid" who liked to hunt, fish, play baseball and was active in the Boy Scouts," Earl Miller said. The tall and thin boy played in the outfield on his baseball team and "with his long legs, he could really go after long fly balls."

Ken's senior report card in 1937-'38 listed his homeroom as 304, run by no-nonsense Adela Klumb, leader of the English department. His first-semester grade for the class called Book was a U for unsatisfactory, and was marked for standard messages such as No. 10, "lack of interest and ambition;" 21, "fundamentals not mastered;" 27, "daily assignments and written work neglected;" and 37, "satisfied with poor work."

His other subjects, however, earned Ken the M mark, for Moderately Sufficient. They were U.S. History, Office Practice, and Non-English 7. All in all, Parker – who would later teach English at the same school and become a department colleague of the same Miss Klumb – said his marks show he was a mediocre student.

Somewhere along the way, at some sort of regional convention of their church, Edith and Willis Miller met Rev. Lowell O. Bodie from Chillicothe, Ill. Bodie apparently arranged for Ken Miller to meet his daughter, Lucille, who was four or five years older. The rest is history – the wedding was on Saturday, June 13, 1942, and Ken was three weeks shy of turning age 22. The service was at 7:30 p.m., with Rev. Bodie officiating and thus marrying off his own daughter. The couple posed for pictures under a large sign that said, "Believe on the Lord Jesus Christ and thou shall be saved." Why the sign said "believe on," instead of "in," is not evident. The reception was held at the home of Ken's parents on North Meade, according to the Appleton newspaper.

A few months later, the paper ran another matter-of-fact story that mentioned Ken – it said he and 51 other draftees entered the Army on Sept. 29, 1942, taking the train from Appleton to Fort Sheridan in Illinois.

Martin Miller

In Fort Sheridan and many other forts and military installations to come, Miller would be around another Miller. On Sept. 2, 1942, the Selective Service System mailed Martin Miller an induction notice requiring him to report at precisely 5:15 a.m. on Sept. 14 at Room 305 of the Washington Building in Madison. He was in the Army, now.

Growing up in the Waunakee and Dane areas a few miles north of Madison, Martin's world was full of these things: siblings, relatives, priests and farming.

Martin was the second of nine children of John Miller and Anna Haeusler. John was from the Dane area and Anna from Milwaukee. They met when she was serving as the housekeeper for her oldest brother, Father George Haeusler, in John's hometown.

Many families around Waunakee and Dane, prime farming areas in Dane County, had bumper crops of kids in that era, and one major reason was necessity – farms needed workers. John Miller was one of 12 children. His mother, Margaret Hein Miller, was age 3 when her family arrived from Wiltingen in western Germany near the Luxembourg border in 1854. On this voyage, her infant brother Peter died and was buried at sea, and the family was shipwrecked for a time in Ireland. She married Peter Miller, who had come by himself as a teenager from the nearby German town of Trassem.

Margaret's 12 children multiplied into an incredible 108 grandchildren, a fertility bonanza that is made even more astounding by the fact there were no twins or any other multiple births. The amount even made the first paragraph of her obituary in 1946 in the local newspaper, and at her funeral, the grandchildren lined both sides of the sidewalk as the coffin was brought to the hearse.

That rich reproduction rate was on the father's side of the family. On Martin's maternal side, the Haeuslers, there were only four first cousins, all of whom were from Plymouth, a few miles west of Sheboygan. Three of them were to become Roman Catholic priests – Lawrence Andre, Raymond Andre and Leonard Andre, all brothers. There also were three uncles – Father George Haeusler, Father

John and Father Joachim, commonly called Father Jochy. And there were dozens of second cousins, the Bunzels, in Milwaukee. So no family gathering was small, or quiet.

Every Fourth of July, the three uncle priests visited their sister, Anna Haeusler Miller, for her birthday and it always was a day of guffawing, cooking and eating for Martin and his siblings. The very Roman Catholic family in a very Roman Catholic area looked up to priests anyway, but when you had some as your own uncles!

"One time we went to Jefferson during the week and a nun heard me calling him Uncle John instead of Father John, and gave me holy hell for being disrespectful to a priest. She figured I was just a local boy," says Herb Miller, the youngest child.

Genevieve Wild, Martin Miller's youngest sister, says Father George "was a sweetheart of a man. Kind, gentle. Nothing shocked him. He heard it all before. In Sun Prairie (where he was pastor), he grew all these beautiful gladiolas. A whole acre of them. That was his hobby, and everyone around Sun Prairie knew about it." Another sibling, Caroline Miller Nye, says: "Father George always said that he felt close to God when he was digging in the dirt."

He also wrote music, one piece of which was played on the organ at the funeral of Pauline Damp, their sister, decades later. In the 1950s, he was made a monsignor. He also loved food like Morell hams and roast beef. "My mom, who was 12 years younger than him, always said he taught her how to cook," Caroline says.

Martin Miller and his brother Robert were well-known for playing euchre at Chambers tavern in Waunakee, and for imbibing in the beverage of the house. Martin would win caramels in board games, and bring them home for his youngest siblings. The bar often was a bigger draw to Martin and Robert than Sunday dinner, and the Miller women finally made it a rule that they would start putting the food away at a certain time if the bar brothers had not come home.

The family moved every few years, because John Miller worked as a herdsman for various farms and had to live on-site. One stop was two miles outside Dane, then it moved into town and John Miller worked for his brother Tony. Then it moved to a farm near Lodi for four or five years. Then back to Dane. "There was always an empty house somewhere for us. We lived in this one house a couple times," says Florence Miller Mueller (yes, she married a man with a name pronounced the same way), the first-born.

The kids attended St. John the Baptist School in Waunakee, walking there every day from the farm, a trek of a couple miles. "I would make Martin run from one telephone pole to another, and then we would walk to the next. Just he and I were going to school. We were the only ones old enough." When the family went to church in winter, it took a horse and sleigh; in the summer, a horse with a buggy.

Amid the Depression, Florence stopped school after eighth grade in 1933 and moved out in order to make money to send home by being a maid and caregiver for a few other families. She was able to come home for a few hours on Sundays. Florence even drove a doctor's convertible and his children to the Gulf Coast of Mississippi, but when the war started the most lucrative work was at Rayovac. Just like their father worked at Allis-Chalmers in West Allis during a previous war boom, Florence and Martin did factory work.

"Martin got to be big like his Dad," co-worker Wilferd Mueller says. "He was a husky guy working in the shipping department at Rayovac, lifting 75-pound batteries. One day he walked into my department, yelling, 'Who is this guy who is going out with my sister?' But he was nice," quite a lively character like the rest of his brothers. And when Wilferd prowled the bars and dance halls in the area, he would see Martin all the time. "Everybody was a friend of his."

Many called him "Ting" because of his time hanging out at Corky Meyer's gas station, and Martin signed all his letters home, "Your brother and son, Ting."

Martin went to one year of high school in Waunakee, but soon thereafter was working on the farm, for other farms, and then went into the Civilian Conservation Corps, the Depression jobs program. Martin was based at Elcho in Langlade County; his sister Genevieve says she had never heard of a porcupine until Martin described one in a letter.

Billie Weiss

Billie Weiss would have told many tales about porcupines and other animals – his childhood in tiny Baileys Harbor was the stuff of pure Americana, from his family's log cabin to the endless tranquil days that the red-haired, freckle-faced boy and his friends spent on Huck Finn-style expeditions of fishing, prowling for frogs and snakes, and gathering Indian arrowheads. The town, then and now, is unincorporated but up sharply during tourist season.

Billie was the youngest of five children of Moritz and Agnes (Pedersen) Weiss, born Aug. 12, 1921, in a log house that had a kitchen, living room, and a ladder to two loft-style bedrooms. The little house was not much fancier than what Laura Ingalls Wilder described in her days on the prairie in Minnesota and South Dakota. "The kids all slept upstairs," says Charles Tischler, a boyhood friend. "The ladder went straight up through a hole in the ceiling, and his mother had a cow in the backyard that she milked daily."

Moritz Weiss worked a small farm for a time, then was assistant keeper at the 1869 lighthouse on Cana Island near Baileys Harbor, still a popular attraction for tourists today. When wartime came, Moritz and many others worked in the shipyards of Sturgeon Bay.

Betty Weiss, a North Dakota native, met Billie's brother Eugene after World War II and married him in 1948. Eugene was in the Army's 32nd Division, the Wisconsin Red Arrow, and fought in New Guinea and the Philippines. They lived next to the site of the Weiss family's log home. The foundation is covered by ferns, and amid the ferns and the tall conifers is a perfectly circular bed for wildflowers, with a stone border that Billie built.

Betty also has a wooden recipe box containing about two dozen arrowheads that young Billie gathered from the soil of the family's garden and in his other meanderings in town and nearby. It has the initials BW (for himself) and BH (for his town) carved into the box. "Where he lived was a sandy ridge. Whenever they plowed for their garden, they found arrowheads," Tischler said.

Cousin Leo Weise, who spells his name differently, calls Billie a "skinny little fella. He got his red hair from his mother. His sister Ruby had freckles like Billie, but no red hair."

Orville Voeks, another pal, says Billie had so many freckles that it was almost one big freckle over his whole face." The story in the Door County Advocate reporting Billie's death used "Red" Weiss in the headline, and the text said he was William "Red" Weiss.

One of Billie's exploits in the 1930s made the newspaper. Under the headline, "See 16-lb. Fish, Go After Tackle and Make Catch," the Advocate reported in a short story datelined Baileys Harbor:

> "It is quite often one sees a big fish swimming in the water, only to find that he is gone when he comes back with tackle and bait to catch him. It was different with Parker Mullen Jr. and William Weiss, local 14-year-olds, last Friday. For their trip home and a little patience, the boys landed a 16-pound pickerel in the harbor here. Their picture was taken with the fish, but it was not finished in time for publication this week."
>
> "Trying to find out the spot such big ones inhabit is like finding a needle in a haystack.
>
> "'That's what everybody asks us,' is the boys' only reply.
>
> "Parker caught the fish casting, and William helped land him, using a spear."

When the photo did run, it showed the two boys each holding the end of a heavy stick with the strong fish hanging from the middle. It is an open question as to which is bigger – the fish or their own smiles.

Tischler chuckles as he recalls how Billie would sneak his father's .22-caliber bolt action Savage rifle, with a five-shot clip, out of the cabin by dropping it down his overalls. The boys used it early and often on red squirrels. Eventually, Voeks says, "His dad bought him a .22. He became an excellent shot with that .22. You could throw a rock and he would shoot it out of the air."

Billie and Orville were inseparable, no matter what was the activity du jour. "We were together from morning to night. He'd come to my place before I was awake. So I tied a string around my big toe, pushed it out the screen, and he'd pull it to make me up," Voeks says. The tug usually came between 6 or 7 a.m.

More than seven decades later, Voeks glowed when talking about his many activities with Red. "Billie gave me a slingshot, a perfect fork of red willow. We were both excellent shots. He also gave me an iron hoop about 10 inches in diameter, and a stick to roll it down the street. I prized them very much."

Harvey Hyllested

Deep within the DNA of Harvey Hyllested or Rice Lake were generations of flower growing and outdoor activities, especially ice fishing in the long winters of northern Wisconsin.

Harvey Edwin Hyllested was the fourth of five children of Hans and Alma Hyllested, born on Nov. 8, 1923. He had three brothers – Robert, Don and the younger DeWayne, and one sister, Camilla, the first-born.

Brother Bob was serving in an Air Force Aviation Engineer brigade in Alaska, the Aleutians and Okinawa, and brother Don also was in the Army, soon to be in the Battle of the Bulge. This comes from Eunice Hyllested of Rice Lake, a Seattle native who was a civilian government employee and met Bob on a troop ship heading to Alaska. She later served in the Women's Army Corps and married him in March 1945 in Seattle. Eunice never met Harvey, but heard many discussions about him in the following decades among his family and cousins.

Hans and Alma owned West Side Greenhouses on Phipps Avenue, right in their yard. It started with one greenhouse in 1927 and blossomed from there, creating and growing spring bedding plants there and selling them to everybody in town. Harvey and all his siblings potted, watered, nurtured and sold the plants.

A 1962 article in the Rice Lake newspaper, The Chronotype, said Hans Hyllested was tearing down his old greenhouses at the age of 69, but would be building one 8 by 16 feet to play around in during retirement, working on creating hybrids of perennials like monkshood and coral bells. It was back to the future in a way, because his first one was the same size, "built of storm windows from the old Tourist hotel after it was gutted by fire."

It noted that "a number of years ago he developed a special tomato strain which produced 3,000 tomatoes per plant but as it turned out the tomatoes ripened a little too late for this area and about the time they were turning, the season was over."

It also said: "He averaged 100,000 plants a year and sold just about all of them. This year he planted 116,000 plants including 5,000 potted plants." His own garden had "beautiful delphinium, some standing nearly eight feet high."

Earlier in his career, the paper said, the senior Hyllested was a cement finisher who helped build Rice Lake High School and laid streets for the Works Progress Administration during the Depression, and was in the Secret Service for seven years, although it did not list where he was based, or say whether he ever directly protected a president. As a younger man he "was employed at the famous Stout Lone Pine estate as gardener and florist."

Stout was Frank Deming Stout, a Wisconsin lumber baron from Chicago. The lodge was a summer retreat on what was known as the Island of Happy Days, was built between 1909 and 1911 and designed by Chicago architect Arthur Huen. Stout, who died in 1927, called the island of "the dearest place on earth" (www.wisconsinhistory.org/hp/register/viewSummary.asp?refnum=95000141)

James Huff Stout, his son, founded what is now the University of Wisconsin – Stout in Menomonie in 1891, worked in his father's lumber business, was a leader in creating traveling libraries, and was a state senator.

The Rice Lake paper said Hans Hyllested once "took Max Schilling, renowned florist; J.C. Penney and Mr. Hershey of the chocolate makers family on a fishing trip on Cedar Lake when they visited the area to attend an auction on the Stout farm. 'The fish were biting very well that day,' he said, 'and I was tickled because they enjoyed the Wisconsin fishing.'"

That was the real James Cash Penney, whose chain of stores started in the early 1900s and went nationwide in the 1920s. He was born in 1875 in Missouri and died in 1971. The Hershey company was founded by Milton Hershey in 1894 in Lancaster, Pa. Hershey was born in 1857 and died in 1945. Guiding a boat of such business tycoons was a sweet day, a milk chocolate day and Hyllested no doubt regaled his sons and daughter with the story for years.

Harvey was born when the family lived in Cedar Lake, and it moved to nearby Rice Lake soon thereafter.

The Hyllested boys were Northwoods strong, in keeping with the heritage of the lumberjacks of a few decades earlier. Don was 6-foot-4 and husky, and Bob was 6-1. "Harvey was tall as they all were, but he was slimmer, had fine facial features and thick, very curly hair," Eunice says.

They would fish in any season, but Harvey had a particular passion for ice fishing, his cousins recall. The boys also were big hunters – deer, rabbits, grouse; anything "to put meat on the table," Eunice says.

They attended Jefferson School, but Harvey was "ill a lot as a boy and missed a lot of school and was old for his class," and did not complete high school. He worked for a time in St. Paul, Minn., in a meatpacking plant.

The family home, about six blocks from Rice Lake the lake, "was a very small white house, a cottage, with three tiny bedrooms," says Eunice, who still lives across the street.

The family attended Bethany Lutheran on West Messenger Street. Harvey's mother was Swedish and Norwegian. The father's side was very Danish, and Eunice notes there is a town named Hyllested in the old country. The town is in Djursland, on the east coast of the Jutland peninsula.

Andy Popielarski

Down in Milwaukee, another family had a son who became an infantryman on Hill 210, and he would not have known much about farming, flowers or adventures in the woods. His stomping grounds were in a solidly working-class, ethnic-immigrant city, where there were two things at almost every intersection: a family-run grocery store and a bar. The fundamental needs of all families, conveniently located. And always within walking distance was a church, each parish organized by and for immigrants from a certain country – one for the Polish, one for the Irish, one for the Germans.

Such was the case at North Bremen Street and East Auer Avenue, a few miles north of downtown. The Popielarski grocery store was run by Vincent and Frances Popielarski (pronounced POP-ill-are-ski), along with their five sons and three daughters, with grandchildren helping out or hanging around. Across Bremen immediately to the east was Benny's tavern. Two blocks away, on Burleigh Street, was St. Mary of Czestochowa church and school, named for the shrine back in the old country, Poland.

Andy was born on Feb. 4, 1924, one of the younger ones in the family, although exactly what number he was has been lost between generations.

Vincent, the father, started the store and Leo, the second son, was to take it over a few years after World War II. The store was on the northwest corner of the intersection, 832 E. Auer, and Leo Popielarski at one time lived on the southeast corner, then moved right above the store. "We were in one of the three apartments; two were upstairs and one in back of the store," says Joe Popielarski of Greenfield, son of Leo and grandson of the founder.

His grandparents lived in a bungalow a block and a half to the north, at 3334 N. Bremen. St. Mary's was one block south and one block west of the store. "All the Popielarski kids, including myself, went through the grade school there," Joe says. "That's a lot of years."

Evie Triscari Schulist, of Milwaukee, went to grade school with Andy for eight years at St. Mary's, but says her most outstanding memory is that there is no outstanding memory. "Andy was a very quiet guy. He would be in the background, not like me. I talk a lot. … He was in my classroom. He was such a quiet guy, not outstanding in a crowd. He was there but not there."

Florence Rosenek Truss also had firm roots at St. Mary's. "I was baptized there, made my First Communion there, made my confirmation there and got married there," says Truss, who was in school with Eddie Popielarski, one of Andy's older brothers, graduating in 1929. When she was first married, she remained in the neighborhood and Leo Popielarski delivered groceries to Truss and her young daughters.

In the fall of 1941, a non-family member was hired – Dolores Tarkowski, who belonged to St. Casimir's parish and had graduated from the public Riverwest High School a few months earlier. Dolores was taking a class in business and heard from her father that the store was looking for a clerk, so she applied and was hired right away. She worked from 7 a.m. to 8 or 9 p.m. six days a week, stocking, carrying out groceries, running the cash register and everything else. At this time, Andy was a junior at Messmer High School, the parochial school that drew a lot of kids from St. Mary's.

What happens to more than a few co-workers eventually happened to Dolores and Andy, sure as kielbasa and beer were popular in Milwaukee. "I just thought he was a nice guy. … He was very quiet and tall and slim. He came from a very good family – honest, hard-working."

Tarkowski, whose last name eventually became Gliszczinski, adds: "We went out a couple times. It wasn't that we could be quite in the open," because her family was not very well-to-do and the Popielarskis not only owned the food store; the father also owned the Pulaski Savings and Loan. Andy went into the military right after graduating from Messmer in 1943, and Dolores wrote a lot and sent packages. This is where the relationship blossomed well beyond what it was in Milwaukee – "Most of it happened while he was in the service."

She went to see him in Virginia in the fall of 1943, just before he went overseas; a visit that her parents allowed only because she went with another local woman. It was there that Dolores and Andy became engaged. Sort of.

"I didn't know if he was coming back," Gliszczinski says, a common fear of brides, brides-to-be, girlfriends and just friends in the war, the same as the prevalent fear in families. "He sent his sister some money around Christmas 1943. I said I would like a cedar chest in lieu of a ring. I was not sure exactly what was going to happen to him."

Messmer High School's 1943 yearbook, the Capitol, lists 41 February graduates and 192 June grads, including Andy. It said he participated in Sodality – one of three religious clubs – band, orchestra and the Polish Club.

Sodality was composed of homeroom representatives and met monthly to discuss what the yearbook calls spiritual and temporal matters. One of its events was "A Day of Spiritual Stimulation." The Polish Club met twice a month with the goal of keeping alive the spirit of Polish traditions. It sang various pieces from the old country and discussed matters about the famous writers of Poland. There were 49 members in Popielarski's senior year.

Andy was a freshman in September 1939, a major date in world history, as Hitler invaded Poland on the first of that month.

The 5 prepare for war

Ken Miller was the only one of the five men who died on Hill 210 to advance beyond private or private first class. His letters home in 1942 and 1943 discuss his gradual climb into more important jobs, such as a runner of messages, a mail clerk and a corporal tech 5. He would die in the hedgerows as a sergeant and leader of a small squad of riflemen. So he clearly was a born leader in terms of the Army field manual. He may have read his Bible at night while other draftees did the things that young men far away from home are apt to do, such as prowl a base and a town looking for liquid refreshment and hot action, but he clearly had a good way of leading. This no doubt came from his work experience in Appleton, and from leadership roles at his church, such as teaching Sunday school. And he already had been married for a few months, so he perhaps had a maturity level higher than most of the unmarried soldiers.

On Oct. 8, 1943, the 28th Division left Boston to go overseas, and arrived in south Wales on Oct. 18. It spent months on maneuvers and various other forms of training preparing for the invasion of Europe.

The St. Mary's Breeze, a special newsletter created by Milwaukee parish during the war, discussed the Popielarskis in several of its issues. In December 1943 it noted: "One of the ushers, Mr. Vincent Popielarski, has three sons in the service, Vincent Jr., Edward and Andrew, they are all across," meaning on the other side of the Atlantic.

The general view of the parish and America was summed up thusly: "We, on the home front, were thankful this year that you boys made it possible for us to 'Hail Mary' instead of 'Heil Hitler.'"

The February 1944 issue reported in the section called Contact Notes: "A bit of news from two of the Popielarski brothers, overseas. Cpl. Edward, stationed somewhere in Northern Ireland, enjoys reading the 'Breeze' and says he is coming along just fine. Pvt. Andy, stationed in England, visited London and had a swell time seeing many interesting and educational places like Westminster Abbey and Big Ben." The April 1944 issue said Vincent sent home a V-mail letter "that they had the pleasure of meeting General Montgomery," meaning that British commander Bernard Law Montgomery was on an inspection tour.

Billie Weiss also reported on a VIP visitor. What is likely the only surviving letter from Weiss was written on April 2, 1944. The day was Palm Sunday, Billie noted in dating the V-mail letter. Weiss' hometown is so small that the post office would easily find his parents, and he addressed it only to: "Mr. Mrs. Moritz Weiss, Baileys Harbor Wisconsin".

"I hope this finds you both well, I didn't get any letters last week. I don't suppose there is much going on around home now anyway. Yesterday we had a chance to see Gen. Eisenhower, something we won't forget for quite a while. There isn't anything doing here on Sunday. About the only thing we can do is go to church and the Red Cross Club, all the other public places are closed on Sunday."

The history of the 28th Division confirms that on April 1, Ike inspected its troops at Margam Castle, Port Talbot, Wales. Two days later, he wrote to Maj. Gen. Lloyd Brown, division commander, that he was "filled with pride at the obvious fitness, appearance and all-around efficiency of the units which I inspected. They impress me as being serious and determined and I am well satisfied that they will give a good account of themselves in the difficult task which lies before us." D-Day was only two months away, and action – and death – were only four months off for these men.

At some point in the spring, Company A posed for a photo. The heads are very small, but siblings remembered where Martin Miller was, and an enlargement of that area shows the bespectacled Ken Miller was only a few feet away.

War was getting closer. D-Day came and went and the 28th Division remained in England. Two weeks later, on June 19, Martin Miller again gave his typical first line but showed boredom, impatience and tension:

> "Dear Sister & All:
>
> "I received your letter and was glad to hear from you again.
>
> "I am just fine and sure am glad to hear that you are also.
>
> "We have very few beautiful days over here it is about time we get some over here.
>
> "There is not a thing to do here also but lay around camp. There is nothing to drink in town at all. The only one over here that gets anything to drink is the priest at mass."

Into the maelstrom

Amid the slow progress after D-Day, with the Allies advancing in a period of weeks a distance that optimistic planners had thought would take only days, Eisenhower considered the possibility of another beach landing elsewhere to take the pressure off Normandy. "The 28th Division, trained for amphibious operations and originally scheduled for the Overlord assault, had remained in England in ... reserve, ready to execute a subsidiary amphibious operation if necessary. The only amphibiously trained force still uncommitted 20 days after the invasion, the 28th Division was released ... to the First U.S. Army Group on 26 June with the condition that it be used only in an amphibious assault" (Blumenson, 1961, p. 187).

On July 13, that proviso was withdrawn, and 10 days later the 28th moved to France. It arrived at Omaha Beach July 26 and 27 – note the short number of days between that date and the fateful Aug. 1.

At about this time, the 900,000 Americans in Normandy were crammed into and behind a front that was only 40 miles wide, roughly the distance between Madison and Janesville or from Appleton to Fond du Lac.

But from mid-July to mid-August 1944, in the span of only a month, the very nature of the war in Europe changed from one in which more than 1 million Allied forces were still bottled up in Normandy to one in which the Germans were on the run, Paris was liberated and victory in Europe seemed to be just around the corner.

During that period, the major crossroads city of St. Lo was seized by Americans after weeks of battle but was demolished by the fighting and months of bombing. And German generals tried to assassinate Adolf Hitler with a bomb, but he was only slightly injured. The German army was encircled in a massive trap at Falaise and although many thousands escaped, many thousands were obliterated.

And Percy, where the 28th Division was heading, was to be one of the next centers of fighting.

Slaughters were becoming more and more frequent, especially from the air as Allied planes pounced on German troop movements. On July 29 and 30, Combat Command B of the American 2nd Armored Division confronted a mass of SS vehicles along a seven-mile stretch of highway between St. Martin de Cenilly to St. Denis le

Gast, “the exact route of retreat that was bring the SS troops on a direct course toward Percy” (Bando, 1999, p. 88). On the evening of July 29, Sgt. John Ponczynski of the 2nd Armored and others were sent up a hill to scout the German movements. “What met their eyes from that vantage point was both unexpected and awesome. … German tanks, and in a cloud of dust, marching columns of hundreds of retreating German troops, rifles slung casually, singing as they marched. … These marching Germans were survivors of the numerous Allied air attacks on the Roncey Pocket, and they believed with the advent of darkness they could reach their new line, west of Percy” (p. 88).

The 116th Panzer Division launched an attack the morning of July 30. “Gen. (Gerhard von) Schwerin’s armor crashed through a … position at Beaucoudray, north of Percy on the Brehal-Tessy-sur-Vire road, but the attack made little progress after that. … it turned out to be a bright, clear day with only scattered clouds and the U.S. planes out in force. … A swarm of U.S. fighter-bombers ruined Gen. Schwerin’s road-bound columns” (Carafano, 2000, p. 252).

On the night of July 31, Winston Churchill and Eisenhower had a champagne toast at 10 Downing St. because things were going so well. “The Normandy front had been cracked wide open, American spearheads were running wild, so spirits were high – in more ways than one” (Breuer, 1985, p. 133).

The leaders were happy, but on the front lines, including at Percy, new soldiers had just started seeing combat – and the final day was coming in the morning for many, such as Weiss, Popielarski, Hyllested, Miller and Miller.

The 28th Division history tells it this way: “The 112th Infantry took up defensive positions to the left (to the east of the hole that the Cobra bombings punched in the German front) for action in event of enemy counterattacks. … The Keystone Division poised in readiness to attack in strength against organized resistance on July 31. Early on July 31 the 110th Infantry, led by Col. Theodore A. Seely, jumped off in the attack due north of Percy. A few hours later the 112th, under the command of Col. Henry Hodes, moved up on the left (northeast of Percy) and took positions near the top of Hill 210. It was then that each regiment met its first strong resistance. …

"Such was the general picture as the 110th and 112th ... struck in strength in their attack toward Percy and on Hill 210 during the first day of August" (28th Division history). The five Wisconsin men were killed on or near this hill – so-named because it was 210 meters above sea level.

"The 112th, jumping off at 0720 hours, was held up 20 minutes later by heavy flanking fire from automatic weapons entrenched on higher ground to the left in the (neighboring) 29th Division zone. "It took nearly 11 hours, but "Hill 210 was finally seized at 1800 after the regiment had engaged in bitter combat and had been subjected to heavy shellfire all day. By nightfall the 110th had maneuvered one battalion to a point beyond the town, although some Germans still held out within Percy itself" (28th Division history).

The division had almost 750 casualties on its first day in combat (Blumenson, 1963, p. 214). Records of 112th Regiment men buried at Omaha Beach (including Popielarski and Weiss) and at the Brittany cemetery at St. James (the two Millers) show that 20 men from around the nation were killed on Aug. 1, three on July 31 and none on July 30. The records also show that 10 members of the 110th Regiment were killed on Aug. 1 (including Hyllested, who is buried at St. James) , five on July 31 and three on July 30.

The big picture to military historians was this: "Though blocked in its effort to drive far to the south, the XIX Corps blocked Kluge's effort to close the gap that Cobra had torn open. By thwarting the German attempt to re-establish a stable defensive line across the Cotentin (peninsula), Corlett enabled the forces on the First Army right to make a spectacular end run. The breakthrough was in the process of becoming a breakout, and the XIX Corps contributed a handsome assist" (Blumenson, 1963, p. 133). Translating all of that, the XIX Corps is a massive group of nine or so divisions that included the 28th. Kluge was German Field Marshal Gunter von Kluge. Cobra featured two days of bombings by dozens of planes, and some bombs fell short of the target and killed Americans. The First Army was a group of more than one corps, so it was much more massive than just plain massive. So Blumenson is saying this was a huge, huge, huge battle and that the 28th did a good job.

The 28th thus essentially acted as a football offensive lineman to help protect the side of the hole that the bombings had created, blocking oncoming defenders so that other infantry and tank divisions could ram through the German line just to the west. The individual soldier knew nothing of that grand scheme of things; it was something for the chess boards of their generals.

Edmund Dziecialowski of Milwaukee was very close to Sgt. Ken Miller on the fatal day. Dziecialowski was a communications sergeant and said Ken, his friend since basic training in Louisiana, was his squad leader (the squad was 12 soldiers). He saw the wounded and unconscious Ken lying on a road but said "I couldn't stop. I had to keep going." The unit was told to move after a heavy German barrage (Mueller, 1984). Ken had a fatal head wound.

Several members of Hyllested's 110th Regiment discussed their first days of combat in letters to author Dorothy Chernitsky, who in 1991 assembled them in the book "Voices from the Foxholes: Men of the 110th Infantry Relate Personal Accounts of What They Experienced During World War II." Her husband, John, was in the anti-tank company of the 110th and she told the author of this book that she had thought about doing hers while sitting at his reunions.

• Charlie Waldrup: "We were all green – it was something different from what we'd ever experienced. Of course, we'd seen a lot of beat-up troops back on the beach, Omaha Beach, and into St. Lo, but this was altogether different because they were shooting at us. We had taken Percy after a pretty fierce fight, lost some troops but we were going out of Percy and one of my buddies said, 'Look at that. There's a dead German.' I said, 'Yes, and if you don't mind, these Germans will kill you, too.' About that time, a burp gun opened up at us. We gave them room; we laid down beside the hedgerows and they were gone in a minute" (Chernitsky, 1991, p. 137).

• Morris Pettit: "My squad and I were in a support platoon as Company B … fell under attack, while moving up a valley. After they became pinned down by machine-gun fire, I received my first mission. We were to attack the German position from the flank. We encountered heavy artillery fire as we moved up the hill; however we continued to advance to a position in which we opened fire on the

Germans. We killed many of the Germans and took several of them prisoner" (Chernitsky, 1991, p. 107).

• Ralph Johnson: Near Percy, "a German patrol slipped by our guards in the wee hours of the morning and, making their way into the Command Post of the First Battalion, captured the battalion commander, Lt. Col. Cummings; his executive officer, Capt. Sweeney of Monongahela, Pa.; … and several key enlisted men – without firing a shot and led them away as POWs" (Chernitsky, 1991, p. 4).

• Staff Sgt. Walter Tauchert of the 110th Regiment received the Distinguished Service Cross for extraordinary heroism at Percy on July 31. The citation said that at 4 p.m., a group came upon a crossroad guarding the approaches to the town, heavily defended by machine-gun emplacements on both sides of the road, by a machine gun and sniper in the attic of a house on the right front and by a half-track on the left front. There also was a heavy artillery barrage.

"From his position at the side of the road, Sgt. Tauchert opened fire upon the machine-gun emplacement menacing his right flank, 75 yards distant, knocking it out with his grenade launcher. Utilizing a machine gun nearby he turned his fire on the machine-gun emplacement on his left flank and quickly silenced that from a distance of 120 yards. Although an air burst from an 88mm exploded with such force as to knock him to the ground and rip the clothing and equipment from his back, Sgt. Tauchert, undaunted by the severe shock, next turned his machine gun on the sniper nest in the attic and proceeded to dispose of it without further delay. He then directed his fire upon the half-track, and by the intensity of this fire forced it to withdraw" (Chernitsky, 1991, p. 117-118).

Others in the 110th also have discussed Percy in other forums.

• Julius J. Kuhn, of West Bend, Wis., the sergeant of the 2nd Platoon in Company B of the 110th, told in his own memoir of someone wearing a priest's clothes who looked suspicious. "Very much alert, we walked through Percy. A priest came toward us holding a small valise. I stopped him and asked what he had in his case. He looked me right in the eye and didn't say anything. We opened the valise and found the uniform of a German officer. I told two of my men to take the Kraut officer behind one of the buildings and shoot him. We didn't feel too bad about it, because that's what he had done to the priest whose clothing he had stolen" (Kuhn, 1994, p. 106).

• Arthur Coon, who was in Company A of the 110th, was a private first class and a native of Andover, Mass., who was wounded and captured. In 1999, the author of this book pieced together Coon's story from several e-mails and phone conversations, plus letters. Coon then read it and approved it from his residence in Walnut Creek, Calif.

"On Aug. 2, at about 2 p.m., I was hit by machine gun fire in Percy and downed. Our squad was on a mission at the edge of town, and seven or eight of us were knocked down. … . One guy got hit in the stomach. This all was behind some buildings, but there was a field of wheat there, too. The machine gun was past the field.

"I was wounded in the right hand, but not badly, although it felt like it was blown to hell. Somehow, I managed to get my little pocket Bible from my shirt pocket and turn to the 23rd Psalm. I think it helped me get through it all! I had spoken to our chaplain before all of this.

"I was captured one-eighth of a mile from the German regimental command post. Although hundreds of Germans were retreating at this time, the command post was still there and they took me right to the command post." He was treated for the wound, although the German doctor kept saying "kaput, kaput." Coon eventually was taken to a hospital in Paris, and was rescued by the French underground when Paris fell in the last days of August.

"Looking into Percy, on our left was a German machine gun near a building. The crew ran away. To the right of that, there was a German tank, which got knocked out with a rifle grenade. We found several French in an underground shelter at a farmhouse. Then off to our far right, but on our side of the main road, a priest came out and asked that I tell our men not to shoot into the parish house." One wonders whether this is the "priest" that Kuhn encountered or the one whose clothes were taken.

• Sgt. Bob Finger of Sheboygan, Wis., was a mortarman in the 110th Regiment. He was a bit behind the front lines, shooting his rounds to help the infantry advance and always in contact with a spotter who ordered adjustments in distance and aim. He was a replacement soldier, meaning someone got killed or wounded before he arrived. Most soldiers in the division had been together a year and a half before the fighting even began.

Interviewed for this book in Sheboygan in October 1998, Finger said: "Well, the first day in action I'll never forget, because in the (United) States for a mortar, you put out three posts – three stakes to sight your guns – 25 yards. We were all given an azimuth, of course. Each gun. So they give us that reading, and so 'put out your stakes,' the lieutenant said. So I put out my stakes, or I had my gunner, second man, that was his duty to do it, to put out the stakes. For sighting. And the lieutenant come along and says, 'Who put out only three stakes?' That's what we did for in the States. For training. That's all we did, is put out – only three stakes. He said, 'FIVE. In combat here, we're putting out FIVE.' So I … I had told the fellows to put out three, so I went out and chopped another branch or two down, three down, so we could put down five stakes. And so I went out and put them out myself. If I told the men one thing and I didn't know the orders, I'll do it myself."

The rest of his initiation to combat was a blur alternating with vivid memories of fear. "Digging in that first day was something else. Of course I tried to find safety behind a stone fence, you know. And I was digging around behind a great big rock, just trying to get down as low as … I was so nervous and so scared, I guess. Not nervous – scared."

In hedgerows, "the brush was piled up as high as this room – eight, 10 feet." His interviewer observed that fighting in hedgerows sounds like it was a giant, confusing mess, and Finger said: "Ohhhhhhh. Especially in your mind, your thoughts. Feelings, you know. Everything else, it's just – you can't imagine, I guess. … Thoughts and anxieties and uncertainty and the fear, the constant fear of what's coming up next, what's going on."

Newspaperman Ernie Pyle was writing about repair of heavy weapons just before Operation Cobra started. Then he stayed with the 4th Division, right next to the 28th Division, in the fateful first days of August.

Pyle told his millions of American newspaper readers: "Surely history will give a name to the battle that sent us boiling out of Normandy – some name comparable with Saint-Mihiel, or Meuse Argonne of the last war. But to us here on the spot at the time it was known simply as "the breakthrough" (Pyle in Nichols, 1986, p. 328). He painted scenes of carnage including "little pools of blood on the roadside, blood that has only begun to congeal and turn black, and the punctured steel helmets lying nearby," plus "the burned-out tanks and broken carts still unremoved from the road" and "cows in the fields, lying grotesquely with their feet to the sky ..." (p. 347).

Pyle also was struck by the "inhuman quiet. Usually battles are noisy for miles around. But in this recent fast warfare a battle sometimes leaves a complete vacuum behind it. ... There is nothing left behind but the remains – the lifeless debris, the sunshine and the flowers, and utter silence" (p. 348).

Bibliography

Army (1946). Historical and Pictorial Review of the 28th Infantry Division in World War II. Atlanta, Ga.

Bando, Mark (1999). Breakout at Normandy: The 2nd Armored Division in the land of the dead. Osceola, WI: MBI Publishing Co.

Blumenson, Martin (1963). The duel for France 1944: The men and the battles that changed the fate of Europe. Boston, MA: Houghton Mifflin Co.

Blumenson, Martin (1961). Breakout and pursuit. Washington, DC: Office of the Chief of Military History, Department of the Army.

Breuer, William B. (1985). Death of a Nazi army: The Falaise pocket. Scarborough House.

Carafano, James Jay (2000). After D-Day: Operation Cobra and the Normandy breakout. Boulder, CO: Lynne Rienner Publishers.

Chernitsky, Dorothy (1991). Voices from the foxholes: Men of the 110th Infantry relate personal accounts of what they experienced during World War II. Uniontown, PA: Dorothy Chernitsky.

Kuhn, Julius J. (1994). I was Baker 2: Memoirs of a World War II platoon sergeant. West Bend, WI: J.J. Kuhn, DeRaimo Publishing.

Mueller, Tom (1984). New chapter added to Millers' tale. Milwaukee Sentinel, Oct. 26, 1984. This was the third story written about Martin and Ken Miller – the first two an May 28, 1984, and Aug. 1, 1984. Respectively, their headlines said "First relative visits grave 40 years after D-Day" and "Akin in more than name, 2 share final resting place." All used with permission of Milwaukee Journal Sentinel.

Nichols, David (ed.) (1986). Ernie's war: The best of Ernie Pyle's World War II dispatches. New York, NY: Random House Inc.

Other reading

Daugherty, Leo (2001). The battle of the hedgerows: Bradley's First Army in Normandy, June-July 1944. St. Paul, MN: MBI Publishing Co.

Delaforce, Patrick (1999). Marching to the sound of gunfire: Northwest Europe 1944-5. Wrens Park Publishing.

D'Este, Carlo (1983). Decision in Normandy. New York, NY: HarperCollins Publishers.

Johns, Glover S. Jr. (2002). The Clay Pigeons of St. Lo. Mechanicsburg, PA: Stackpole Books.

Miller, Robert A. (1988). August 1944: The campaign for France. Novato, CA; Presidio Press.

Chapter 8:

A nurse who served and died

German planes dropped the bombs 4,000 miles from Wisconsin, but the attack struck a powerful blow that echoed through the state's history: An Army nurse became the first Wisconsin woman to be killed by enemy fire in a 20th century war, if not ever.

The bombs at the Anzio beachhead in Italy on Feb. 12, 1944, fatally wounded 2nd Lt. Ellen G. Ainsworth, 24, a native of Glenwood City in St. Croix County in the northwestern corner of the state. She was the first and last female from Wisconsin killed by enemy fire in that war, but there were others from non-battle injuries. For example, another chapter of this book discusses the case of 2nd Lt. Eleanor Nelson of Rock County, who is buried in Hawaii.

And there have been others killed by enemy fire since: One woman in the Persian Gulf war in 1991, six in Iraq and one in Afghanistan as of the spring of 2009.

Ainsworth died four days after the bombing and is buried at the Sicily-Rome Cemetery near Nettuno and Rome.

She received the Silver Star for gallantry, because two days before being injured she had led efforts to protect patients at the 56th Evacuation Hospital amid an extremely heavy artillery barrage that left some of the unit's tents in tatters. Also receiving the Silver Star were Elaine Roe, a native of Whitewater, and two other nurses at Roe's nearby 33rd Field Hospital. Those attacks were quite heavy, but the nurses went through three full months of almost-daily barrages of some kind; whether they were artillery, bombs or both. All of that was occurring because Allied forces were stalled at Anzio and the beachhead was very small and cramped, so hospitals were quite close to loading areas, ammunition areas and even the front line.

In 1986, Ainsworth was the focus of the Milwaukee Sentinel's Memorial Day story by the author of this book, and Roe was

Ellen Ainsworth,
Glenwood City,
Anzio, Italy

interviewed. Ainsworth's sister, Lyda, 76 at the time, reported what other nurses wrote to her family: As Ainsworth had done during the earlier artillery barrage, the nurse supervised efforts to protect patients by placing them on the dirt floor of the tent, with their beds over them.

The Feb. 12 bombing did not last as long as the artillery barrage had lasted and only slightly damaged the hospital. When the all-clear sounded, Ainsworth "dared leave for a minute, to run back to her hut and get something," Lyda reported. But just as she got there, another bomb fell, and the fluke scored a direct hit on her tent and left the nurse paralyzed with severe back wounds.

In the four days before she died, Ainsworth kept asking about the patients and whether anyone else was wounded. "Her one concern was for other people," Lyda said. One letter reported she had asked a colleague: "Mary, tell me the truth. Was anyone else hurt?"

Ainsworth was one of only 16 women killed by enemy fire in the war, Maj. Cynthia Gurney, Army nurse historian, said in 1986.

A total of 59,000 American women served as nurses during World War II, with almost 30,000 in combat zones. A total of 201 died as a result of illnesses or accidents (Monahan & Neidel-Greenlee, 2003, p. 458). About 70 were held as POWs by the Japanese after the 1942 surrender in the Philippines.

Gurney reported that 264 nurses died in World War I, but all the cases were caused by the flu pandemic and other diseases. Four Air Force nurses died during the Korean War, but none was blamed on enemy fire. And in Vietnam, nine women died, but only one case was due to enemy fire, Gurney said.

Ainsworth's life began in a setting right out of Norman Rockwell. Glenwood City, with a population of 1,200 today, calls itself "the city of 57 hills."

In the family home on Pine Street, Ainsworth showed her future calling at an early age. "She was going to be a nurse from the time she was a tiny tot dressing wounds on her dolls," said Lyda, who was nine years older. "If a doll's arm was limp, she'd tie it up with a handkerchief or anything like that."

Ainsworth teamed up with two cousins her age to become what was known around town as the TT – "Terrible Trio." One time, the girls had a Halloween party at a local lake. "I don't know what happened there, but they always called it the TT Lake," Lyda said.

Ainsworth went to nursing school in Minneapolis and was a floor supervisor in a hospital there when she entered the service on her 23rd birthday. Her family never saw her again.

"Every time she was scheduled for a leave, it was canceled because they were moving her," said Lyda, who was a teacher and journalist in several cities around the state, including Muskego, Waupun, Waunakee and Ashland.

The U.S. and British invasion at Anzio was designed to outflank strong German defenses to the south. The Allies had landed on the Italian mainland at Salerno in September 1943 but quickly became mired down. The goal at Anzio was to help the Allies finally crack the defenses and seize Rome, about 35 miles away.

The invasion went well when it started on Jan. 22, 1944, but the forces opted to secure their beachhead instead of driving inland immediately. Maj. Gen. John P. Lucas feared having the invaders stretched too thin to face German counterattacks. But his hesitation gave the Germans more time to react and build up strong defenses near Anzio.

The slow pace was one of the war's greatest controversies, and British Prime Minister Winston Churchill said: "I expected to see a wildcat roaring into the mountains – and what do I get? A whale wallowing on the beaches!"

It wallowed four months, constantly exposed to enemy artillery fire from the hills and to air attacks until an immense assault from the south caused the German defenses to collapse. By that time, 59,000 Allied troops had been killed or wounded at Anzio.

More than one-third of the American women killed by enemy fire in the entire war died there – Ainsworth and five other nurses.

Lt. Gen. Mark Clark, commander of the Fifth Army, said the nurses "were tremendous builders of morale at a time when it badly needed building. They went about their work wearing helmets and facing danger as a great as anyone else on the beachhead. They worked with the doctors and in the operating rooms through bombardment of all kinds, day and night. It seemed to be that they were among the real heroes of Anzio" (Monahan & Neidel-Greenlee, 2003, p. 238).

Col. Florence Blanchfield, superintendent of the Army Nurse Corps, told Ainsworth's parents in a condolence letter: "She typifies the very finest in American womanhood. Had she known that it was to be thus, she would still have said, 'I must go. It is my duty.' The nurses are like that in this war. They fear nothing. They beg to go forward as far as possible because they feel they are needed so urgently" (Monahan & Neidel-Greenlee, 2003, p. 6-7).

The citation for the Silver Star honored Ainsworth for "calmly directing the placing of surgical patients on the ground to lessen the danger of further injury during the enemy shelling of the hospital. By her disregard for her own safety and her calm assurance, she instilled confidence in her assistants and her patients, thereby preventing serious panic and injury" (Monahan & Neidel-Greenlee, 2003, p. 272).

Elaine Roe was 67 and living in Mount Morris, Ill., when interviewed for the 1986 newspaper story. Her last name was Pieper.

Her job at Anzio consisted of surgery shifts that frequently ran around the clock. "I don't think any of us went to bed for three nights. You're so busy you don't think about the fact you need rest yourself," she said.

Pieper received her Silver Star for actions the same week as Ainsworth's during the artillery barrage on her 33rd Field Hospital, which killed two of her colleagues and wounded three officers and enlisted men. Using flashlights, Pieper and other nurses worked in total darkness amid the heavy shelling, which included many air bursts, to evacuate 42 patients to safer quarters.

Shelling in the area had been frequent, but not intensive, and the hospital staff did not understand the immensity of the problem that particular day until the soldier patients – much more familiar with imminent danger – said the unit should begin an immediate evacuation or prepare to get hit.

"They called it incoming traffic," Pieper said. "We were very blasé about what was going on" until that warning.

After the havoc, "there were quite a few holes in our tent." Pieper added that she still did not realize how bad it was until seeing pictures of the scene after the war that relatives had saved from newspapers.

"The attack seemed like it lasted several days," said Pieper, who was chief of the unit's surgical department and was not injured.

One of those killed was her head nurse, 1st Lt. Glenda Spelhaug of California – "an excellent nurse and leader. We all thought an awful lot of her." Like Ainsworth, Spelhaug is buried at Sicily-Rome.

Pieper's job bore some resemblance to that portrayed in the television series "MASH," from the Korean War. "I only wish we had it that easy – that we had that much fun. I don't think you can know how terrible it was until you've been there."

The unit's work ranged from amputations to broken bones and wounds to the head, chest and abdomen.

The Anzio tents were marked with big red crosses for medical facilities, but that did little good because their closest neighbors were ammunition and gasoline dumps, a radar station, an airfield and antiaircraft batteries (Sarnecky, 1999, p. 224). The hospitals were one mile from any of the military targets, and the Germans were given the coordinates of the medical facilities under the assumption they would not be shelled. Fat chance – some of the nurses say the wounded men told them it was safer out at the front (Monahan & Neidel-Greenlee, 2003, p. 266).

The nursing teams were brought ashore on Jan. 28, four days after the invasion, and arrived amid a German air raid.

The entire beachhead was under German observation and could be reached by its artillery. "The officers who chose and planned the site told us that because the hospitals were all in one area, and every tent was clearly marked with a red cross, we would be so safe that we wouldn't even need foxholes," said Lt. Claudine Glidwell, one of the nurses (Monahan & Neidel-Greenlee, 2003, p. 256-57).

Everyone was to find out every day for months how flatly wrong that was. There were artillery bombardments, strafing raids, aerial bombardments and more.

On Feb. 7, a German plane that had conducted a raid was being chased by a British Spitfire and jettisoned five bombs in order to gain maneuverability – the jettisoning occurred right over the 95th Evacuation Hospital. Three nurses were killed, along with 25 other people, and about 50 were wounded – including nurse Ruth Buckley of Elmwood, Wis., although the book calls it Elmswood – in Pierce County (Monahan & Neidel-Greenlee, 2003, p. 262). Soldiers volunteered to dig foxholes inside the tents of nurses.

On Feb. 8, amid an overall German offensive at Anzio, the legendary "Anzio Annie," a 170mm gun mounted on a railroad car and rolled inside a cave to hide it between firings, began a long series of shooting. Two nurses at the 33rd Field Hospital were killed – this is the attack in which Pieper's boss, Spelhaug, was killed, and in which Pieper's work earned the Silver Star along with two other nurses – and 11 staff members were wounded.

On Feb. 10, artillery shells also hit Ainsworth's 56th Evac Hospital. But no one was seriously injured, because of the actions by Ainsworth, who was on duty in the surgical ward.

Two days later, however, the story was quite different, and Ainsworth's number was up. At 18:30, German planes waged an attack on the harbor that lasted about 90 minutes, during which time a bomb fell into the officers' living area of the 56th Evac, and Ainsworth was struck by fragments in the chest and abdomen. She had a tear in her left lung, lacerations of the right side of the diaphragm and spleen, and a stomach wound (Monahan & Neidel-Greenlee, 2003, p. 274-275)

Lyda Ainsworth said her sister "always said she belonged with the boys, the soldiers," so after the war, the family abided by that wish. She is one of 7,862 troops buried at Sicily-Rome. Lyda visited the grave in 1960.

Although the Silver Star was issued only three months after Ainsworth died, other honors came a few decades later when the feminist movement was well under way. "There was a long stretch in there where they didn't recognize women at all," Lyda said.

The first honor came in 1978, when the health clinic at Fort Hamilton in New York was named for Ainsworth. Then in 1980, Army Secretary Clifford Alexander Jr. dedicated the Ainsworth Conference Room in the Pentagon near his office. It is used as a briefing room and has about 100 seats.

In 1977, American Legion Post No. 168 in Glenwood City expanded its name to the Curry-Ainsworth Post. Stephen S. Curry had been killed in World War I.

Bibliography

Monahan, Evelyn M., and Neidel-Greenlee, Rosemary (2003). And if I perish: Front-line U.S. Army nurses in World War II. New York: Alfred A. Knopf.

Mueller, Tom (1986): Enemy fire killed one servicewoman from Wisconsin. Milwaukee Sentinel, May 26, pages 1, 14. Used with permission of Milwaukee Journal Sentinel.

Mueller, Tom (1986): Whitewater native describes her ordeal in WWII. Milwaukee Sentinel, page 14. Used with permission of Milwaukee Journal Sentinel.

Sarnecky, Mary T. (1999). A history of the U.S. Army Nurse Corps. Philadelphia: University of Pennsylvania Press.

Other reading

Clark, Lloyd (2006). Anzio: Italy and the battle for Rome – 1944. New York: Atlantic Monthly Press.

Tomblin, Barbara Brooks (1996). G.I. Nightingales: The Army Nurse Corps in World War II. Lexington, Ky.: The University Press of Kentucky.

Chapter 9:

A chaplain is KIA

Wearing his Army uniform, the Rev. Raymond Hansen had one last duty to perform in his Evangelical United Brethren Church in Augusta in Eau Claire County on Thursday, May 21, 1942:

Perform the wedding of Wilfred Wood and Lorraine Walker.

The ceremony was at the church at the corner of Spring and Grant Streets, the reception was at the Walker family dairy farm southwest of town on Pettis Road, and the pastor and his wife of one year joined in the pictures being taken out on the lawn. And then the 29-year-old first lieutenant was off to the Army's chaplain school in Pennsylvania.

Hansen had come to Evangelical United in 1938, when he was 25 or 26.

The Army assigned Hansen to the 8th Regiment of the 4th Infantry Division, which trained in Georgia and wound up being one of the invasion forces on D-Day, June 6, 1944. The bloodiest of the five beaches was Omaha, but there were deaths where the 4th arrived at Utah Beach – including that of Army combat engineer Gerald Rehfeldt of Appleton, whose story is told elsewhere in this book.

Chaplain Hansen, a captain, was killed on June 11, five days after D-Day, and is buried at Omaha Beach, as is Rehfeldt. The pastor died a month short of his 32nd birthday.

A monument on Chaplains Hill at Arlington National Cemetery honors a total of 134 Protestant chaplains, including Hansen, who were killed in World Wars I and II. It does not list them individually, but a total of 70 Roman Catholic priests who were killed in World War II are listed on another monument there. In World War II, eight Jewish chaplains died, including one in Normandy.

Chaplain Raymond Hansen of the United Brethren Evangelical Church of Augusta in Eau Claire County died in Normandy on June 11, 1944. Two years earlier, his last act in Augusta was to conduct the marriage ceremony for Wilfred Wood and Lorraine Walker. Hansen and his wife, Leona, stand behind the happy couple in this photo at their wedding reception. At the left is maid of honor Esther Heideman, sister of the groom, and at right is best man Gordon Wood, one of the groom's brothers.

A chaplain often was in the line of fire, as he helped the wounded, retrieved bodies, buried bodies in temporary graves quite close to the battlefield, etc. He also conducted religious services, gave confession and absolution individually or en masse, provided individual counseling to members of all faiths and served as morale officer to units, organizing activities like ballgames and bingo to take their minds off of war or to defuse tension and boredom during training.

Hansen was born July 15, 1912, and was accepted for chaplain duty on April 25, 1942, just a few weeks before the Augusta wedding, according to records of the U.S. Army Chaplain Museum at Fort Jackson, S.C., provided by Marcia McManus, director. There is evidence in Augusta that Hansen was from Denmark in Brown County.

Wilfred Wood, 28, married Lorraine Walker, 25, on that Thursday in Augusta. She made her own wedding dress, which looks fairly elaborate for a time in which the world had many scarcities of products because of the war, and many people had little money in the wake of the Depression. "I still have it, too," up in the attic, says their daughter, Celia Bethke, of rural Augusta.

The maid of honor was Esther Heideman, sister of the groom, and the best man was Gordon Wood, one of the groom's brothers. The others in the wedding party were Beatrice Walker, the bride's sister who was 13 years younger; Elaine Poor, a longtime friend; and Marshall Walker, another brother of the groom.

Wilfred and his brothers were attired in pinstripe, double-breasted suits.

In his time in Augusta, Hansen picked up a reputation: He loved Jell-O, the jiggly, inexpensive and flexible product that could be a salad-type serving with the meal or a dessert. Heat up water, stir in the granulated goodness, mix it up real good, add cold water, mix it up some more and then stick it in the icebox or refrigerator. Say H-E-L-L-O to J-E-L-L-O.

This is what Harold Burrows of nearby Fairchild remembers most about him. The William and Hilda Burrows family had moved to a 60-acre dairy farm near Fairchild in 1939 from Norwalk in Monroe County to the south. Harold was 14 and had an older brother; his two older sisters had been married in a double ceremony a year earlier. The first thing the Burrows family did in Fairchild was to start going to the nearest branch of their Evangelical United Brethren church, as they had done at Norwalk – and at their new home, the church was a few miles to the west in Augusta. They hopped in their 1937 Ford '85 for the drive.

"Back then the pastors made the rounds to their parishioners' homes two or three times a year. He just loved Jell-O. Every time we had Rev. Hansen here, we had a big bowl of Jell-O," Burrows chuckles.

"He loved Jell-O like Ronald Reagan liked jellybeans."

However, Jell-O in the 1940s did not come in nearly the rainbow of seemingly dozens of flavors like a pot of jellybeans. "Way back then it was pretty much just red Jell-O that we had," Burrows said.

The dinners with the reverend at the Burrows dining room table were held during the week, not after church on Sunday. Hilda Burrows just used her regular dishware for these occasions, because Hansen was "regular folk just like us," Harold says.

"Rev. Hansen was quite a fun-loving person, not an old sourpuss," Burrows says. "He was a fairly well-built man; a little taller than average, stocky but not heavy-set."

Augusta, with a population of about 1,500 today, is framed in a way by West Lawn Cemetery on the western edge and East Lawn Cemetery on the other edge, both on the combined Highways 27 and 12. Those going through town will pass Stone Street, Crocker Street, Pond Street and Sand Street, among others, and can go on nine miles to Fairchild to the east, or turn and go 19 miles to Cadott on the north, perhaps stopping at Coon Fork County Park.

The Walker dairy farm had been in the family for two generations already and is now officially designated by the state as a farm owned by that family for a century. It is run by Bethke's cousins. The

Century Farm program was launched in 1948 in conjunction with the state's centennial celebration. There are currently more than 7,400 such farms and homes across the state.

"Chaplain Hansen baptized my Mom a month before her wedding," Bethke says. The Walkers probably attended church only infrequently, going to Thompson Valley Methodist near their house, but her mother possibly never had been baptized in any faith, she said. Wilfred Walker and all of his family were Evangelical.

Hansen had been commissioned at Fort Snelling, Minn., as a first lieutenant just before the wedding.

According to a clipping from the Augusta newspaper from sometime in the spring of 1943, he had just arrived at Camp Gordon, Ga., with what it called the 4th Motorized Division.

> "Camp Gordon is a new camp, developed entirely since last September and now is directing military training for more than 20,000 soldiers, which is one-third of the men which will be trained in the camp at one time in a short time," the article said.
>
> It continued: "Chaplain Hansen has been assigned in the 4th Division to service in special troops including two full battalions of medical and engineer troops. Besides these there are three companies of men assigned in signal, military police and headquarters, which with the two battalions include more than 2,500 men to be ministered in moral and spiritual affairs every week.
>
> "The division is scheduled to leave on extensive maneuvers early in July to include divisions in the entire First and Second Army, duplicating conditions as near to actual war as is possible to produce in the Carolina swamps. The chaplain's work is made most difficult during these two months, but presents a tremendous challenge to meet the deepest need of the solider, and opens the way to genuine service in the actual fighting front which follows soon. Chaplain

Hansen expects to remain with the 4th Division throughout the war," the article finished.

The camp was near Augusta, Ga., so Hansen traveled more than 1,000 miles and wound up living near a town of the same name as his Wisconsin home. But he was definitely getting lots of reminders of the South – Camp Gordon was named for a Confederate general.

Hansen came back to Wisconsin in August 1943, a few months before leaving for England with the 4th Division. On Aug. 29, he came to a dinner at the house of Ida Schneider in Augusta; also attending was his wife, Leona, and her father, the Rev. Marks, an older minister who had replaced Hansen in Augusta. People just called him "Rev. Marks," and no one really remembers his first name any more.

Schneider's daughter, Lael, found that date in her mother's diary. The diary also says Leona Hansen was teaching school in Neillsville, and that the Hansens also were going to cross the state to visit his parents in the village of Denmark, which is in Brown County 15 miles south of Green Bay.

Schneider says her mother's notes reported that Hansen had married Leona on April 14, 1941.

Schneider says that at some point before D-Day, Hansen ran in to her husband, Verne, and Augusta native Bill MacLachlan in England, and they posed along with another soldier in front of a barracks or some such building with a tar-paper roof. Hansen had presided at the marriage of MacLachlan back in Augusta. Each soldier is wearing a jacket, so one can assume it was winter or early spring.

Four decades after the war, the Evangelical United Brethren denomination merged with the Methodist denomination and is now the United Methodist Church nationally and in Augusta.

The Augusta United Methodist Church observed its 150th anniversary in 2008 (Augusta was founded in 1856). It is located at 137 W. Brown St., right off the main drag of Lincoln Street. Hansen's old church is about two blocks away from the current one. It is now a house; a second floor was added with three big skylights, the old, high church windows were replaced with regular, smaller windows and the old bell tower removed.

In order to become a chaplain, Hansen or any minister or priest first had to ask permission from his church denomination, and the denomination then made its recommendations to the Army or Navy.

How often did chaplains get in danger? The better question is how often did they not. In a comprehensive book reviewing the service and sacrifice of Roman Catholic priests, Father Donald Crosby says that on Guadalcanal, and in Sicily, and on the Italian mainland, chaplains were shot at as they tried to bury the dead (Crosby, 1994, p. 43-44, 92 and 100).

Crosby says that in the Marine invasion of Betio and Tarawa in the Gilbert Islands of the Pacific in November 1943, Joseph Wieber, a Catholic priest, was in the command boat in the first assault wave. A Japanese shell smashed the vessel, killing all the other officers and technically leaving Wieber in command, except that it was forbidden under regulations. The landing craft of John Laughlin, a Protestant chaplain, got stranded on the coral reef for 24 hours, and for some reason the Japanese could not, or did not, fire at it again. Laughlin worked to help wounded Marines all around him, and eventually took medical supplies to the men on shore.

Another chaplain was killed on the beach in the 1942 invasion of North Africa, and Catholic chaplain Albert Hoffman of Dubuque, Iowa, lost a leg when he stepped on a mine on the beach arriving in Italy. Others in Italy were wounded by bombs or by German 88-mm shells at night. Chaplains were taken prisoner in the Battle of the Bulge in December 1944 and January 1945.

Cornelius Ryan, in his 1959 masterpiece, "The Longest Day," told about two things that happened on D-Day right in Hansen's own 8th Regiment of the 4th Division:

• As assault boats headed for the coast, "one boat carrying Lt. Col. James Batte and the 4th Division's 8th Infantry Regiment troops threaded its way through the dead bodies (floating offshore), Batte heard one of his gray-faced men say, 'Them lucky bastards – they ain't seasick no more'," (Ryan, 1959, 1984, p. 205).

• The 4th Division's Brig. Gen. Theodore Roosevelt, 57-year-old son of the former president, the only general to land in the first wave, walked around on his cane, giving orders, examining the terrain and aiding the wounded, like Hansen no doubt was doing, too. "Sgt. Harry Brown of the 8th Infantry saw him 'with a cane in one hand, a map in the other, walking around as if he was looking over some real estate.' Every now and then a mortar burst on the beach, sending showers of sand into the air. It seemed to annoy Roosevelt; impatiently, he would brush himself off" (p. 232). German artillery fire blasted about a dozen men, and "seconds later, a lone figure emerged from the smoke of the artillery burst. His face was black, his helmet and equipment were gone. He came walking up the beach in complete shock, eyes staring. Yelling for a medic, Roosevelt ran over to the man. He put his arm around the soldier. 'Son,' he said gently, 'I think we'll get you back on a boat'" (p. 272).

Roosevelt is best known for his reaction to landing at the wrong place amid the massive invasion, high seas and enemy fire: "We're going to start the war from here" (p. 273). He earned the Medal of Honor for his leadership on D-Day, and died of a heart attack in his sleep on July 12. He is buried at Omaha Beach, like Hansen and several others in this book.

The colonel who ran the 8th Regiment, and thus would have been well-acquainted with Hansen, was James A. Van Fleet. The leader of the 12th Regiment, another part of the 4th Division, was Col. Russell Reeder, but on June 11 it was changed to James Luckett. It is not clear why this happened, but it came on the very day that Hansen was killed. Leadership of regiments changed for many reasons, including death, injury, failure to advance as fast as generals wanted, promotions, etc. (www.history.army.mil/documents/eto-ob/4ID-eto.htm).

From June 10 to 20, division headquarters was at the town of Le Bisson (www.history.army.mil/documents/eto-ob/4ID-eto.htm), and the 359th Regiment of the 90th Infantry Division was attached to Hansen's 4th Division for a few days, but was reassigned on June 11 from positions near Fresville and moved to Barneville (Colby, 1991). All of this was a few miles from the town of Ste. Mere Eglise, where the 82nd Airborne paratroopers had landed in the first hours of D-Day.

So somewhere amid all of that, and the dense hedgerows of Normandy, Hansen was killed on June 11. What could he have been doing? Probably the same things that other chaplains went through in Normandy, some fatally.

"Paratrooper padre" Father Francis Simpson jumped with the 101st Airborne in the first moments of June 6. So did others with the 101st and 82nd Airborne. At bloody Omaha Beach, Father John Kelly arrived 40 minutes after H-Hour, as did Father Joseph Lacy.

Father Ignatius Maternowski parachuted and landed in a heavily defended area at the confluence of two rivers, and was killed by German fire as "he bended down to help a wounded solider lying on the causeway. ... The German troops later apologized, saying they would have held their fire had they known that Maternowski was a chaplain and insisting they had been unable to see his chaplain's identification in the darkness" (Crosby, 1994, p. 126).

Also killed in the first days in Normandy was Father Philip Edelen, who at 11 p.m. on June 9 was "with his unit in the city of Trevieres when an artillery shell exploded on top of him, blowing off most of his left leg. He soon suffered a cerebral hemorrhage as well" (p. 133), and died at 3 a.m. June 10. This is only one day before Hansen was killed, and not too many miles from where the 4th Division was fighting.

And Father Dominic Ternan died June 19 when his battalion in the 315h Infantry Regiment ran into heavy machine-gun fire. "Almost everyone was hit except Ternan, who, thinking that the firing had stopped, ran to a wounded sergeant lying in a ditch by the side of the road. A German sniper saw Ternan, fired and hit him," (p. 134), and he died immediately. "Once again, a German infantryman expressed his deep regret that he had slain a chaplain, but he insisted that the raincoat Ternan was wearing had hidden his chaplain's insignia and his Red Cross arm band. Both the Army and the chief of chaplains treated his apology with contempt, condemning it as an exercise in arrogance and self-service and unworthy of a serious response."

The most famous chaplain deaths in the war were the four men aboard the USS Dorchester in the north Atlantic who gave up their life vests for other men after it was torpedoed by a U-boat and sank in only 25 minutes. They last were seen on the deck of the sinking ship, with arms linked and praying.

In the Navy, a Roman Catholic chaplain, Lt. Cmdr. Joseph O'Callahan, was awarded the Medal of Honor, the nation's most prestigious, for many acts of sacrifice in the invasion of Okinawa in 1945. After a Japanese aerial attack on his aircraft carrier, the USS Franklin, in which nearly 1,000 men were killed, O'Callahan comforted the injured and led damage control parties, including dumping ammunition into the ocean before it could explode and make things even worse.

The medal citation, reported by the Navy Historical Center, said:

> "A valiant and forceful leader, calmly braving the perilous barriers of flame and twisted metal to aid his men and his ship, Lt. Cmdr. O'Callahan groped his way through smoke-filled corridors to the open flight deck and into the midst of violently exploding bombs, shells, rockets and other armament.
>
> "With the ship rocked by incessant explosions, with debris and fragments raining down and fires raging in ever increasing fury, he ministered to the wounded and dying, comforting and encouraging men of all faiths; he organized and led firefighting crews into the blazing inferno on the flight deck; he directed the jettisoning of live ammunition and the flooding of the magazine; he manned a hose to cool hot, armed bombs rolling dangerously on the listing deck, continuing his efforts despite searing, suffocating smoke which forced men to fall back gasping and imperiled others who replaced them.
>
> "Serving with courage, fortitude and deep spiritual strength, Lt. Cmdr. O'Callahan inspired the gallant officers and men of the Franklin to fight heroically and with profound faith in the face of almost certain death and to return their stricken ship to port" (www.history.navy.mil/photos/pers-us/uspers-o/j-ocalln.htm).

In March 1942, Chaplain George E. Rentz, a Presbyterian, died after giving up his life jacket to a wounded sailor. They had been on the USS Houston, a heavy cruiser, which was torpedoed multiple times in the Battle of the Sunda Strait in the Java Sea. This battle was described in the chapter on the worst days for Wisconsin in the war.

Rentz and others converged on a floating piece of wreckage, which became dangerously overcrowded. Rentz, 59, who also had been a World War I chaplain, prayed and led the men in singing hymns, then placed his life jacket near a wounded sailor and quietly slipped into the sea to his death. Rentz was the only Navy chaplain in the war to receive the Navy Cross (www.edow.org/news/window/july2004/ww2.html). The sinking killed about 700 men.

In 1942 in the Philippines as Japanese invaders flooded in, Father William Cummings kept the staff calm during a bombardment and strafing of a hospital on April 7. Amid widespread screaming and panic, Cummings stood on a metal table and began leading the "Our Father."

"The screaming stopped. Men quieted. Some joined in. The work of the nurses and corpsmen became easier. But the raid wasn't over. In fact, it really hadn't begun. Lt. Juanita Redmond, on duty in one of the open-sided, tin-roofed, converted motor pool sheds, known as a general medical ward, heard someone outside yell, 'They're coming back!' Bearing down on the mess hall and the doctors' and nurses' headquarters, the Japanese scored direct hits on both. Again the concussion knocked people down. Again patients bounced like rubber balls off their beds onto the hard cement floors.

"Miraculously, Father Cummings was able somehow to ride out the blasts on top of his makeshift pulpit in the middle of the orthopedic ward. Standing there, arms still outstretched, paying little attention to what was happening, he no doubt instilled the helpless patients with courage. The ward remained calm" (Young, 1992, p. 270-271). He was wounded not long thereafter but survived.

One of the eight Jewish chaplains killed in the war was Rabbi Irving Teppler of Chicago, hit by bomb splinters in the end stages of the battle of Normandy on Aug. 13, 1944, while serving with the 60th Regiment of the 9th Infantry Division (Bergen, 2004).

Wisconsin's Hansen no doubt felt the same motivation to be a chaplain as the Rev. Paschal Deputy Fowlkes and Father Anthony Conway, both of whom also died in service to the country and the Lord.

Fowlkes was a 26-year-old Episcopal minister when he enlisted in the Army as a chaplain in 1942, saying he felt a duty to join "the battle for the preservation of democracy and freedom and justice." Fowlkes served in the invasion of North Africa, Sicily, D-Day and in the Battle of the Bulge. On March 24, 1945, in the final weeks of the war, Fowlkes jumped with history's largest paratroop assault, and was killed by gunfire near Wesel, Germany. He was with the 507th Parachute Infantry Regiment and is buried in the Netherlands (www.edow.org/news/window/july2004/ww2.html).

Conway, a Marine chaplain, said in a letter written to his parents one day before being killed on Guam on July 21, 1944: "If the worst should happen to me, that is God's will, and I gave my life for the Church and the God who rules it. I took the vow at ordination to obey. My work here is obedience at its best" (Crosby, 1994, p. 188). Conway is buried in Honolulu.

Chaplains served in other countries, too, including German clergy ministering to German troops before and during their invasions. Bergen (2004) has photos of German priests holding masses for troops before the invasion of Poland in 1939, and recounts chaplains serving in the invasion of Russia.

Bibliography

Army (1945). Order of battle of the United States Army World War II: www.history.army.mil/documents/eto-ob/4ID-eto.htm.

Bergen, Doris L. (ed.) (2004). The sword of the Lord: Military chaplains from the First to the Twenty-first Century. Notre Dame, Ind.: University of Notre Dame.

Colby, John (1991). War from the ground up: The 90th Division in World War II. Austin, Texas: Nortex Press.

Crosby, Donald F., S.J. (1994). Battlefield chaplains: Catholic priests in World War II. Lawrence, Kan.: University Press of Kansas.

Episcopal Diocese of Washington, D.C. (undated). Exhibit honors World War II's chaplains. www.edow.org/news/window/july2004/ww2.html

Navy Historical Center, www.history.navy.mil/photos/pers-us/uspers-o/j-ocalln.htm

Ryan, Cornelius (1959, 1984). The longest day. New York, NY: Simon & Schuster.

Young, Donald J. (1992). The battle of Bataan: A history of the 90-day siege and eventual surrender of 75,000 Filipino and United States troops to the Japanese in World War II. Jefferson, N.C.: McFarland & Co. Inc.

Other reading

Brody, Seymour (undated). Rabbis as chaplains in America's military: A tradition of service, dedication and bravery. www.library.fau.edu/depts/spc/brody_chaplains.pdf

Catholic Chaplain's Monument at Arlington National Cemetery, www.arlingtoncemetery.net/catholic.htm

Chaplain's monument at Arlington National Cemetery, www.arlingtoncemetery.org/descriptions/chaplains_hill_monument.html

Evangelical Lutheran Church in America (undated). By their side: Lutheran military chaplains. www.elca.org.

Chapter 10:

Bullets, torpedoes and deaths on Christmas

Monuments, chapels and MIA walls at cemeteries run by the American Battle Monuments Commission feature inspirational quotations about sacrifice, duty, honor, country and God.

For example, at the Honolulu Memorial, this inscription honors MIAs from World War II, Korea and Vietnam: "These men were part of the price that free men have been forced to pay to defend human liberty and right / To these men we owe a debt to be paid with grateful remembrance of their heroism."

The MIA Memorial Court in Manila says: "Some there be which have no sepulchre / their name liveth for evermore / Grant unto them O Lord eternal rest / who sleep in unknown graves." Another, at a mosaic there, says: "To their memory their country brings its gratitude as flowers forever living."

At the Brittany American Cemetery in France, a sculpture bears this Bible verse from 2 Timothy: "I have fought a good fight / I have finished my course / I have kept the faith."

And then there is this, inside the chapel at the Sicily-Rome Cemetery at Nettuno, Italy: "Peace on earth / good will among men."

Actually, despite what the angels in the Gospel of Luke proclaimed with glorias and a giant star, Christmas Eve and Christmas Day frequently saw the exact opposite – plenty of killing and death for Wisconsin soldiers – on Christmas Eve in every year of the war, and Christmas Day in 1942, 1943 and 1944.

A total of 17 Wisconsin men who are buried overseas or MIA died on Christmas Eve over the years, and the Christmas Day number is 22.

These dates also featured an absolutely shocking event; one that is seldom if ever memorialized or written about today but was the topic of an excellent 1963 book "A Night Before Christmas," by Jacquin Sanders. Seven of the Wisconsin men killed on Christmas Day 1944 were in the 66th Infantry Division and died after a German submarine torpedoed a troop ship full of replacements heading across the English Channel and into the Battle of the Bulge. The attack occurred just before 6 p.m. on Christmas Eve, a time when many family parties usually are getting started.

The seven men are on the MIA walls at the Normandy cemetery and at Cambridge, England. The attack killed about 800 men overall.

Across the world two years earlier, on Christmas Eve 1942 in New Guinea, the lack of peace and good will was marked by battles so severe that two Wisconsin members of the Army's 32nd Division, the famed Red Arrow that originally was a Wisconsin and Michigan National Guard unit, received the Medal of Honor for sacrificing their lives to save those of others.

It is not very hard to find dates that were more "peaceful" than Dec. 24 and 25 among Wisconsin soldiers buried overseas or MIA. For example, on June 25, one Wisconsin man was killed in 1942, zero in 1943, four in 1944 and zero in 1945.

On Sept. 25, no Wisconsin men were killed in 1942, none in 1943 and eight in 1944. For March 25, two Wisconsin men were killed in 1942, none in 1943, two in 1944 and zero in 1945, according to the ABMC database.

Examining different days in different months across the span of the war, on July 10 no Wisconsin men were killed in 1945 in the ABMC database, three in 1944, four in 1943 and one in 1942. On Oct. 20 in 1944, five men died, two in 1943 and none in 1942. And on April 5 in 1945, six were killed, four in 1944, one in 1943 and none in 1942.

In any of the ABMC cemeteries, there are many Stars of David over graves instead of crosses. They are one of the first things that a visitor will notice. To the Jewish, Christmas Eve and Day were just regular days. But here's betting that the day of Hanukkah, which is different every year, also saw plenty of deaths.

Torpedoing of the Leopoldville

The seven men from Wisconsin who were killed on the Belgian troop-transport ship Leopoldville as it made an 18-hour trip across the English Channel were in the Army's 66th Infantry Division; most of them were in the 262nd Regiment of that division.

They are Army Pvt. Douglas Brady, Walworth County; Pfc. Raymond Gaudynski, Milwaukee County; Pvt. Irving Grant, Milwaukee County; Pfc. Dean McHugh, La Crosse County; Pvt. Howard Peters, Milwaukee County; Pfc. Einar Pettersen (the spelling of his last name is correct), Racine County; and Pfc. William Schulz, Milwaukee County.

Schulz was in the 264th Regiment, which also was part of the 66th Division. Six are on the MIA wall in Normandy; McHugh is on the MIA wall at Cambridge, England.

In addition, a Navy man, Fireman Second Class Gerhard Kluewer of Oconomowoc, is on the MIA wall at Cambridge from that date and thus may have been on the Leopoldville in some capacity.

For some reason, the dates on the MIA walls for these men all say Dec. 25. The torpedo was just before 6 p.m. on Christmas Eve, killing some men immediately, and the ship sank in two hours. But many more men died aboard lifeboats, in life preservers, etc.

Nine more Wisconsin men are listed as killed on Dec. 26, 1944, by the ABMC, but none was in the 66th, so the ship's toll likely was complete as of Dec. 25.

The group of veterans and retired seamen called the U.S. Navy Armed Guard and World War II Merchant Marine has a Web site that discusses the Leopoldville, and says it was "never subjected to enemy fire in her 24 (previous) channel crossings, safely delivering 120,000 troops. This was just expected to be another routine crossing from England to France" (www.armed-guard.com).

"A Night Before Christmas" is not a version of the poem about Santa's arrival on the rooftop and down the chimney by

Clement C. Moore, but rather a recounting of this disaster by Jacquin Sanders, who was a member of the 66th Division aboard the other troop ship that evening, the SS Cheshire. There were 2,000 men on each ship, en route from Southampton, England, to Cherbourg, France.

Sanders says the troops were irritated about being moved during Christmas – "There was defiance, even sullenness, in the way these soldiers clung to the idea that Christmas should 'be itself,' even in wartime, even for infantrymen ... This is not to say that the outfit resented being sent into combat. On the contrary, the men expected and in many cases even looked forward to physical danger. It was only the timing they quarreled with" (Sanders, 1963, p. 14-15). They had observed Thanksgiving in the middle of the Atlantic, en route to England.

Soon after the Leopoldville and Cheshire left Southampton with four destroyers as their escorts, they were ordered into a zig-zag pattern to evade submarines, which had been sighted in the past two weeks. The ships went into at least two alerts, manning battle stations and firing depth charges. This was more than three hours before the actual attack. But there was no general alert to the troops aboard.

Then it happened. The German submarine U-486, commanded by Oberleutnant Gerhard Meyer, fired.

"In the forwardmost troop compartments the explosion of the torpedo was a soft thud, removed as the sound of a truck backfiring on a distant highway, an easy bump, like a rowboat jarring a submerged rock. Some men felt the ship give a small shudder; others were conscious of an increased rocking movement. One group had gathered in a corner to sing Christmas carols. 'O Little Town of Bethlehem' quavered questioningly for a moment or two, then resumed strength and pace" (Sanders, 1963, p. 66).

But farther back on the ship, there was no doubt – 300 men were killed instantly in the compartments that took the direct hit. The ship was one hour from Cherbourg, which was only 5.5 miles away. But it was Christmas Eve, and skeleton crews were operating in the port, while higher officers were attending parties complete with liquor, music and 40 members of the Women's Army Corps. Some had left orders not to be disturbed.

Sanders makes a complete deconstruction of the incident, examining the actions of Capt. Charles Limboor of the Leopoldville, the Belgian crew, dozens of ship hands from the Congo who did not speak English, the infantrymen and their lack of major seagoing training even though they had just crossed the Atlantic, the lack of a clear "abandon ship" order, how American officers ordered their men to stay onboard, those operating the Cherbourg harbor facilities, crews of the destroyers, how the first message about the torpedoing went back to England and through channels rather directly than to those in the French harbor who could have ordered an emergency, and on and on.

Fort O'uest, at the entrance to the Cherbourg harbor, thought something was wrong because the Leopoldville had stopped and then began drifting out of shipping lanes toward a minefield, so the fort began flashing inquiries via blinkers. But they were not answered for a crucial half-hour. Then, for another half-hour, good soldiers and Navy men tried to follow the chain of command and get approval from higher-ups to proceed with rescues or at least sailing out to the halted vessel. But it was hard reaching the bosses on Christmas Eve, and some who answered the phone were disbelieving and refused to send the call up the ladder.

The combination of the holiday, parties, command inertia and undermanned command posts and the fact that few harbor craft actually were on station to set out for an emergency on Christmas Eve made for a disaster. The top Army man at the fort, Lt. Col. Tom McConnell, "couldn't – by ordinary requests or even demands – get past the various junior officers and noncoms manning all the headquarters. This was Christmas Eve, he was told. The brass was not to be disturbed except for important emergencies" (Sanders, 1963, p. 189). It also was getting darker by the minute. Finally, a Navy ensign got the attention of Lt. Cmdr. Richard Davis to come to duty and Davis did enough swearing at those in other military branches, and magically some PT boats at last fired up and headed out toward the Leopoldville. "His force and fury helped save hundreds of lives" (p. 192).

Aboard the Leopoldville, hundreds of men were trapped down below because the blast had destroyed ladders. Shockingly, multiple soldiers saw dozens of the Belgian or Congolese crewmen hurrying into their own lifeboats with "valises, attaché cases, bulging canvas bags" (Sanders, 1963, p. 124), and even a parrot in a cage. This rather than save space for some of the 2,000 passengers or to stay behind and direct their military guests to safety. The captain and his top officers did not leave, but their leadership was spread much thinner without a full crew and with panic beginning to rise.

A British destroyer, the Brilliant, was able to come alongside despite high waves in order to begin rescues. Many men fell into the sea, were hurt jumping onto the heaving deck of the destroyer, were crushed in the sea between the two ships, failed to cope with swinging on ropes, etc., but the Brilliant did rescue about 500 or 600 – until it had to depart for fear of being overloaded and capsizing.

Although the Leopoldville's captain reportedly said early-on that there was no doubt the ship was going to sink, that never was announced, even when the ship began to list more and more. Two hours after the torpedoing, by Sanders' estimate, 1,200 of the original 2,237 people on board were still aboard. This was at 8 p.m., and it went under soon thereafter.

Roughly 800 died and 1,400 survived. Of the ship's crew of 230, only five were lost (p. 244).

Ray Clark of Wyoming, who was a staff sergeant, was the subject of a story in the Sheridan Press newspaper on the 45th anniversary of the sinking. Clark is a Mason and so the story is posted at the Masonic Web site of www.scottishrite.org.

> "It was a terrible stormy night," he says. "The waves were 20 feet high. Ships that pulled alongside couldn't rescue us because the water was too rough."
>
> When the torpedo hit, "I was in my hammock one deck down, about the center of the ship. I suspected right away that we'd been hit by a torpedo because it was a large explosion that rocked the ship pretty good." Ray went on deck immediately, and "I

> was sure the ship was going to sink because she was listing pretty hard."
>
> Just before it sunk, it "rolled over on its side," Clark says. "I ran down the side until I got to the water. Then I started swimming as hard as I could." Clark swam until he was exhausted, and when he looked back, he was only about 40 feet from where he'd gone into the water. The suction of the sinking ship was pulling him back.
>
> "I had to keep swimming as hard as I could just to keep afloat. ... My life preserver was soaked with oil from the ship and was starting to lose its buoyancy. I'd been in the water over six hours when a French tug pulled me out."

Besides the Leopoldville, the Christmas 1944 toll is so high because of the Battle of the Bulge,which is a far better-known story and thoroughly memorialized in history – the general's famous "Nuts" answer to the German demand to surrender, Germans disguised in American uniforms and with American jeeps, the massacre in the snow at Malmedy, etc.

Comprehensive books about the Bulge abound. But some that were checked for information about the Leopoldville – including Gerald Astor's 1992 book "A Blood-Dimmed Tide: The Battle of the Bulge by the Men Who Fought It" – had nothing on the Christmas Eve disaster in the index. However, "A Time for Trumpets: The Untold Story of the Battle of the Bulge," by Charles B. Macdonald (1985), has a few pages, all of them based on Sanders' book.

The battle started with the German attack on Dec. 16 and ran into late January 1945. Other than the Leopoldville, the Wisconsin men killed on Christmas Eve 1944 were from groups like the 5th Infantry Division, the 836th Bomber Squadron of the 487th Bomber Group (Heavy), the 705th Tank Destroyer Battalion and 75th Infantry Division.

All the men on the accompanying list that are buried in Europe but were not on the Leopoldville certainly were in the Battle of the

Bulge. Those killed on Christmas Day 1944 were, variously, from units like the 3rd Infantry Division, 3rd Armored Division, 106th Infantry Division, 80th Infantry Division and 101st Airborne Division.

Buna, New Guinea

On the other side of the world, the fighting by Wisconsin's 32nd Division and the Australians in the final months of 1942 and early January 1943 represented the first major Allied land victory in Asia in World War II. The Marines had invaded Guadalcanal in August 1942, but the island "was not declared won until Feb. 9" (Mayo, 1974, p. 180). However, when the author of this book wrote that phrase in the Milwaukee Sentinel in 1985, a Marine quickly called to challenge that, gruffly noting that his unit already had been pulled out of Guadalcanal and replaced by Army troops, who finished the remnants of fighting.

At Guadalcanal there were 1,600 Allied deaths, and at Buna there were 3,095, plus thousands more lost to malaria, dysentery, dengue fever or scrub typhus (Mayo, 1974, p. 180).

Japan had invaded New Guinea on March 8, 1942. It already had invaded Rabaul in the Bismarck islands in January 1942 and seized Singapore the next month, and the Allies feared that the continent of Australia was next if New Guinea were to fall. When the Japanese captured the villages of Salamaua and Lae in New Guinea, they were only 400 miles away from the northernmost point of Australia.

The 32nd Division had been a Wisconsin and Michigan National Guard unit before it was federalized in 1940. The division consisted of infantry companies, artillery units, medical groups and the like scattered all over the state – Oshkosh, Waupaca, Menasha, Rhinelander, Oconto, Ripon, Edgerton, Eau Claire, Chippewa Falls, River Falls, West Bend, Marshfield, Beaver Dam, Platteville, Baraboo, and many more points, including multiple units from Milwaukee and Madison. In fact, the Wisconsin rosters as of when the 32nd was federalized span 68 full pages in "The 32nd Infantry Division in World War II," by Maj. Gen. H.W. Blakeley (1957), the official history of the division. He was not part of it in the war (he served in Europe) but reviewed all materials after the conflict. The Michigan rosters in the book span 39 pages.

Elements of the division were sent to New Guinea in September 1942 along with Australian troops. The 32nd was very ill-equipped in terms of weapons, gear and even clothing for a jungle that featured huge bugs, tropical diseases, dysentery, incredible rainstorms, chills, heat, impenetrable swamps, swiftly flowing rivers, chronically wet firewood, "blood-sucking bats; rats as large as collies; wild boars; snakes; crocodiles; monitor lizards over six feet long; diseases that could make a man's scrotum swell up to the size of a pumpkin; and hungry cannibals who enjoyed the practice of eating living meat" (Campbell, 2007, p. 79). On top of that, the intelligence about the number of Japanese forces and their defenses was severely wrong.

Gen. Douglas MacArthur, Southwest Pacific commander, became unhappy that his orders were somehow not successfully carried out despite the fact that conditions on the ground were far different than what was assumed in the comfort of headquarters – that the troops had the proper equipment, that the Japanese defenses could be easily overcome with light weapons, and on and on. MacArthur relieved Maj. Gen. Edward Harding of command on Nov. 30 and replaced him with Lt. Gen. Robert Eichelberger, who found much the same difficulties and the same impatient MacArthur. Many wound up saying, in essence, that it was a lot easier to sit on your khaki butt at a typewriter in a faraway headquarters than it was to actually carry out the orders.

In a story told again in "The Ghost Mountain Boys," a 2007 book by James Campbell, some parts of the 126th Infantry Regiment had to slash their way through the jungle for 130 miles over the Owen Stanley mountains, which featured impossibly steep and inhospitable terrain, huge insects, tropical diseases, legends about ghosts that scared natives who were hired to help carry gear, razor-sharp kunai and elephant grass, and so on. Capt. William Fleischer, quoted in the history by Blakeley (1957), said it thusly: "It was a grueling march on a line paralleling the Kokoda trail, and the men who made it will remember it forever as a living, wide-awake nightmare. For 42 days they climbed, scrambled, clawed and suffered – many times cutting their own trail through some of the most awesome territory in the world" (p. 46).

Then it came time to face the enemy! And when the enemy was not to be seen, its snipers frequently took over.

In his memoirs, Eichelberger called the few pieces of civilization at Buna "godforsaken little places on the inhospitable northern coast of New Guinea. A few score native huts and the coconut plantations around them represented, before the war, Buna's sole claim on an indifferent world's attention" (Blakeley, 1957, p. 53). By this time, MacArthur had flown to the New Guinea capital of Port Moresby, on the southern coast, and his headquarters had a shady porch from which he issued his orders that had little to do with actual conditions on the north coast.

A medical officer reported to Eichelberger on the day the general took over that the beleaguered men "looked like 'Christ off the cross'," (Campbell, 2007, p. 220).

The Allied force in New Guinea was divided into two prongs, named the Warren Force and the Urbana Force.

This book's account will focus primarily on the 127th Regiment – which was flown from Australia to Port Moresby on Thanksgiving and then to the north coast on Dec. 11 – because of its losses on Christmas. But other units of the Red Arrow were pounded all during the weeks of fighting, including the 126th Regiment and the 128th.

The 127th Regiment entered the fray on Dec. 14 at Buna Village, but found the Japanese had pulled out to Sananánda or to Buna Government Station, leaving behind extensive damage from artillery and other weapons. MacArthur's headquarters immediately trumpeted this advance as the "first major offensive victory over the Japanese for Gen. Douglas MacArthur" (Mayo, 1974, p. 145). However, the main objective was Buna Government Station, and that attack began a week before Christmas, with both the Warren and Urbana forces.

Books and the division veterans' detailed Web site (www.32nd-division.org/history) say that on Dec. 24, the 127th Regiment – under Col. John Grose, who had been installed by Eichelberger – tried to drive across the former rubber plantation known as the Government Gardens at Buna.

"The troops had to cross in succession the so-called Gardens – actually an area overgrown with kunai (tall jungle grass that was as sharp as a knife) – then a swamp some 125 yards wide and finally the coconut grove known as Government Plantation. The whole area was well-prepared for defense with the usual mutually supporting bunkers and fire trenches" (Blakeley, 1957, p. 104).

The two Medal of Honor incidents, both fatal, on Christmas Eve were the only ones for the division in the Buna campaign (the 32nd would earn nine more in the war).

One such incident came when a Japanese grenade fell close to the captain of Company I, Michael Ustruck. First Sgt. Elmer J. Burr of Menasha threw himself on the grenade.

In military-esque language, the posthumous citation read: "For conspicuous gallantry and intrepidity in action above and beyond the call of duty. During an attack near Buna, New Guinea, on 24 December 1942, 1st Sgt. Burr saw an enemy grenade strike near his company commander. Instantly and with heroic self-sacrifice he threw himself upon it, smothering the explosion with his body. 1st Sgt. Burr thus gave his life in saving that of his commander" (www.32nd-division.org/history).

When a group from Company L of the 127th Regiment was held up by enemy fire on the outskirts of the Gardens, Sgt. Kenneth E. Gruennert, who was in the lead, eliminated two pillboxes that were holding up the advance. Burr, of Helenville in Jefferson County, also received the Medal of Honor posthumously.

The citation said:

> "For conspicuous gallantry and intrepidity in action above and beyond the call of duty. On 24 December 1942, near Buna, New Guinea, Sgt. Gruennert was second in command of a platoon with a mission to drive through the enemy lines to the beach 600 yards ahead. Within 150 yards of the objective, the platoon encountered two hostile pillboxes. Sgt. Gruennert advanced alone on the first and put it out of action with hand grenades and rifle fire, killing three of the enemy.

> "Seriously wounded in the shoulder, he bandaged his wound under cover of the pillbox, refusing to withdraw to the aid station and leave his men. He then, with undiminished daring, and under extremely heavy fire, attacked the second pillbox. As he neared it he threw grenades which forced the enemy out where they were easy targets for his platoon.
>
> "Before the leading elements of his platoon could reach him he was shot by enemy snipers. His inspiring valor cleared the way for his platoon which was the first to attain the beach in this successful effort to split the enemy position" (www.32nd-division.org/history).

The bodies of both Burr and Gruennert were returned home after the war and thus are not in the database of the American Battle Monuments Commission, which is used for this book. The Christmas deaths who are buried overseas, in Manila, are Sgt. Louis Wierzelewski, Milwaukee County (killed on Christmas Eve) and four men killed on Christmas Day: Sgt. Ervin Michalak, Milwaukee County; Sgt. Robert Smith, Marinette County; Pfc. Bernhard Stegemeyer, Sheboygan County; and Pvt. Lester Van Der Weele, Sheboygan County. All are from the 127th Regiment.

Eichelberger said in a note to MacArthur written on Christmas Day that "I think the all-time low of my life occurred yesterday" (Blakeley, 1957, p. 107). But the attack was ordered to continue on the 25th, and one company advanced to within 300 yards of the seashore.

"Capt. James W. Workman, commanding Company C, was killed while leading an attack on a bunker. He was later awarded the Distinguished Service Cross. Sgt. William Fale, Pfc. William Balza and Pvt. Gordon W. Eoff, all of Headquarters Company, 127th Infantry, also won the DSC for their efforts to get telephone wire forward to companies which were out of communication with regimental headquarters" (Blakeley, 1957, p. 107).

That all was action on the Urbana Front. On the Warren Front, early on Dec. 24, four tanks crossed a bridge built and repaired by engineers. An all-out attack by Australians and Americans initially showed promise, but was soon reduced to a very slow and costly advance, at the loss of three of the tanks (www.32nd-division.org/history).

From Dec. 24 to 28, "Warren Force was to experience bitter fighting, marked by fanatical Japanese resistance, futile attempts to struggle through the swamps on the enemy's flanks, and many examples of individual courage and devotion to duty" (Blakeley, 1957, p. 97).

When the battle finally ended on Jan. 22, the division as a whole had lost 690 killed in action and 1,680 wounded, with untold hundreds greatly weakened by the disease (Blakeley, 1957, p. 125). Campbell (2007) says the casualty rate was more than 90 percent – from deaths, wounds, injuries and illness – out of nearly 11,000 troops, there were 9,688 casualties (p. 270), of which 7,125 were from the jungle diseases.

As for the 126th Regiment, when it finally left New Guinea on Jan. 9, it had fewer than 200 soldiers still capable of fighting, compared with 1,400 when it began in November (Mayo, 1974, p. 170).

Logistically, the division's 1942 experience was a lesson to the Army as it sent its first division into combat. It was very poorly equipped, not trained for jungle warfare, artillery was of no use in the dense tree canopies of jungle, intelligence about the number of Japanese and the nature of their defenses was poor, and on and on. The main factors were "the interference of senior commanders, and sometimes of their staff officers, in the operations of lower units sometimes several command echelons below them; the international quality of the chain of command and finally, the continued extensive mixing of combat units. The common factor in these matters seems to have been the constant pressure of, first, the situation as it existed, and second, General MacArthur himself" (Blakeley, 1957, p. 126).

After the losses at Buna, the 32nd was re-staffed and revitalized during all of 1943, and returned to combat at Saidor in New Guinea in the first days of 1944. It also fought at Aitape in New Guinea, Morotai in the Indonesian islands, Biak island, and the huge Philippine islands of Leyte and Luzon.

Bibliography

Blakeley, H.W., Maj. Gen. (1957). 32nd Infantry Division in World War II. Madison, Wis.: 32nd Infantry Division History Commission, State of Wisconsin.

Campbell, James (2007). The Ghost Mountain boys: Their epic and terrifying battle for New Guinea – the forgotten war of the South Pacific. New York: Crown Publishers.

Mayo, Lida (1974). Bloody Buna: The grueling campaign in New Guinea that thwarted the Japanese invasion of Australia. Garden City, N.Y.: Doubleday and Co. Inc.

Red Arrow Division's history at www.32nd-division.org/history/ww2/ww2.html

Sanders, Jacquin (1963). A night before Christmas. New York: G.P. Putnam's Sons.

Sheridan (Wyo.) Press (1999). A Christmas Eve he will never forget. Dec. 24. Article posted at www.scottishrite.org/council/journal/dec00/clark.html

World War II U.S. Navy Armed Guard and World War II U.S. Merchant Marine. www.armed-guard.com/leopold.html

Deaths at Christmas

This list is compiled from the database of the American Battle Monuments Commission and cross-referenced with the 1946 official booklets of Navy / Marine losses (including hometown) and of Army / Air Force casualties (which lists only counties), and with Army enlistment records. This list gives a hometown for Army / Air Force men if it was found via other processes. If serviceman is on an MIA monument, it is noted; otherwise he is buried.

Dec. 24, 1941

Army Capt. Walter H. Write, Rock County, MIA wall in Manila

Dec. 24, 1942

Army Sgt. Louis Wierzelewski, Milwaukee County, buried in Manila

Dec. 25, 1942

Army Sgt. Ervin Michalak, Milwaukee County, buried in Manila

Army Sgt. Robert Smith, Marinette County, Manila

Army Pfc. Bernhard Stegemeyer, Sheboygan County, Manila

Army Pvt. Lester Van Der Weele, Sheboygan County, Manila

Dec. 24, 1943

Air Force 1st Lt. George Jameson, Oconto County, buried in North Africa

Dec. 25, 1943

Navy Aviation Machinist's Mate 3rd Class Dennis Paquette, Park Falls, MIA wall in Manila

Army Pvt. Robert Nelson, home county not found, Sicily-Rome

Dec. 24, 1944

Air Force Tech Sgt. Robert Behrens, Sheboygan County, MIA wall in Manila

Army Pvt. Earl Erickson, Manitowoc County, buried in Henri-Chapelle, Belgium

Army Pfc. Harry Frese, Clark County, Luxembourg

Army Staff Sgt. Kermit Gunderson, Dane County, Henri-Chapelle

Air Force 1st Lt. Robert Harriman, Dane County, Henri-Chapelle

Army Pvt. Joseph Mueller, Winnebago County, Manila

Army Pfc. George Patrica, Milwaukee County, MIA wall in Ardennes

Air Force Sgt. Edward Riesing, Milwaukee County, Cambridge, England

Army Technician 4th Class John Schmitz, Marathon County, MIA wall Ardennes

Army Pvt. Victor Schneider, Winnebago County, Luxembourg

Air Force Flight Officer Joseph Shuster, home county not found, Henri-Chapelle

Air Force Cpl. Charles Teipner, Langlade County, MIA wall in Manila

Army Pvt. Forrest Trantham, home county not found, Luxembourg

Dec. 25, 1944

Army Pvt. Leonard Bolinski, (not on Army list, but serial number shows he was from Milwaukee County and enlisted in Kentucky), Lorraine Cemetery, St. Avold, France

Army Pvt. Douglas Brady, Walworth County, MIA wall in Normandy

Seaman First Class Russell Damiano, Milwaukee, MIA wall in Honolulu

Army Pfc. Raymond Gaudynski, Milwaukee County, MIA wall in Normandy

Army Pvt. Irving Grant, Milwaukee County, MIA wall in Normandy

Navy Fireman 2nd Class Gerhard Kluewer, Oconomowoc, MIA wall at Cambridge

Army Technician Fifth Class Aloys Husting, Ozaukee County, Henri-Chapelle

Army Pfc. Dean McHugh, La Crosse County, MIA wall at Cambridge

Army Pfc. David Mueller, Milwaukee County, Henri-Chapelle

Army Pvt. Howard Peters, Milwaukee County, MIA wall in Normandy

Army Pfc. Einar Pettersen, Racine County, MIA wall in Normandy

Army Pvt. Lloyd Scheller, Racine County, Luxembourg

Army Pvt. Leonard Schilz, Milwaukee County, Epinal

Army Pfc. William Schulz, Milwaukee County, MIA wall in Normandy

Army Sgt. Roy Sprister, Outagamie County, Luxembourg

Air Force Staff Sgt. Andrew Sutter, Marathon County, Henri-Chapelle

Dec. 24, 1945

Army 1st Lt. Robert A. Mitzner, Jefferson County, Lorraine

Chapter 11:

The big brass

Brig. Gen. Richard Andersen, Racine

Air Force Brig. Gen. Richard Andersen had finished a major task, creating bases and runways for waves of B-29 superbombers on the island of Guam to attack Japan. They were joining B-29s already flying from nearby Tinian and Saipan, and the Guam additions meant the attacks would become even more pulverizing and widespread.

On Feb. 25, 1945, the B-29 Superfortress flew its first combat missions from Guam, from the airfields that Andersen had worked months to create. The very next day, Andersen, a 1926 West Point grad from Racine, and his boss, Lt. Gen. Millard Harmon, left Guam on a flight to Hawaii for a meeting to help plan the forthcoming invasion of Japan (www.globalsecurity.org/military/facility/andersen.htm).

Andersen and Harmon never arrived. The B-24 Liberator bomber carrying them and eight other men vanished sometime after its intermediate stop at Kwajalein.

Both Andersen and Harmon are on the MIA wall at Honolulu. Andersen was 41; Harmon was 57.

The Racine Journal-Times newspaper reported on March 5, 1945, that the military said that "when last heard from, the bomber reported ample fuel to complete the flight and was traveling in good weather over calm seas. When the plane failed to respond to communications ... all available naval ships and planes were dispatched to join the search. ... Later indications point to the search as the greatest since the hunt for Amelia Earhart and Capt. Eddie Rickenbacker."

That is a reference to the female air pioneer who disappeared on an attempted flight around the world in 1937, and to the World

Brig. Gen. Richard Andersen, Racine, Air Force on Guam

Cmdr. Bertram Prueher, Bloomer, Navy squadron leader

War I Ace of Aces, who was on a tour of overseas installations in 1942 when his B-17 plane vanished on a flight from Hawaii to New Guinea. He and six other survivors were finally found after 24 days aboard life rafts.

The Racine newspaper said Andersen's wife, Esther, and their two children, Nancy Jo and Jay, were living in Washington, D.C., and her parents were Mr. and Mrs. F.H. Hau, formerly of 715 Cleveland Ave. in Racine, but were now living in Fond du Lac.

Andersen and Harmon were part of the leadership in the Headquarters of Army Air Forces, Pacific Ocean Area. Harmon, a three-star, was commanding general of the organization, and deputy commander of the 20th Air Force. Andersen was his chief of staff, according to Harmon's official Air Force biography at www.af.mil/bios/bio.asp?bioID=10235.

Andersen had been a brigadier general, a one-star, for only one month. But because of his work to create B-29 fields at Guam, one of them was named for him a few years after the war, and today it remains Andersen Air Force Base, a centerpiece of American defenses in the Pacific. Its Web site is www.andersen.af.mil/.

The B-29s from Guam soon were involved in some of the biggest actions of the war, including the infamous March 9-10 fire-bombing of Tokyo by 334 Superfortresses that killed more than 80,000 people. Each B-29 carried 1,520 firebombs (Glusman, 2005, p. 376).

The two B-29s that dropped the atomic bombs on Japan in August 1945, and ended the war, flew from Tinian.

The Superfortress was specifically designed for the war against Japan. It was 50 percent larger than any other heavy bomber, could carry twice the weight that a B-17 bomber could, and fly twice as far. (Coffey, 1982, p. 334). The behemoth plane finally was ready for combat in 1944, and was first put in India, and then China. But Japan was at the edge of its maximum range and flying over mountains to get there was difficult. It became much more feasible once Saipan, Tinian and then Guam fell after long battles on land, and runways and air facilities could be constructed on those islands.

Now the B-29s were about 1,500 miles from Japan, and when Iwo Jima fell, crippled planes had a place to land instead of ditching at sea while trying to make it all the way back to the Marianas.

The first B-29s arrived in the Marianas on Saipan in October 1944. Within a month, 111 of them were on a mission against Tokyo.

The atomic bomb could be flown only in a big plane such as this – the device weighed 6,000 to 7,000 pounds. Only the highest of Air Force personnel knew the bomb was coming – Air Force Chief Henry "Hap" Arnold was told in late 1944 or early 1945 (Coffey, 1982, p. 356-357), because crews had to be trained to drop it.

The successful test was conducted July 16, 1945, in New Mexico, and the bombings at Hiroshima and Nagasaki came three weeks later.

Andersen was born in Racine on May 10, 1904, and graduated from Racine High School in 1922, a few years before it was replaced by Washington Park High School.

In his high school yearbook, the Kipikawi, his name was given as James Anderson, with an 'o.' He was senior class secretary, and the clever line by each graduate's photo said for him, "He's fickle – but who cares?" Page 97 lists him as associate editor of the Enicar magazine.

Many of the newspaper clippings at the Racine Heritage Museum spell his name with an 'o' instead of an 'e.' So do all the references to him in the 1922 yearbook, and those when he was an underclassmen. The two spellings of the name are easily confused by those who are listening but not careful with the letters, but one would think the "fickle" Andersen would have insisted his fellow students spell his name right. There were dozens of both versions in the city, but the spelling with 'o' was more common – the 1921 City Directory had three full columns of Andersen families and eight full columns of Andersons.

After Racine, Andersen's next stop was the U.S. Military Academy, and he graduated in 1926, ranking No. 37 out of 152 in his class, according to the records in the West Point Library (www.library.usma.edu/archives/special.asp). That put him in the upper 25 percent of the class.

Another newspaper story, from 1937, reported Andersen's graduation from Air Corps Advanced Flying School at Kelly Field in Texas, and said their children were ages 8 and 2, and that they would be coming home to Racine to visit the Hau family and Andersen's brother, Morris, who lived on Roe Avenue, and sister, Mrs. Fred Hanson, who lived on Clarence Avenue. Andersen was a captain at that time.

One of Andersen's next career steps was as an instructor in the Department of Chemistry and Electricity at West Point, and the first director of Stewart Field, the new air training field at West Point. Until Stewart Field was established in 1942, all cadets trained at Kelly Field in Texas.

In 1944, as a colonel, he went to Hawaii as chief of staff for an Air Force group. He was the principal planner for the move of the headquarters to Guam, which was accomplished in January 1945. That same month he was promoted to brigadier general.

The following history about Andersen's work on Guam is compiled from www.globalsecurity.org/military/facility/andersen.htm and other sites:

The Air Force built and maintained three airfields there – North Field (the one named for Andersen a few years later), a B-29 facility; Depot Field, a B-29 depot and maintenance base (later renamed Harmon Field in honor of the lieutenant general); and Northwest Field, a combined B-29 /fighter base.

Construction of North Field had begun in November 1944, carving it out of forest and brush on the northern end of the island. It also must be noted that the Japanese had attacked Guam on Dec. 8, 1941, and it surrendered two days later. But U.S. Marines invaded it in July 1944, a few weeks after Marines and the Army invaded nearby Saipan, and won it back the next month.

On Feb. 3, 1945, one of the two runways was completed, and the first B-29 landed on the field that day with Maj. Gen. Curtis E. LeMay Jr. at the controls. This was three weeks before Andersen was killed.

The 314th Bomb Wing began operating from Guam in February 1945. Its units were the 19th, 29th, 39th and 330th Bomb Groups.

In 1947, North Field was renamed North Guam Air Force Base. On Oct. 7, 1949, it was renamed Andersen AFB in honor of Andersen.

The Racine Journal-Times reported the news about the renaming ceremony on April 25, 1950. The article said Andersen's wife attended the ceremony with her son, James Roy Andersen, and "presented a large portrait of her late husband to Air Force officials."

As for his boss, Millard Fillmore Harmon Jr. was born Jan. 19, 1888, at Fort Mason, Calif., and graduated from West Point in 1912 (his father graduated in 1880). The son's Air Force biography says that two years later, he was detailed to the newly organized Aviation Section of the Signal Corps, and accompanied the Punitive Expedition into Mexico (led by Gen. Black Jack Pershing) and did aerial patrol work along the border. Wilbur and Orville Wright made their landmark flight at Kitty Hawk, N.C., in 1903, barely a decade earlier. Harmon was attached to the French 13th Group de Combat as a pilot during World War I.

In January 1942, he became chief of the air staff, Army Air Forces. In July 1942, he was appointed commanding general of U.S. Army Forces in the South Pacific area, an area that was under Navy command. In November, Adm. William (Bull) Halsey assumed command of the South Pacific, and they worked together. In 1944, at the end of his mission, Halsey wrote, "I was particularly fortunate in having Harmon as commanding general of the Army Forces; his sound advice and wholehearted cooperation in attaining the common goal were outstanding contributions to the joint effort" (www.af.mil/bios/bio.asp?bioID=10235).

On Feb. 2, 1943, Harmon was promoted to lieutenant general and kept moving up the command ladder. In 1944, he was designated deputy commander of the 20th Air Force, under the command of Gen. Henry H. (Hap) Arnold. Under his command, the B-29s began their bombardment of Japan from Guam, Tinian and Saipan.

Arnold always called him "Miff" Harmon, according to a biography of Arnold (Coffey, 1982). The biography has less than one line on the loss of Harmon, saying only that his "plane had just disappeared on a routine flight" (p. 361).

Cmdr. Bertram Prueher, Bloomer

One does not often hear about the coast of Brazil being a scene of intense fighting in World War II, but it was.

Navy Cmdr. Bertram Prueher was a pilot and the leader of a squadron that patrolled the Atlantic against German U-boats lurking along shipping routes from a major American supply base in Brazil. The submarines had sunk many vessels in the months preceding August 1943, and Prueher's squadron had sunk several U-boats.

Prueher's plane was shot down by gunfire from one or more U-boats on Aug. 11 or 12, 1943, in the Atlantic off the coast of Natal, now a resort city of about 800,000, in the state of Rio Grande de Norte in northeastern Brazil. His name is on the East Coast Monument in New York City, as are those of several other servicemen discussed in this book.

The American Battle Monuments Commission gives his date of death as a year later, as is the case with several other Navy men and is standard recordkeeping during and after the war.

Prueher – the name is pronounced in his native Bloomer as PREER – was a 1933 graduate of the U.S. Naval Academy, and was about three weeks short of his 31st birthday when he was killed. He was the father of three small children.

A private Web site devoted to Navy Patrol Squadrons, www.VPNavy.org, says Prueher was from "Blommer, Wis.," which led the research of this book to Bloomer in Chippewa County. A call to Bloomer High School seeking information quickly led to Jim Kouba, a military veteran who had helped organize the creation of a large memorial listing all veterans from the town who have served in the military. The memorial was dedicated in 2008, and Prueher's three children attended, traveling from their homes in California, Missouri and Virginia.

Prueher spent some years in Tennessee, and in fact the Navy's 1946 booklet of deaths lists him under that state. The booklet says the next of kin was his wife, Mrs. Farrell Prueher, Warner Pl., Bellmeade, Nashville. This is not totally accurate: his wife's full name was Jean Farrell Prueher, and she lived in the posh area of Belle Meade.

When the time came to put him and a state on the East Coast Monument, it was Wisconsin.

Prueher was commander of Bombing Squadron 107 (VB-107 in Navy lingo). It originally was VP-83, but on May 15, 1943, the number was changed. Its standard plane, beginning in May 1943, was the PB4Y-1, "flying the Army version of the B-24D Liberator, redesignated P4BY-1 by the Navy," according to the Dictionary of American Naval Aviation Squadrons (www.history.navy.mil/avh-vol2/chap3-6.pdf).

The unit was based first in Norfolk, Va., beginning in September 1941, then in Natal from March to June 1942, then back in Norfolk briefly, and finally to Natal beginning in June 1943.

The squadron's record includes attacks on surfaced U-boats in several months of 1943 before the fateful day for Prueher. In January, two U-boats were sunk, and in April, two planes sunk a U-boat by dropping depth charges, some from a height of only 50 feet. On July 12, a little more than two weeks before Prueher was shot down, another flyer was shot down by a sub and all aboard were killed. Two weeks before that, a PD4Y-1 made a night attack on a surfaced U-boat and one engine was shot out (www.history.navy.mil/avh-vol2/chap3-6.pdf).

The German subs were inflicting a toll, too. In March 1943, a U-510 torpedoed eight ships in three hours off the coast of Brazil, in what was called the most successful single U-boat action of the war (www.worldwar-2.net/timelines/war-at-sea/atlantic/battle-of-the-atlantic-index-1943.htm). In June 1943, a U-513 sank four ships off the coast, and the next month, a U-185 bagged three merchant ships.

On his final flight in August, Prueher left Natal with extra fuel in order to conduct a long search. "Three surfaced U-boats were attacked in the afternoon," according to the Aviation Squadron dictionary. "Subsequent testimony of German naval personnel captured at a later date indicated that Lt. Cmdr. Prueher's aircraft was shot down by the combined AA (antiaircraft fire) of the submarines during his second bombing pass" (www.history.navy.mil/avh-vol2/chap3-6.pdf).

This article gives his name as B.G. Prueher (the list of commanders a few pages later correctly has it as B.J.), and his rank evidently was elevated after his death. He assumed command in January 1943 and was replaced a few days after his death by Lt. Cmdr. Renfro Turner Jr. The same article gives his date of death as Aug. 12, while most others give Aug. 11.

The comprehensive, but privately organized Web site of uboat.net says of the fatal day: "After failed meeting attempts due to constant airborne patrols, U-185 and U-604 finally met in the morning of 11 August, the crew of the latter starting at once the transfer of remaining provisions, oil and spare parts to U-185. After several hours of strenuous work, U-172 also arrived on the scene at 18.00. Detected by HF/DF localization, the meeting was crashed soon after by a Navy PBY-4 Liberator, piloted by the commanding officer of squadron VB-107, Lt. Cmdr. B.J. Prueher. Prueher took off with extra fuel tanks, knowing the targeted U-boats were on the edge of his plane's maximum range; after a 1,000-mile flight, he sighted the hoped-for U-boats. While U-604 lay helpless with most of her crew on the deck, and U-172 successfully crash-dived, the AA crew of U-185 opened fire on the Liberator, which did two attack runs without inflicting damage, before being shot down out of control on the third, killing all aboard" (www.uboat.net).

In 2008, the Website NashvillePost.com carried a Memorial Day salute to several area men, and included this:

"We remember Bertram Joseph Prueher.

"Bert Prueher told Naval Academy classmates that he had civilian ambitions. His 1933 Annapolis yearbook reported: 'His ambition is to retire young with a large tract of land and an appreciable income.'

"When war came in 1941, Wisconsin native Prueher went from a fine home in Belle Meade to the cockpit of an antisubmarine patrol aircraft. Commanding a squadron stationed at Natal in northern Brazil, Lt. Cmdr. Prueher regularly encountered German U-boats seeking to disrupt Allied shipping. While diving to attack a submarine on Aug. 11, 1943, his aircraft tumbled into the sea. The bodies of those aboard were never found."

(www.nashvillepost.com/news/2008/5/26/nashville_now_and_then_the_last_full_measure).

The base at Natal served as a transit point for American goods going overseas before the Allied invasion of North Africa in 1942. Natal was regarded as a "trampoline" for supplies from America to North Africa (Wolf, undated, http://history.sandiego.edu/gen/st/~johnw/Trampoline.htm).

Natal was the largest U.S. air base outside American territory, and the U.S. Fourth Fleet was based at Recife. Brazil also "sent its navy in pursuit of German U-boats and provided an expeditionary force and a fighter squadron on the Italian front ...."

(McCann, undated, http://warandgame.wordpress.com/2008/10/14/brazil-and-world-war-ii-the-forgotten-ally).

Earlier, in mid-August 1942, "10 U-boats went into action against coastal shipping, attacking in quick succession six vessels off Segipe and Bahia. In five days the Germans cut maritime communications with the northeast, and succeeded in doing what diplomacy had been able to do only superficially, namely, uniting Brazil against them. One ship, the Baependi, went down with 250 soldiers and seven officers, along with two artillery batteries and other equipment. The army cried for revenge. Another vessel sank with pilgrims en route to a Eucharistic Congress in Sáo Paulo," the McCann article said.

All in all, "Brazil took an active part in World War II as a supplier of strategic raw materials, as the site of important air and naval bases, as a skillful supporter of the United States in pan-American conferences, [and] as a contributor of naval units, a combat fighter squadron and a 25,000-strong infantry division. It lost 1,889 soldiers and sailors, 31 merchant vessels, three warships and 22 fighter aircraft" (McCann, undated, http://warandgame.wordpress.com/2008/10/14/brazil-and-world-war-ii-the-forgotten-ally).

Cmdr. Robert Bonin, Milwaukee

This book found only one Wisconsin war death in which the serviceman was the skipper of a vessel – the submarine USS Gudgeon, which vanished in April 1944. Cmdr. Robert Bonin's date of death as listed by the ABMC is Jan. 15, 1946, but that is merely a post-war closing of the books.

The 1946 Navy book of casualties says he was from Milwaukee, with the next of kin being his wife, Regis Barbara Bonin, 921 S. 29th St. He was a 1936 graduate of the U.S. Naval Academy at Annapolis.

Cross-indexing the sub's crew list with the ABMC index of Wisconsin men with the posted death date of Jan. 15, 1946, and with the Navy booklet of war deaths, shows two state men were on the submarine with him: Radioman 2nd Class Kenneth Krueger of New London and Fireman 2nd Class Robert Taylor of Lake Mills. Like their commander, they are on the MIA wall at Honolulu.

Bonin had been on seven submarine patrols on the USS Grayling, including some as executive officer, and earned the Silver Star while on the Grayling (Ostlund, 2006, p. 340). He graduated from Boys Trade and Technical High School (p. 339) and attended college for one year before going to Annapolis. Assuming he was 20 when he arrived there and 24 when he graduated in 1936, he was 31 or 32 when he was killed on the Gudgeon.

Bonin was the fifth captain of the Gudgeon, which had made 11 previous patrols and sunk a total of 24 ships, one of the best records of the submarine fleet. On the final patrol, the skipper was a new face on the boat, as was the executive officer and 10 other crew members out of 78.

The Navy Historical Center says the Gudgeon was sunk by Japanese depth charges and/or bombing. (www.history.navy.mil/library/online/sublosses/sublosses_gudgeon.htm). It left Pearl Harbor on April 4, 1944, destined for the northern Mariana islands. The Historical Center tells the story:

"She left Johnston Island on 7 April 1944, after having topped off with fuel, and was never heard from again.

"Originally scheduled to leave her area on 16 May, she was ordered on 11 May to depart her area in time to take station for a special assignment. An acknowledgment for this message was required and when none was received, it was asked for again on 12 May.

"... On 18 April, enemy planes claimed that they dropped bombs on a submarine. 'The first bomb hit the bow, the second bomb direct on bridge. The center of the submarine burst open and oil pillars rose.' The position given for this attack is 166 miles ... from 'Yuoh' Island. No island approaching the spelling or sound of this word can be found in the Pacific, and it is assumed that a mistake has been made either by the Japanese or in translation of the position. If the island referred to could be Maug, the position given would be in the middle of the area in which Gudgeon should have been at the time specified ...

"On 12 May 1944, a number of submarines patrolling the Marianas reported that the enemy engaged in intensive antisubmarine tactics.

"... The probability as to the cause for Gudgeon's loss is that she was depth-charged, bombed, or both."

However, a fuller story of the submarine is told in the 2006 book "Find 'Em, Chase 'Em, Sink 'Em: The Mysterious Loss of the WWII Submarine USS Gudgeon," by Mike Ostlund, whose uncle was a lieutenant junior grade on the sub. The Gudgeon's motto was used in the title.

Ostlund found the word "yuoh" means sulfur in Japanese, and the word island is "Jima" in that language. Ostlund deduced that the pilot may have been referring to Iwo Jima which, because of its volcanic history and smells, was often called Sulfur Island. An acquaintance in Japan obtained and helped translate Japanese pilot information for Ostlund.

Ostlund mapped the sub's assigned patrol zone and found that it was 166 miles from Iwo Jima. He says the Navy merely split the difference between different possibilities of when and how the submarine disappeared.

At any rate, the sea is 4,000 feet deep in the area that Ostlund has surmised the Gudgeon sunk in.

The Gudgeon was built at the Mare Island Navy Yard in California, and was launched on Jan. 25, 1941. It sank 25 ships (one more than Ostlund's tally), totaling 166,400 tons, and damaged eight more, for 41,900 tons. She headed out to war four days after the attack at Pearl Harbor, and in January 1942, sunk the Japanese submarine I-73, becoming "the first United States submarine in history to sink an enemy combatant ship" (www.history.navy.mil/library/online/sublosses/sublosses_gudgeon.htm).

The first skipper was Lt. Cmdr. Elton W. Grenfell, followed by Lt. Cmdr. Hylan Lyon, Lt Cmdr. William Stovall Jr., and Lt. Cmdr. William S. Post Jr. for patrols seven through 11, and finally Bonin.

The Navy says Bonin's old sub, the Grayling, also had its luck run out – it disappeared on its eighth patrol, in September 1943. The captain at that time was Cmdr. Robert Brinker of Illinois (www.valoratsea.com/losses1.htm).

Cmdr. Raymond Hansen

This next officer was on the heavy cruiser USS Vincennes and was one of the 332 men killed on that ship Aug. 9, 1942, in the disastrous Battle of Savo Island off of Guadalcanal.

The nighttime battle – featuring a long list of Navy blunders, command errors, and bad luck – killed 1,275 Americans overall. Two other American heavy cruisers and an Australian cruiser were sunk, all in a matter of minutes (Warner & Warner, 1992, p. 211). "Four invaluable cruisers had been lost, and the U.S. Navy had suffered the worst open-sea defeat in its history" (p. 3).

The ABMC lists Cmdr. Raymond Hansen's date of death as Aug. 10, 1943, but that is one year and one day after the sinking, a standard way of declaring someone dead. He is on the MIA wall at Manila.

Hansen was a 1922 graduate of the U.S. Naval Academy, according to the Annapolis school, but it could not dig up his Wisconsin hometown, nor could the Wisconsin Veterans Museum or this author. He is not in the 1946 Navy booklet of deaths from Wisconsin. Perhaps his case is like that of Lt. Cmdr. Bertram Prueher, in which he was living in another state, but his native Wisconsin was the one that went on the MIA wall. If Hansen was age 22 when he graduated from Annapolis, he would have been 42 or 43 when the Vincennes was lost.

The Vincennes' skipper was Capt. Frederick Riefkohl, and the executive officer was Cmdr. W.E.A. Mullan. Other high officers were Lt. Cmdr. R.L. Adams, gunnery officer; Cmdr. A.M. Loker, navigator; Lt. Cmdr. Cleverland Miller, another navigator; Lt. Cmdr. R.R.

Craighill, another gun control officer; Lt. Cmd. Edmund DiGiannatonio, assistant engineering officer, and Cmdr. James Blackwood, chief medical officer. Hansen would have been intermingling every day with all these men, who were detailed in Warner & Warner (1992).

The Vincennes had been involved in some of the most significant actions of the war to date, according to the Dictionary of American Naval Fighting Ships. It was one of the ships protecting the USS Hornet on April 18, 1942, when the aircraft carrier launched the planes of Jimmy Doolittle's daring raid on Tokyo. It also was firing in the Battle of Midway in June 1942, and screened the USS Yorktown when the carrier was attacked and disabled by Japanese bombers. The Vincennes underwent repairs in Hawaii and had just returned to war in early August, shelling targets on Guadalcanal.

Then came the night of Aug. 8-9. The Vincennes and its sister American cruisers, the Astoria and Quincy, and the Australian cruiser Canberra ran into a force of Japanese cruisers shortly after midnight. In a brief battle featuring naval gunfire and torpedoes, all four Allied ships were devastated, and the Vincennes was so quickly crippled that it was being evacuated only 22 minutes into the battle (Warner & Warner, 1992, p. 202).

The Vincennes found itself caught in beams from Japanese spotlights and opened fire to try to shoot them out.

"... Almost at that moment enemy shells began landing on the Vincennes; at least three of the Japanese cruisers were attacking her. The port side of the Vincennes' bridge was destroyed by a shell. A dozen shells knocked out most of the small guns. Capt. Riefkohl turned hard right, and ran into three torpedoes ..." (Hoyt, 1982, p. 43).

Miller, standing next to Capt. Riefkohl on the bridge, was killed along with two men in the pilot house (Warner & Warner, 1992, p. 148). Hansen may well have been on the ship's bridge at this time. "Other shells exploded in the carpenter shop, the hangar and the antennae trunks. Planes on the Vincennes' hangar deck burst into flames" (p. 148).

"Losing steering control five minutes later, Vincennes was dead in the water within minutes. Rapidly hitting shells quickly reduced the ship's gun power to a fraction of its original strength and before long, snuffed it out entirely. Like a pummeled and reeling challenger in the boxing ring, Vincennes wallowed to a halt, hit at least 57 times by 8- and 5-inch shells, and began listing more and more" (www.history.navy.mil/danfs/v3/vincennes-ii.htm).

It went under the water just before 3 a.m. The survivors included Riefkohl, Loker, Adams and Craighill. The dead included Hansen, Miller and Dr. Blackwood. A total of 332 men on the ship were killed, roughly half of its crew.

A list of MIAs from the ship, published on Sept. 3, 1942, includes 12 officers, of whom Hansen, as a commander, is the highest ranked. In addition, there is one lieutenant commander. (http://familytreemaker.genealogy.com/users/m/a/g/Stephen-Arthur-Maggiora/PHOTO/0026photo.html)

While he survived, Riefkohl, who ran the Vincennes but also was commander of the group of other cruisers and their accompanying destroyers, was faulted in a Navy investigation as "far from impressive" in terms of leadership (Warner & Warner, 1992, p. 223).

The four ships were the first to wind up at the bottom of the sea in a series of battles off Guadalcanal that lasted until February in an area that would become known as "Iron Bottom Sound" because of all the ships that were sunk there (www.history.navy.mil/photos/sh-usn/usnsh-v/ca44.htm, and Hammel, 1987). Each side was trying to bring more troops and supplies to its men on Guadalcanal, which had been invaded by U.S. Marines on Aug. 7.

Hansen was in the same graduating class as some famous names from the military and title-winners in sports. The best-known member of the Class of 1922 was Hyman G. Rickover, who became a submariner and the father of the nuclear Navy in his 64 years of active military service. Six classmates were part of the Navy crew team that won the gold medal in the 1920 Summer Olympics in Antwerp, Belgium.

When Hansen arrived at Annapolis, the academy superintendent was Capt. Archibald Scales, who had taken office in February 1917. But just before Hansen's senior year, a new superintendent came aboard: Rear Adm. Henry Wilson, effective in July 1921 (www.usna.edu/VirtualTour/150years/1920.htm).

Bibliography

Andersen Air Force Base, Guam, official site: www.andersen.af.mil.

Andersen Air Force Base, Guam, history: www.globalsecurity.org/military/facility/andersen.htm.

Coffey, Thomas M. (1982). Hap: The story of the U.S. Air Force and the man who built it: General Henry H. "Hap" Arnold. New York: The Viking Press.

Dictionary of American Naval Fighting Ships, http://www.history.navy.mil/danfs/v3/vincennes-ii.htm.

Glusman, John A. (2005). Conduct under fire: Four American doctors and their fight for life as prisoners of the Japanese 1941-1945. Viking. New York: The Penguin Group.

Hammel, Eric (1987). Guadalcanal: The carrier battles. The pivotal aircraft carrier battles of the Eastern Solomons and Santa Cruz. New York, N.Y. Crown Publishers Inc. This book has excellent blow-by-blow, man-by-man, job-by-job accounts of multiple attacks on carriers.

Harmon, Lt. Gen. Millard. Official Air Force biography at www.af.mil/bios/bio.asp?bioID=10235.

Hoyt, Edwin P. (1982). Guadalcanal. Briarcliff Manor, N.Y.: Stein and Day.

McCann, Frank D. (undated). What did you do in the war, Zé Carioca? University of New Hampshire. http://warandgame.wordpress.com/2008/10/14/brazil-and-world-war-ii-the-forgotten-ally/.

NashvillePost.com, www.nashvillepost.com/news/2008/5/26/nashville_now_and_then_the_last_full_measure.

Navy, Dictionary of American Naval Aviation Squadrons, www.history.navy.mil/avh-vol2/chap3-6.pdf.

Navy Historical Center, www.history.navy.mil/photos/sh-usn/usnsh-v/ca44.htm.

Navy Patrol Squadrons, private Web site, www.vpnavy.org/vp83_1941_1943.html.

Navy submarine USS Gudgeon, www.history.navy.mil/library/online/sublosses/sublosses_gudgeon.htm.

Ostlund, Mike (2006). Find 'em, chase 'em, xink 'em: The mysterious loss of the WWII submarine USS Gudgeon. Guilford, Conn.: The Lyons Press.

U-boat information: www.uboat.net.

U-boats off of Brazil: www.worldwar-2.net/timelines/war-at-sea/atlantic/battle-of-the-atlantic-index-1943.htm.

U.S. Military Academy Library, www.library.usma.edu/archives/special.asp.

U.S. Naval Academy, www.usna.edu/VirtualTour/150years/1920.htm.

USS Vincennes, partial list of dead: http://familytreemaker.genealogy.com/users/m/a/g/Stephen-Arthur-Maggiora/PHOTO/0026photo.html.

Valor at Sea Web site, www.valoratsea.com/losses1.htm).

Warner, Denis and Peggy, with Sadao Seno (1992). Disaster in the Pacific : new light on the Battle of Savo Island. Annapolis, Md. Naval Institute Press.

Wolf, John (undated). "Trampoline to Victory" U.S. relations with Brazil during World War II 1937-1945. http://history.sandiego.edu/gen/st/~johnw/Trampoline.htm.

Chapter 12:

The many pawns

Electrician's Mate 3rd Class Eugene Laux, Menasha

Eugene George Laux was a crewman on a submarine whose prior history included sinking several ships and having several escapes from disaster with Japanese ships and "friendly fire" from American forces right after Pearl Harbor. His vessel's luck finally ran out.

Laux, 21, an electrician's mate third class, and the rest of the 77 crewmen on the USS Pompano were killed in either late August or in September 1943 when it presumably hit a mine off the coast of Japan and sank immediately. The American Battle Monuments Commission gives the date as Jan. 4, 1946, for the entire crew, but that was just a formal record-clearing day for the crew after the war.

Laux was born Oct. 12, 1921, grew up at 228 Broad St. in Menasha and enlisted in the Navy in 1942. He may have volunteered for the submarine fleet because it had higher pay, according to his sister, Rita Compton. Contrary to popular belief that only small men were on submarines due to their extremely tight quarters, Laux was tall and heavy-set, Compton said.

His job was tending the electric motors of the sub, made by Allis-Chalmers of West Allis. John Neiding of South Milwaukee, president of the southeastern Wisconsin chapter of the Wisconsin Submarine Veterans of World War II, said in 1990 – when the author of this book gathered this material for a private project – that Laux's job would have included work on these motors, and that there would have been eight or nine other electrician's mates. A sub used the silent electronic motors when submerged, and its diesel engines when running on the surface. Its speed was much faster when on the surface.

Eugene Laux,
Menasha,
submarine USS Pompano

John Jerstad,
Racine,
Ploesti, Romania

Roy Harms,
Grafton,
Ploesti, Romania

Carl Zeidler,
Milwaukee,
ship off of South Africa
Milwaukee Sentinel photo

Dennis Venne,
Tomahawk and Milwaukee,
Germany

Laux was on more than one sub patrol, and Compton does not recall him being on anything other than the Pompano. His first patrol came in late 1942 or early 1943, more than a year after the sub's first mission.

Earl Kreitzmann of Mukwonago was an 18-year-old fireman on the Pompano on its sixth war patrol, the last one that it completed safely. He said the sub went to heavily mined shipping lanes off of Honshu, the main Japanese island, where the Pompano also was patrolling on its final journey.

"They had to be careful," Kreitzmann says. "We did almost get our fanny blown off."

After the sixth patrol, he was rotated off the sub in order to train to become an electrician's mate. But his name never was removed from the Pompano's crew list, so Kreitzmann's family was advised he was missing when the submarine did not return from patrol. He had to send special cables from Midway, where he was stationed, to straighten things out.

A 1949 Navy report said the Pompano left Midway on Aug. 20 on the seventh and final patrol and never was heard from again. Her orders were to patrol off of Honshu from about Aug. 29 to Sept. 27. "In view of the evidence given, it is considered probable that Pompano met her end by an enemy mine," the report said. "Operational loss or loss by an unreported attack are alternate possibilities," but were considered less likely.

The Pompano's war service and crew can be found at www.history.navy.mil/library/online/sublosses/sublosses_pompano.htm. It was launched in 1937 at the Mare Island Navy Yard in San Francisco and was one of six subs in its generation, named the Perch class after the first one. A total of 28 submarines were built later in Manitowoc, Wis.

In 1941, the Pompano and four other subs underwent an extensive refurbishing in San Francisco and were supposed to arrive at Pearl Harbor at 8 a.m. on Dec. 7, which would have put them right in the middle of Japanese attack. But they had been slowed by bad weather and still were 125 miles northeast of Oahu, running on the surface. The subs were spotted by a Japanese scout plane and dove to escape. One sub, the Plunger, was attacked.

When the subs arrived off of Pearl on Dec. 9, the jittery U.S. commander ordered planes to attack them out of fear they were

Japanese. But Rear Adm. Thomas Withers Jr., a submarine fleet boss, knew better and ordered the attack to be scrubbed.

The Pompano and three other subs were quickly ordered out on a reconnaissance mission to the Marshall Islands, and the Pompano was the very first to leave Pearl. It was attacked by U.S. pilots on Dec. 20, when it was two days out of Pearl. A Navy patrol plane bombed it and then radioed the aircraft carrier USS Enterprise that a Japanese sub was in the vicinity, so three dive bombers from the Enterprise joined in.

"Happily, the bombers were more eager than accurate," Rear. Adm. Harley Cope and Capt. Walter Karig say in their 1951 book "Battle Submerged – Submarine Fighters of World War II." The bombs slightly damaged one of the sub's diesel fuel tanks and left an oil slick in its wake for the rest of the patrol, something very dangerous for a submarine. It was not aware of its slick until after the sub was rattled several times by depth charges "and all hands wondered at the mysterious ability of the Japanese to detect" it, Cope and Karig say.

Clay Blair writes in the 1975 book "Silent Victory: The U.S. Submarine War Against Japan," that the Pompano narrowly escaped an attack by a Japanese destroyer after being caught on the surface on Aug. 9, 1942. An engine exhaust valve broke loose and seawater rapidly poured in, rising above the engine room floor plates. The water had to be pumped out, but the sound of the pumps brought on more savage depth-charging. Then the Pompano ran aground on an underwater shoal.

Capt. Willis Manning Thomas was ready to go to the surface, evacuate and scuttle the sub, but top officers prevailed on him to try one more time to escape. The Pompano surfaced only 1,000 yards from the Japanese coast and somehow managed to get out of the area in one piece.

That, however, was before Laux joined the crew.

The Pompano made more trips to the area and in July 1943, the mission that Kreitzmann was on, Blair says it fired torpedoes at a freighter, a small convoy of three destroyers, another convoy, a tanker and a freighter. All either missed or exploded prematurely.

The mine that the Pompano presumably hit could have been on the surface or submerged, Kreitzmann says. In fact, the subs Runner, Pickerel and Golet had been lost in this period. "The mines were lethal. That was terminal. They were opened up like a sardine can by the blast. There were rarely survivors," he adds.

The submarine fleet boss, Rear Adm. Charles Andrews Lockwood Jr., decided not to go back to that area for a time after the Pompano was lost. Blair's book says postwar records from the Japanese indicate the Pompano sunk two ships, the Akama Maru of 5,600 tons and the Taiko Maru at 3,000 tons, on the final trip.

On its seven missions, the Pompano sank 10 enemy ships and damaged four, according to the Commander Submarine Force, U.S. Pacific Fleet (www.csp.navy.mil).

Besides the Pompano, 51 American subs were lost during the war – 24 sunk by surface ships, and mines probably responsible for the rest. The U.S. death toll was 3,505, a total of 16 percent of the officers in the program and 13 percent of the enlisted men like Laux.

Maj. John Jerstad, Racine, and 1st Lt. Roy Harms, Grafton

The lives of Army Air Force Maj. John J. Jerstad and 1st Lt. Roy C. Harms ended during a daring air raid on Romania two years before the end of World War II, but the flower of freedom did not blossom in that land until nearly five decades later.

Jerstad, 25, of Racine, flew a crippled B-24 bomber that led one of seven American strike forces in the raid – sometimes at treetop level and sometimes even lower – through a thicket of antiaircraft fire around the important, German-held oil refineries at Ploesti, 35 miles north of Bucharest.

The bomber, named Hell's Wench, took staggering hits in the cockpit and elsewhere, and the pilots could have aborted the mission and bailed out or veered off and tried to land somewhere because the plane was in flames. But the bomb run was at a critical point and the fliers continued to lead the 22 planes in their section to the target. That heroism resulted in the conferring of the Medal of

Honor – the nation's highest military award – to Jerstad, who was the co-pilot but was flying the plane, and to Lt. Col. Addison E. Baker, who was the group commander and was in the pilot's seat.

Harms, 26, of Grafton, was the pilot of another B-24 in that group whose plane was shot down and crashed, leaving only one survivor in the 10-man crew. That survivor said Harms had reported, "it looks rough, but here goes," according to the 1962 book "Ploesti: The Great Ground-Air Battle of 1 August 1943," by James Dugan and Carroll Stewart. Harms' plane had a four-foot hole in the left vertical stabilizer, shells shattered the nose and tail, and a fire broke out in the fuselage. Harms received the Distinguished Flying Cross.

The massive operation was code-named Tidal Wave, and a total of 178 American bombers, carrying 1,733 crew members, took off on Aug. 1, 1943 from Libya to hit a target 1,200 miles and seven hours away. Then they had to fly back to Libya, if they could make it that far. Most did not.

A total of 310 crewmen were killed. About one-third of the planes were lost in less than a half-hour over Ploesti. Harms is one of 1,409 names on the MIA wall at the American cemetery near Florence, Italy, as is Baker, the pilot of Jerstad's plane. Jerstad is buried at the U.S. Ardennes Cemetery in Belgium.

Jerstad and Harms went to war after growing up as models of civic involvement in their Wisconsin communities. Jerstad set up a summer camp for boys and girls along Lake Michigan to pay his way through college, and Harms was the co-leader of a Boy Scout troop.

Jerstad and fellow Medal of Honor recipient Marine Pfc. Harold C. Agerholm (his story is told in the June 1944 chapter of this book) were honored with a school in Racine (the Jerstad-Agerholm Elementary and Middle School), and the American Legion post in Grafton is named for Harms and a World War I veteran.

Jerstad, called Jack by his family and Jerk by others, taught elementary school for one year in Racine before entering the military, his sister, Mary Jacobs of rural Jackson County, said in a Memorial Day story in the Milwaukee Sentinel (Mueller, 1990). He ran a youth facility named Camp Norshore, teaching swimming and handicrafts, and used his pay for tuition at Northwestern University, where he was a drummer in the marching band.

In Grafton, LeRoy Paulin, who was a member of Harms' Scout troop in the late 1930s, said in the 1990 story that "his family had the grocery store downtown. He knew every kid in town. He would ride a horse around town all the time."

The reddish-brown horse was named Bonnie, according to Virginia Harms Horton of Kirkwood, Mo., one of Harms' three sisters. She also said that instead of going to college, he went to the West Coast on a faster form of travel – a motorcycle.

He was in the National Guard at the time of Pearl Harbor, and selected pilot training, completing that program in June 1943. A mere two months later, he was in the big raid.

Harms was in the 329th Bomber Squadron of the 93rd Bomber Group, Heavy, dubbed the Traveling Circus. Jerstad was in the headquarters of the 2nd Bomber Wing. Baker and Jerstad's plane was the one that recognized the mission leader had taken a wrong turn and got it back on course.

The Medal of Honor citation for Jerstad said:

"For conspicuous gallantry and intrepidity above and beyond the call of duty. On 1 August 1943, he served as pilot of the lead aircraft in his group in a daring low-level attack against enemy oil refineries and installations at Ploesti, Rumania. Although he had completed more than his share of missions and was no longer connected with this group, so high was his conception of duty that he volunteered to lead the formation in the correct belief that his participation would contribute materially to success in this attack.

"Maj. Jerstad led the formation into attack with full realization of the extreme hazards involved and despite withering fire from heavy and light antiaircraft guns. Three miles from the target his airplane was hit, badly damaged, and set on fire. Ignoring the fact that he was flying over a field suitable for a forced landing, he kept on the course. After the bombs of his aircraft were released on the target, the fire in his ship became so intense as to make further progress impossible and he crashed into the target area. By his voluntary acceptance of a mission he knew was extremely hazardous, and his assumption of an intrepid course of action at the risk of life over and above the call of duty, Maj. Jerstad set an example of heroism which will be an inspiration to the U.S. Armed Forces" (www.history.army.mil/html/ moh/wwII-g-l.html).

The medal citation for Baker said "he led his command, the 93rd Heavy Bombardment Group, on a daring low-level attack against enemy oil refineries and installations," and after the bombs were released, "his valiant attempts to gain sufficient altitude for the crew to escape by parachute were unavailing and his aircraft crashed in flames after his successful efforts to avoid other planes in formation. By extraordinary flying skill, gallant leadership and intrepidity, Lt. Col. Baker rendered outstanding, distinguished, and valorous service to our Nation"

(www.medalofhonor.com/WorldWarIIA-C.htm).

Wisconsinites Harold F. Korger and Boyden Supiano had front row seats, stationed in the noses of their B-24s as bombardiers. In fact, Korger WAS the front row, because his plane was the leader of one of the seven strike forces.

Korger, from Eau Claire, and Supiano, who became principal at J.I. Case High School in Racine, were second lieutenants in the 98th Bomb Group, the Pyramiders.

In the long flight to Romania from Libya, elements of their group became separated in dense clouds over the mountains. Then the force was attacked by fighter planes and ran into heavy flak from disguised positions in haystacks and railroad cars. It also discovered that other parts of the attacking wave took wrong turns near the oil refineries and bombed the 98th's own targets, leaving Korger and Supiano facing exploding American bombs, oil fires and dense smoke in their low-level attack. Some B-24s were shot down, smashing right through walls of buildings and out the other side. Others were badly damaged and ran out of fuel while trying to limp back to Libya, landing at sea or in enemy or neutral territory.

How did they survive all of that? "Luck, luck, luck," Supiano said. Korger credited "the Almighty" and "probably 98 percent luck. They couldn't hit everybody" (Mueller, 1990a).

Korger's pilot was Col. John R. "Killer" Kane, who led the group of 48 Pyramiders and received the Medal of Honor for the mission, like Jerstad and Baker in another group. Two other men received the medal. Jerstad and Baker were the only fatalities receiving the Medal of Honor:

In his extremely vulnerable position in the first wave of his group, Korger said, "you'd think they would have hit us. But the three in the first wave made it through. We thought a good many times we were going to go down." Korger said that as his group arrived at its own target, the biggest of the refineries at Ploesti, the bombs dropped by other planes that had taken the wrong path were just starting to explode, having been armed with time-delay fuses in order to let following waves have a clear shot. "We flew right through an exploding oil tank," Korger said. "We thought we had bought the farm at that point. We got slightly singed by it" (Mueller, 1990a).

Korger dropped his four 1,000-pound bombs and Supiano, his three. The bombardier in the wingman of Kane's plane was killed by antiaircraft fire, but Korger said he was too busy getting things ready to notice that. As his plane rose as it adjusted after the bombs were dropped, it was hit and lost one of its four engines. The propeller tips on another one were damaged.

Amazingly, the only injuries to anyone on Korger's plane, the Hail Columbia, were bumps and bruises upon landing at a British facility on the island of Cyprus. But Supiano, who in the raid was one row behind Korger on the left side of the formation, was wounded in a leg just as he released his bombs. He said the navigator was covered with red fluid, but it turned out to be hydraulic fluid, except for a bleeding wound in an arm. Supiano's plane was one of 88 that made it all the way back to Libya.

Going home, Kane flew the crippled plane at ground level to make a tougher target for fighter planes. Several German and Romanian fighter planes attacked or were spotted, including an old Romanian biplane, which Korger said "brought a little element of humor into an otherwise sober situation" (Mueller, 1990a). The crew tossed out equipment and guns to save weight, and the definition of this kept expanding as the crisis grew. "We threw everything out, including the guns, parachutes, bomb gear, everything that moved.

We made it, but just barely." He said the plane was flying so low that it "picked up corn stalks in our bomb bay."

It was able to make it to Cyprus, making a night landing at a British facility and losing the landing gear when it hit a ditch at the end of the runway. Korger said the plane would have caught fire, but there was not enough fuel for it to burn.

Lt. j.g. Carl Zeidler, Milwaukee

The following story is told every few years in Milwaukee, but it bears repeating in this book about Wisconsin men lost at sea or killed overseas. The mayor of Milwaukee, who was elected in 1940, resigned in 1942 to serve in the Navy in the war. He was dead by the end of the year.

Carl Zeidler was elected mayor in a stunning upset of long-term incumbent Daniel Hoan, a Socialist who had led the city since 1916. Zeidler was all of 32 at the time; Hoan was 59. Zeidler was known as the "blond baritone" because of his swinging-bachelor status, "his Teutonic good looks and a golden singing voice" (Gurda, 1999, p. 303). One of his standard tunes was "God Bless America." He had been an assistant city attorney in the Hoan administration. His campaign emphasized change and new ideas, and in the last years of the Depression, it sold well. He won nearly 53 percent of the vote, a margin of almost 12,000 out of the 212,000 cast.

That, however, was a year and a half before Pearl Harbor. Zeidler decided in early 1942 that his country needed him. He became a member of the Navy Armed Guard, which meant he was stationed on a merchant vessel carrying war supplies in order to help defend it against attacks by German submarines, ships, and planes. He became leader of a gunnery crew.

Lt. j.g. Zeidler, 34, was killed when his ship, the La Salle, was torpedoed by a U-boat 350 miles off the tip of South Africa. Zeidler and all 12 other members of the Navy Armed Guard aboard were killed, along with all 39 members of the crew, who were in the Merchant Marine.

All of the above is what is told every few years. Here are some new wrinkles:

The ABMC database says Zeidler was killed on Nov. 2, but the Merchant Marine says it was Nov. 7, and the Pentagon's Prisoner of War/Missing Personnel Office says it was Oct. 11. Check it out at www.abmc.gov, www.usmm.org and www.dtic.mil/dpmo/WWII_MIA/NAV_M_Z.HTM.

Various reasons for that disagreement are that the La Salle sank immediately and thus may have not had time for an SOS, that it was not in a convoy, that it was far out to sea, or that it was under radio silence. The Pentagon date is so far from the other two that Oct. 11 may just be when the ship left one of its stops.

The final word on the date goes to U-boat records. The private Web site of www.uboat.net is run by Gudmundur Helgason of Iceland, and contains voluminous records and sorts them via ship, via nationality, via month and more. It says the La Salle was sunk on Nov. 7 (http://uboat.net/allies/merchants/losses_year.html?qdate=1942-11&string=November+1942).

The site says the ship was sunk at global position 40.00S, 21.30E – Grid GR 7599, which it shows is about 300 miles off South Africa in the area where the Atlantic and Indian Oceans meet.

The La Salle's route was from New York to Guantanamo, Cuba; to Balboa in the Panama Canal Zone on Sept. 26, to Cape Horn and then to Capetown, South Africa. The ship was carrying 6,116 tons of trucks, steel and ammunition, the site says.

"At 22.50 hours on 7 Nov, 1942, the unescorted La Salle was hit by one torpedo from U-159 about 350 miles southeast of the Cape of Good Hope. The U-boat had followed the ship for five hours and already missed with a stern torpedo at 21.19 hours. The torpedo ignited the cargo of ammunition and the ship exploded, creating a fireball hundred meters high and completely destroyed the vessel. Bits of wreckage fell around the ship for several minutes afterwards and slightly wounded three men on watch in the conning tower of the U-boat. It is reported that the explosion was heard clearly at Cape Point Lighthouse over 300 miles away" (http://uboat.net/allies/merchants/losses_year.html?qdate=1942-11&string=November+1942).

Because the U-boat had been following the ship for hours, and because one torpedo already had missed, the La Salle and Zeidler must have been at battle stations for some time.

It said the captain of the U-159 was Helmut Witte, who had the rank of kapitänleutnant and was age 27 at the time. On a previous patrol, the U-159 was a part of the wolfpack Eisbär, which operated in the waters off Capetown beginning in September 1942. He sank two dozen ships during the war, 10 of which were in June 1942. He served on the U-boat until June 1943 (http://uboat.net/men/witte.htm).

A month after that, the U-boat got its comeuppance: it was sunk in the Caribbean Sea south of Haiti, by depth charges from an American aircraft (VP-32, P-1). All 53 on board were killed (http://uboat.net/men/witte.htm).

Zeidler's name is on the East Coast Memorial of the ABMC, the same site where the Coast Guardsmen and passengers on the USS Dorchester who are discussed earlier in this book are honored. The memorial is in Battery Park, at the southern end of Manhattan, and overlooks the Statue of Liberty.

One other Wisconsin man on the East Coast Memorial from the same date that the ABMC lists for Zeidler (and the identical other date that the Pentagon office gives for Zeidler) is Seaman 2nd Class Frank Gorney of Superior. His address in the 1946 book of Navy casualties is given as 1421 N. 5th St. in that city. Zeidler's address is given as 504 N. 33rd St., Milwaukee, the home of his parents, given as Mr. and Mrs. Michael W. Zeidler.

A total of 33 Wisconsin men serving in the Navy Armed Guard were killed in the war (www.armed-guard.com). The Web site is run by veterans of the group and says: "We were NOT guards. We WERE U.S. Navy gun crews consisting of gunners, coxswains and boatswains, radiomen, signalmen, an occasional pharmacist and, toward the end of the war, a few radarmen, who served at sea on merchant ships. The Merchant Marine sailed the ships while the Armed Guard provided gunnery protection and communications services. The Armed Guard crews were small, our hearts were large."

According to the Merchant Marine, the year in which Zeidler met his fate, 1942, was the worst year of the war for merchant ships sunk and mariners killed – 4,363 seamen were on 571 ships that were sunk or damaged (www.usmm.org). But for members of the Navy Armed Guard like Zeidler, 1943 was the worst year for deaths – there were 1007 dead, compared with 622 killed in 1942.

In the entire war, a total of 1,614 merchant ships were sunk or damaged, 8,421 members of the Merchant Marine were killed, and 2,193 members of the Navy Armed Guard were killed.

2nd Lt. Eleanor Nelson, Rock County

Army nurse 2nd Lt. Eleanor Nelson was from Rock County, although exactly where is a mystery to the Historical Society of that area, to the VFW in Janesville, to the library in Edgerton, and even to the Army Nurse Corps.

This much is known for sure: Nelson is on the Rock County list of those who died in the Army in the war, and it was from "non-battle injuries." The ABMC says she died Oct. 19, 1945, more than two months after VJ Day, and is buried in Honolulu. Her tombstone says she served with the 148th General Hospital, and that hospital was based on Saipan and Guam in the last year of the war.

A total of 201 members of the Army Nurse Corps died as a result of illnesses or accidents (Monahan & Neidel-Greenlee, 2003, p. 458).

The Army Nurse Corps was asked to help dig for any information about Nelson's case. This was its answer to the author of this book after a few days of searching: "I am sorry to say I do not have any information on this nurse … but I was wondering if you are willing to give me any information you have collected/found/written on any nurses. We are always trying to increase our collection. We are unfortunately only as good as the information we either obtain or are given."

That message came from Lt. Col. Cheryl Y. Capers, Army nurse historian, acting chief of the Office of Medical History of the Nurse Corps.

The 148th was a general hospital, not an aid station right on the battlefront, nor a field hospital right behind the field of battle. Nor was it an evacuation hospital, which was farther back and sent soldiers on for more-thorough care on a non-crisis basis. But on Saipan and Guam, conditions were hardly sedate no matter where any facility was, and it definitely was not a scene from the musical "South Pacific."

"Malnutrition was common and disease endemic. ... Early admissions to the hospital were in such poor condition that 10 to 12 patients a day succumbed to their wounds" (Tomblin, 1996, p. 57). Head and body lice were chronic, and the same flies that feasted on unburied bodies and trash were landing on island residents and on the medical people.

The invasion of Saipan by Marines and the U.S. Army was launched on June 15, 1944 – the stories of two Wisconsin Marines who were killed, Merlin Mosey and Willis Oftedahl, are told earlier in this book – and Guam followed a week later. Both are islands in the Marianas chain. Basically, Nelson's hospital moved in when the islands were secured and other islands like Iwo Jima were attacked.

The first nurses to arrive on Saipan were the 369th Station Hospital, and Nelson's 148th and the 176th Station Hospital followed. The 148th set up in the first week of August, less than two months after the invasion – right amid an outbreak of dengue fever spread by mosquitoes. "Army medical personnel were thoroughly exhausted by this influx, 20,000 dengue cases, which did not abate until October 1944" (Tomblin, 1996, p. 57).

There were "five admissions for disease to every battle casualty. Half the nurses on the island suffered from dengue fever. The epidemic was controlled only after the Army sprayed DDT across the entire island in September, according to the Nurse Corps (www.history.army.mil/books/wwii/72-14/72-14.htm). Add to that the fact that there were plenty of Japanese stragglers still on the island, causing trouble and drawing fire from Americans, who sometimes got jumpy and fired at their own. There also were some strafing raids by Japanese planes in 1945, but no injuries, and there was such a severe shortage of pure water that it had to be rationed and hand carried to wards from outside drums, the Nurse Corps says.

In February 1945, the Saipan hospital began receiving hundreds of casualties from the invasion of Iwo Jima, and quickly was overloaded – there were round-the-clock shifts, low supplies, plus continued severe shortages of water. Then on March 5, an epidemic of food poisoning struck. Tomblin (1996) quotes nurse Mary Sherman of the 148th as saying the hospital was so short of personnel that it put MPs to work to care for the sick. A total of 746 nurses, doctors, and other hospital personnel fell ill (p. 58).

Conditions were not much better on Guam, where Nelson and the 148th later were stationed along with other hospital units.

The Army's Office of the Surgeon General published in 1964 a review of surgery experiences. Although it is not clear who wrote this report, it said this for Saipan on Dec. 7, 1944:

"Today, with Col. Eliot Colby, MC, Surgeon, Army Garrison Force, Island Command, Saipan, we had a hurried preliminary survey of the island, which is far more attractive than I had anticipated. There was a Japanese air attack this morning, and on getting up I was a bit disconcerted to find no foxholes. Found the colonel in charge of ATC digging a foxhole, asked him why, and he pointed to his teeth marks on the floor.

"The 148th General Hospital is still in tents although prefabricated buildings are under construction. Headquarters is built in quonset huts, and the labor has been used to improve this and other sites. Colonel Colby says that hospitals have "No. 1" priority, but then "No. 1" becomes subdivided into "a, b, c, et cetera."

The report also said there was a large number of civilian wounded, even on the beaches. "One platoon of the 31st Field Hospital was designated as a civilian hospital. This platoon with 100 beds soon had 880 patients." (http://143.84.107.102/booksdocs/wwii/actvssurgconvol2).

One month before Nelson's unit arrived on Saipan, an Army surgeon, Capt. Ben. Salomon, 29, who grew up in Milwaukee and graduated from Shorewood High School but was working and living in California before the war, earned the Medal of Honor for an incident in which he was killed. Salomon was in the 105th Infantry

Regiment of the 27th Infantry Division. The medal was not presented until 2002 and a site devoted to Jewish achievers says this was because "as medical personnel he was considered ineligible. (It was after) numerous attempts during the half-century following the war that he was finally awarded with the honor" (www.www.j-grit.com/military-and-spies-ben-salomon.php).

The citation told of the events of July 7, 1944:

"The Regiment's 1st and 2d Battalions were attacked by an overwhelming force estimated between 3,000 and 5,000 Japanese soldiers. It was one of the largest attacks attempted in the Pacific Theater during World War II. Although both units (battalions in the 105th Infantry) fought furiously, the enemy soon penetrated the battalions' combined perimeter and inflicted overwhelming casualties.

"In the first minutes of the attack, approximately 30 wounded soldiers walked, crawled, or were carried into Captain Salomon's aid station, and the small tent soon filled with wounded men. As the perimeter began to be overrun, it became increasingly difficult for Captain Salomon to work on the wounded.

"He then saw a Japanese soldier bayoneting one of the wounded soldiers lying near the tent. Firing from a squatting position, Captain Salomon quickly killed the enemy soldier. Then, as he turned his attention back to the wounded, two more Japanese soldiers appeared in the front entrance of the tent. As these enemy soldiers were killed, four more crawled under the tent walls. Rushing them, Captain Salomon kicked the knife out of the hand of one, shot another, and bayoneted a third. Captain Salomon butted the fourth enemy soldier in the stomach and a wounded comrade then shot and killed the enemy soldier. Realizing the gravity of the situation, Captain Salomon ordered the wounded to make their way as best they could back to the regimental aid station, while he attempted to hold off the enemy until they were clear.

"Captain Salomon then grabbed a rifle from one of the wounded and rushed out of the tent. After four men were killed while manning a machine gun, Captain Salomon took control of it. When his body was later found, 98 dead enemy soldiers were piled in front of his position. Captain Salomon's extraordinary heroism and devotion to duty are in keeping with the highest traditions of military service and reflect great credit upon himself, his unit, and the United States Army" (www.cmohs.org/recipients/salamon.htm).

Salomon entered the Army via California after graduating from the University of Southern California. He is not buried overseas.

While not much could be found about Nelson, the Wisconsin State Historical Society has a collection of two albums of memorabilia from another nurse from Rock County: Marcia Gates of Janesville, who was a POW in the Philippines.

Gates volunteered in 1941, at age 26, and was sent to the Philippines where she treated the wounded at Bataan, and later at Corregidor. She was taken prisoner there when American forces surrendered on May 6, 1942, and interned at the Santo Tomas prisoner of war camp in Manila until Feb. 6, 1945. (http://content.wisconsinhistory.org/cdm4)

Pfc. Dennis Venne, Tomahawk and Milwaukee

A grateful stranger in the Netherlands cared deeply enough about a fallen soldier from Wisconsin to write letters and make overseas phone calls to learn more about the Army man.

The soldier was Pfc. Dennis I. Venne, who was in the 36th Tank Battalion of the 8th Armored Division, part of Gen. George Patton's powerful 3rd Army. The 34-year-old GI was wounded in Germany and died a month later, on April 4, 1945, in a hospital in Holland. This was one month before VE Day and about two weeks before Venne's birthday.

The grateful stranger was John H. Vervoort of Eijsden, who adopted the grave of Venne in the Netherlands American Cemetery at Margraten, about 12 miles from Vervoort's home. Vervoort wrote to the Wisconsin Veterans of Foreign Wars in 1985 to inquire how to find Venne's family, and the VFW referred it to the author of this book, because of his past work involving the group. The author started calling people named Venne in Tomahawk – one said she was a relative but that his sister lived in Milwaukee and was named Bielinski – and wrote this story for the Milwaukee Sentinel (Mueller, 1985).

Venne was a native of Tomahawk who moved to Milwaukee in 1942 because of abundant wartime factory work. He tried three times to enlist in the Army, only to be rejected because of physical problems, including poor eyesight, missing teeth and foot trouble. But late in the war, manpower needs became more acute and he was finally accepted for service in 1944.

Vervoort and other citizens of the Margraten area adopt graves of American soldiers to show they are "grateful because they helped us get our freedom back." Adopting a grave means taking flowers there six or seven days a year, such as Memorial Day and the soldier's birthday, Vervoort says. Vervoort met this author at the grave in 1988 while I was on a trip to Germany, and he said he loves the cemetery because it is such a peaceful place. He eagerly recounted many facts about it that he had learned in his visits.

Irene Bielinski of Milwaukee, Venne's sister, said in the 1985 story that she was touched by his efforts.

She said the only thing her family knew about Venne's death was from a letter that her father received from a lieutenant who was wounded at the same time. It said "his tank took a direct hit … while they were running for cover, they caught shrapnel fire."

Venne and the lieutenant were captured by the Germans, and she was not clear in her own mind years later whether Venne died in an American facility or a German hospital. Bielinski said that the family was notified that he was wounded but did not learn of his death until a month after VE Day.

Bielinski said Venne had worked on several farms in the Tomahawk area and came to Milwaukee to work in a factory "because work up there was scarce and didn't pay much." He was shy and a loner, "who hated school with a passion. He'd crawl out the window and hitch a ride on the wood wagon" to get out of school.

Bielinski named one of her nine children for her brother – Dennis Ivan.

The official Web site compiled by veterans of the 8th Armored Division, www.8th-armored.org/division/8histmar.htm, says the biggest fighting in early March was at Lintfort and Rheinberg, Germany. On March 5, "heavy fighting in and around Rheinberg resulted in 199 casualties and the loss of 41 tanks while the Germans suffered 350 men killed and 512 taken prisoner." The next day, the main fighting was between Rheinberg and Ossenberg. "The area (nicknamed '88 Lane') was under direct anti-tank and heavy artillery fire, and each house had to be cleared by dismounted infantry. Several 8th Armored men received the Silver Star and other medals for fighting on March 5. This is likely to be is when Venne was wounded.

In his 1970 history of the battalion at www.8th-armored.org/books/36tk/36h-pg03.htm#top, veteran Fredrick Slater entitled a chapter "Bloody Rheinberg." It began: "The blood-red clouds in the sky that greeted the sun on the morning of 5 March 1945 were a forecast of the shedding of the blood of men of the 36th who were to die that day on German soil. The tankers were to meet an overwhelming force, yet in spite of great odds, they were to emerge victorious from the ordeal."

Slater also said: "The next morning the battered but proud battalion reassembled in Rheinberg and took count of itself. We had lost 41 tanks and 131 men were either dead, missing, or wounded. Rheinberg doesn't look like much of a place on a map but it is written indelibly on the hearts of the men of the 36th because it was there that they received their baptism of blood and proved themselves worthy of the title of 'Soldier.' Refusing to give up when things were darkest, they battled on forward against a fiercely resisting and well-dug-in enemy."

Staff Sgt. Raymond Olson, Vernon County

On a quiet road atop a hill facing the cold breezes from the Pacific Ocean near San Francisco's Golden Gate Bridge is a little-noticed monument to servicemen who were killed along the West Coast of North and South America and whose bodies were never recovered.

This is the West Coast Memorial of the American Battle Monuments Commission. It is at the Presidio of San Francisco, near the southern edge of the Golden Gate. It is a curved gray granite wall decorated with bas relief sculpture and a statue of Liberty (but not the famous one in New York) on its right side.

Three men from Wisconsin are among the 412 on the monument – Air Force Staff Sgt. Raymond P. Olson from Vernon County, Navy Seaman Second Class Jerry Hoffman of Plymouth, and Navy Lt. Benjamin Frankel of Cudahy.

Hoffman was killed Dec. 10, 1943. His parents were Mr. and Mrs. Henry Hoffman of 213 Collins St. in Plymouth, according to the Navy's booklet of war deaths and injuries. Frankel died on April 13, 1945, in the last four months of the war in the Pacific. His mother was Fannie Frankel of 3753 E. Armour Ave.

Relatives by those names in those towns and areas could not be found. There were no big sinkings of ships on those dates, or noteworthy accidents in waters off the West Coast.

But much more is known about Olson's death on May 21, 1945, thanks to members of his unit – the 29th Bomber Squadron, Heavy – who have put it on the Internet. He died in the crash of a B-24 Liberator near the Galapagos Islands off the coast of South America. There were five other deaths, but two survivors. The Army/ Air Force listing of casualties lists Olson as dying of non-battle injuries. The unit says it was a training flight.

The squadron's Web site of www.geocities.com/Pentagon/Bunker/4215/index.html says the unit was part of the VI Bomber Command and the 6th Air Force.

Army records at the National Archives say Olson enlisted Oct. 21, 1941, even before even Pearl Harbor, and was born in 1923, so when he died he was 21 or 22. He went into the military via Milwaukee, had four years of high school, and his job was an actor, according to the Air Force records. He was single.

The bomb squadron's Web page says the data was collected by Charles E. Meketa, squadron historian, and printed in 1992.

The 29th conducted anti-submarine patrols in the Caribbean, and participated in defense of the Panama Canal. It was based in Panama and later in the Galapagos Islands, which are about 500 miles off the coast of Ecuador, and are where Charles Darwin studied what became his theory of evolution.

The Web site says that on May 21, 1945, a B-24 Liberator, serial number 44-41641, was reported missing on a training flight that was supposed to last nearly 2.5 hours. The plane was last seen by another squadron plane in the area of San Cristobal Island. Planes searched for it for several hours until dusk, resuming the next day from dawn to dusk.

Finally, on May 23, oxygen bottles and one survivor were sighted at Bahia Rosa Blanca. That search plane did not have a working radio, so it returned to base and another went back, dropping supplies and equipment and finding another survivor about a quarter-mile from the first, according to the Web site.

The second survivor was Cpl. Richard A. Tremper. The first was Cpl. Walter S. Beebe. The next day, "a ground party under the command of Capt. E.F. Herrington was sent to the scene to continue the search. Statements from the survivor able to talk said other survivors were highly unlikely. After further searching with no positive results the search was terminated with the returned of the search party on 25 May 1945." (www.geocities.com/Pentagon/Bunker/4215/index.html).

Bibliography

Army (undated). The Army Nurse Corps. www.history.army.mil/books/wwii/72-14/72-14.htm

Army (1964). Activities of surgical consultants, volume II. Prepared and published under the direction of L.; Gen. Leonard D. Heaton, Surgeon General, U.S. Army.

Blair, Clay (1975). Silent victory: The U.S. submarine war against Japan. Philadelphia: Lippincott.

Cope, Harley Francis, and Karig, Walter (1951). Battle submerged; submarine fighters of World War II. New York, Norton.

Defense Prisoner of War / Missing Personnel Office: www.dtic.mil/dpmo/WWII_MIA/NAV_M_Z.HTM

Dugal, James, and Stewart, Carroll (1962). Ploesti: The great ground-air battle of 1 August 1943. New York: Random House.

Gurda, J. (1999). The making of Milwaukee. Milwaukee, Wis.: Milwaukee County Historical Society.

Medal of Honor citation for Maj. John Jerstad, www.history.army.mil/html/moh/wwII-g-l.html

Medal of Honor citation for Lt. Col. Addison Baker, www.medalofhonor.com/WorldWarIIA-C.htm

Medal of Honor citation for Capt. Ben Salomon, www.cmohs.org/ recipients/salamon.htm. Discussion of his actions also at www.j-grit.com/military-and-spies-ben-salomon.php

Merchant Marine: www.usmm.org

Monahan, Evelyn M., and Neidel-Greenlee, Rosemary (2003). And if I perish: Frontline U.S. Army nurses in World War II. New York: Alfred A. Knopf.

Mueller, Tom (1990). Young lives ended in the hell over Ploesti, Milwaukee Sentinel, May 28, p. 1, 6. Used with permission of Milwaukee Journal Sentinel.

Mueller, Tom (1990a). Survival is credited to "luck, luck, luck." Milwaukee Sentinel, May 28, p. 6. Used with permission of Milwaukee Journal Sentinel.

Mueller, Tom (1985). Dutchman seeks out fallen GI's kin. Milwaukee Sentinel, Dec. 12, page 1, Part 3. Used with permission of Milwaukee Journal Sentinel.

Navy, Pompano record. www.history.navy.mil/library/online/sublosses/sublosses_pompano.htm

Navy, Commander Submarine Force, U.S. Pacific Fleet. www.csp.navy.mil

Navy Armed Guard veterans: www.armed-guard.com

Slater, Fredrick (1970). History of the 36th Tank Battalion
www.8th-armored.org/books/36tk/36h-pg03.htm#top

Tomblin, Barbara Brooks (1996). G.I. Nightingales: The Army Nurse Corps in World War II. Lexington, Ky.: The University Press of Kentucky.

U-boat information: www.uboat.net

Wisconsin State Historical Society, albums of Army nurse Marcia Gates. Summary at http://content.wisconsinhistory.org/cdm4

8th Armored Division veterans, www.8th-armored.org/division/8histmar.htm

29th Bomber Squadron, Heavy: www.geocities.com/Pentagon/Bunker/4215/index.html

Chapter 13:

Telegrams and funerals – and then, the news gets even worse

Across the state, families received the telegrams that they had been dreading in 1941, 1942, 1943, 1944, 1945 and even beyond. Some who learned a family member was MIA received second telegrams, which they were fearing more than the first, but at least offered some formal closure.

Some families received an unthinkable third, even after VE Day or VJ Day.

The messages came from leaders like the Marine Corps commandant, the commander of the Coast Guard, the adjutant general of the Army, and other high-ranking figures in Washington.

In Kewaskum, the family of Coast Guard Machinist's Mate 2nd Class Ray Buddenhagen got a Western Union telegram, which was dated 2:04 a.m. June 17, 1943, reporting that he had been "killed in action" and "his body has not been recovered. … To prevent possible aid to our enemy, please do not divulge the name of his ship or station."

The Coast Guard cutter Escanaba, whose crew had an unusually large complement of Wisconsin men because it had been based on Lake Michigan before the war, had been sunk in the North Atlantic on June 13. A total of 101 men were killed, and only two survived.

On Aug. 2, 1944, teenager Genevieve Miller sent her brother Martin a letter, not knowing or sensing what had happened in the hedgerows of Normandy only one day earlier, and penned these lines: "I guess it's about time I was slinging a little ink in your direction, huh? I haven't heard from you for a little while but I imagine I'll be getting a letter one of these days."

Paul Hartzheim,
Juneau,
crashed in
Mediterranean
died two years after
cousin

Vincent Popielarski,
Milwaukee,
Germany
killed three months
after brother

Four weeks after she sent the note, a telegram arrived Aug. 27 at her family's latest residence, a farm near Basco in southern Dane County, south of Verona and north of Belleville. It said: "The secretary of war desires me to express his deep regret that your son Private Martin Miller has been reported missing in action since One August in France. If further details or other information are received you will be promptly notified. J.A. Ulio, the adjutant general."

A few months later, Genevieve's note of Aug. 2 would be returned to her as undeliverable because Pvt. Miller was MIA.

On June 5, 1945, Bernice Howe of La Crosse received this word about her brother: "Deeply regret to inform you that an official finding has been made that your friend (why it used that word is not certain, but it probably was standard when going to someone with a different last name) Private First Class Willis O. Oftedahl who was previously reported missing in action was killed in action 15 June 1944 at Saipan Island Marianas Islands in the performance of his duty and service of his country. Please accept my heartfelt sympathy." The telegram was from Gen. A.A. Vandegrift, commandant of the Marines.

"My grandmother NEVER gave up hope of one day finding him alive," says Kay Burke of Viroqua, Oftedahl's niece and a daughter of Howe. "She and the family searched every war picture, book, news, and film. He was her youngest child, the apple of her eye and supported her financially, as her husband died when Willis was 10."

Vandegrift knew full well the perils and sacrifices of Saipan. His son, Lt. Col. Alex Vandegrift Jr., had been the battalion commander of Cpl. Merlin Mosey in the Marine division that joined Oftedahl's group in the attack. Mosey was killed the same day as Oftedahl. And the father himself had been a commander at Guadalcanal, receiving the Medal of Honor for leadership there and elsewhere in the Solomon Islands.

In Milwaukee, one of the clerks in the Popielarski family grocery store was Dolores Tarkowski, who had developed a romance with co-worker Andy Popielarski. When the Red Cross went to Andy's home of 3334 N. Bremen in mid-August 1944 to report that he had been killed in Normandy, the parents were not there because they were out shopping. So the telegram was brought to the backup address – the grocery store. Older brother Leonard Popielarski also was out at the time, so Tarkowski took the sad news directly.

Joe Popielarski, son of Leonard, was about age 9 and his family was living above the store at the time. The boy heard sounds of screaming and grief that he had never heard before from adults. "She went into absolute hysteria," Joe says. "She came screaming into the hall. I was taken aback. I didn't know what to do."

On or about the same day in Door County, Catherine McArdle was working in the Sturgeon Bay shipyards, building LSTs and other landing craft. She came home to hear the whole town of Baileys Harbor talking about Billie Weiss, news that was doubly horrible because it came only two months after the loss of his boyhood pal Carl Zahn in the 32nd Division in New Guinea, the same place where Billie's brother Eugene also was fighting in the same division. The town and the county had many men at war, including another boyhood chum, Orville Voeks, who was piloting B-17s that were bombing Germany day after day.

"The whole town felt it. In a small town, our tragedies are one another's tragedies, and our happiness is one another's happiness," McArdle says. "Billie was a very lovely young man, a high-caliber young man."

The Advocate newspaper, located in Sturgeon Bay, headlined its top front-page story on Aug. 25, "Door Co. Boy, World War Victim," with a deck adding that "'Red' Weiss of Baileys Harbor Killed in France Aug. 1." There also was a headshot of Weiss. The article said Billie was the 15th Door County man killed in the war.

"Outdoor life was his hobby, and he spent many hours boating, fishing and hunting. Fishing was particularly his favorite sport, and his ambition, never fulfilled, was to take a trip to the Canadian wilds for trout. Of a cheerful disposition, he was well-liked by all who knew him," the story said.

In Appleton, Ken Miller's cousin Carol Parker was 6 at this time, but "the impact was so great that I can remember it today."

The family had been told that Ken was MIA, most likely at the end of August, and the final telegram came on a very cold Sunday morning, Parker says, remembering that jackets were worn, doors were closed and storm windows were on. The date was Oct. 29.

Lucille Miller – Ken's wife had moved back home to Illinois at some point after he was drafted – got the final telegram and called Earl Miller, Parker's father, about 10 a.m., "while we were getting ready for church. We went over to Ken's home. My parents told us to wait out in the yard." This was young Carol and her brothers, David, 3, and Jim, 1. "We tried to look in the living room window as we stood on the porch to see what was happening. We knew it was something awful.

"They went upstairs and got Grandma and Grandpa (Charles and Anna Miller) and Edith and Will (Ken's parents). I heard Aunt Edith screaming. I remember watching my father's face as he had this horrible task. I only saw my father cry twice in his life. This was one; the other was when his father died."

When the kids finally were let inside, "I ran to my Grandma to hug her." The North Meade Street neighbors quickly materialized for comfort. And the blue star that hung in the window, signifying a son or daughter in the service, soon was replaced by a gold one – signifying the ultimate sacrifice.

"I still can get tears in my eyes and a lump in my throat over that whole thing. His death so profoundly affected everyone I loved. And I was just a little kid. ... I've always believed I've been more aware, than others my age, of what the effects of the war were, because of Kenny's death," Parker says.

Ken's memorial service was held at 3 p.m. the next Sunday, Nov. 5, at the Christian and Missionary Alliance Tabernacle. Officiants were the Rev. Earl A. Gulbranson of the Alliance, and the Rev. J. Raymond Chadwick of the First United Methodist Episcopal Church, the family's first congregation. Chadwick read 1 Corinthians 15: 50-58 (about the Resurrection of the Dead; "Death has been swallowed up in victory. Where, O Death, is your victory? Where, O Death is your sting?") and Revelation 21: 1-4 (the last book of the New Testament, about Judgment Day and the new kingdom: "Death will be no more; mourning and crying and pain will be no more ...").

The soloist, a Mr. Sigl, sang "What If It Were Today" and "The Love of God."

The program noted: "And we know that all things work together for good to them that love God, to them who are called according to His Purpose," a quote from Romans 8:28. A remembrance card carried a placid drawing of a stream and trees, with a church steeple in the background, and was entitled "Beside Still Waters." Inside was the 23rd Psalm, which ends with, "and I will dwell in the house of the Lord for ever."

The funeral of Martin Miller, who was in the same regiment and company as Ken and Billie Weiss and Andy Popielarski, was held two weeks later, on Monday, Nov. 18, delayed so that his sister Caroline could return from California and the Marine Corps. The Millers had the same last name and been killed the same day in Company A of the 112th Regiment, both being MIA for more than two months and then both being declared dead. Martin's family was notified on Oct. 25; Ken's on Oct. 29.

The weeks since the first telegram had dragged on, and turned into months. Every time a car drove slowly past their country lane, the family feared the worst, that it was another sad telegram being delivered. "My mother's hair turned white overnight," said Florence Mueller, the oldest child, and the family began losing whatever hope it did have. Martin Miller's 25th birthday came and went on Oct. 14.

Now the family faced another crisis – a very happy event was coming up: the first mass of a newly ordained priest cousin, Lawrence Andre, in Plymouth, Wis. But the Millers were obviously in no mood for smiling, much less partying.

"Dad didn't want to go. We didn't want to spoil the event for the Andres," Florence said. On the other hand, all the Milwaukee-area Haeusler and Bunzel relatives would have wondered what had happened to Anna Haeusler Miller's family if nobody came. Mary Andre, the new priest's mother, was the only sister of Anna.

So a compromise was reached between the two impossible extremes, but the compromise was not very easy, either. The family would attend, but "we just wouldn't say anything about Martin," Florence said. That stiff upper lip did not last long – cousin Ray Andre, who would become a priest himself and would be a groomsman at her wedding a year and a half later, asked a routine question about whether the family had heard anything more about Martin. She could not lie – she asked to see him privately.

She asked him to keep quiet for a day or so. He said he had heard many cases of the bad news coming about three months after the first bit of news.

The family's church now was St. William in the town of Paoli at the crossroads of Highway 69 and County PB in Dane County. The solemn high mass was celebrated by Martin Miller's three uncles, Fathers George, John and Joachim Haeusler, and the brand-new Father Lawrence Andre, his cousin, was the master of ceremonies, as the Waunakee newspaper put it. Many of the same Haeusler and

Bunzel relatives who were at the Plymouth celebration came to this sad event.

Martin's fiancee, Clara Kelter, who at one point had been a neighbor in Waunakee, of course was a centerpiece of the mourning. Nearly six decades later, Florence Mueller broke down when she related how her sister Caroline was able to get a surprise leave from the Marine Corps at Goleta Air Base in Santa Barbara, Calif., to come home to Martin's memorial, and how the family kept the plan from Anna Haeusler Miller until Caroline arrived, because they did not want the grieving mother to be worrying about travel connections during the three-day train trip. "The Red Cross made it possible for me to come home for Martin's funeral, and they lent me the money for the trip," Caroline says.

It was a very sad day. But better ones were to come: A year and a half later, Father George would preside over the wedding of Florence and Wilferd Mueller in this same church, and in the months that followed, Caroline and Genevieve also would march down that same aisle to marry Marine Robert Nye of Massachusetts and Paoli native William Wild, respectively.

In Rice Lake, a headline in The Chronotype reported on Sept. 6: "Pfc. Harvey Hyllested Killed in Active Duty." The one-paragraph story – the news must have come right on its deadline given the brevity – said he was killed in early August in France, serving with an infantry division. The top story on the page, right above Hyllested's death, said five sons of the Sever Miller family were now in the military.

A week later, the newspaper printed a longer item with Harvey's picture, and this time the headline said: "Harv. Hyllested Killed in France." There was a subheading giving more information: "Has Two Brothers in Service; Father in Secret Service During World War I."

The story gave his date of death as Aug. 1 and said he worked at the Cudahy Co. in St. Paul before entering the Army in March 1943. His basic training was at Camp Robinson, Ark., and Camp Pickett, Va.

For many years thereafter, "His mother and his sister would get tears in their eyes if his name was even mentioned," says Eunice

Hyllested of Rice Lake, who met and married Harvey's brother Bob during the war, and did not know Harvey.

In Viroqua, the memorial service for Marine Willis Oftedahl was held on July 1, 1945, more than a year after the invasion of Saipan, and nearly a month after his death was confirmed. The local newspaper reported Pastor O.M. Kleven gave "a strong sermon on 'More than Conquerers'."

The phrase is from a passage in the New Testament, Paul's letter to the Romans, (8:35-37).

It says: "Who will separate us from the love of Christ? Will hardship, or distress, or persecution, or famine, or nakedness, or peril, or sword?

"As it is written, 'For Your sake we are being killed all day long; we are accounted as sheep to be slaughtered.'

"Nay, in all these things we are more than conquerers (the spelling was changed in newer versions of the Bible) through Him who loved us. For I am convinced that neither death, nor life, nor angels, nor rulers, nor things present, nor things to come, nor powers, nor height, nor depth, or anything else in all creation, will be able to separate us from the love of God in Christ Jesus our Lord."

The obituary continued: "The men's octette sang, and the Viroqua American Legion took part in the service." The hymns began, "A mighty fortress is our God" and "God bless our men in air, on land and sea!"

The obituary said Oftedahl had been baptized by Rev. L.F. Hammer, and had been confirmed by Kleven – who presided at the funeral – in 1936 at the same Bethel Lutheran Church.

For William Hartzheim, killed in the sinking of the USS Dorchester along with the four chaplains who were put on a U.S. postage stamp, the town of Juneau in Dodge County gathered to mourn nearly three months later, on Friday, April 30, 1943. The Independent newspaper bannered it across the top of page 1 that afternoon.

The mass was held at 8:30 a.m. at St. Mary's Roman Catholic Church and was celebrated by Father Joseph B. Webber with assistance from Juneau Post No. 15 of the American Legion.

Hartzheim was the first serviceman from Juneau to be lost in the war. "Regrettable as the news has been to all our people, circumstances will embalm his memory in the tomb of the nation's military heroes," said the newspaper story, which had no byline.

The paper said Juneau Mayor Hugo Werblow had requested that all business in the city be suspended that morning for one hour, and that "all people of the community in general attend the requiem as a testament of patriotic tribute," as the paper put it.

The mayor said: "The people of this community are deeply touched by the tragic ending of this young life and extend in full measure to the members of the family their sincere sympathy." The paper printed the proclamation alongside the story.

After these funerals, the Wisconsin families went on with their mourning and their tears and tried to continue their lives.

But then, incredibly, horribly, awfully, the Grim Reaper of the telegram world came knocking again for some of them:

* Andy Popielarski's older brother, Pfc. Vincent Popielarski, 29, was killed not even four months later, on Nov. 17, 1944, while serving with the 36th Armored Infantry Regiment of the 3rd Armored Division. He is buried at the Henri-Chapelle Cemetery in Belgium.

• WIlliam Hartzheim, who had been on the USS Dorchester, lost a cousin in an absolutely unthinkable way. Army Technician 4th Class Paul Hartzheim, 28, and more than two dozen other servicemen were killed when their plane crashed in the Mediterranean on Aug. 1, 1945, while on the way home from Italy to be discharged. The plane had a mechanical failure.

Repeat: Paul Hartzheim survived the war, but died in an ACCIDENT nearly three months AFTER hostilities in Europe ended while ON THE WAY HOME. His name is on the MIA wall at the Sicily-Rome Cemetery.

Two Hartzheims. Two deaths at sea: one on a ship and one on a plane. One very early, in 1943, and one very late, after the war was won in Europe. Both very sudden and very unexpected. Another page one story in the Juneau newspaper. Two spots on MIA walls, on the East Coast Memorial and at Sicily-Rome.

Paul's younger brother Joe, age 18 at the time, had entered the Army right after graduating from Juneau High School in May 1945, and was based in St. Louis. Because it was after VE Day, he was prepared for his family to notify him when Paul would be safely home. In fact, the Jefferson Barracks in St. Louis was a discharge center, and Joe and others were working from 8 a.m. to midnight processing the returning vets.

But when the word from his family came, it was via telegram, and it was like a sock in the gut. A big wallop.

"I was sitting on a tree stump outside the barracks. I read the telegram eight times. I couldn't believe it," Joe Hartzheim said. "I cried like a baby. I couldn't get over it."

Paul was well-known for his athletic prowess and lineage. As the local paper said in reporting his death, he "graduated from Juneau High School in 1935 with a fine scholastic record and an athletic history that still ranks with the best in the school's private hall of fame. He was a fast, high-scoring forward on the basketball team, a shifty halfback with the grid squad, a consistent point-getter as a distance runner with the track team and an effective pitcher on the baseball nine. He was one of the very few graduates who was awarded 11 athletic letters during their high school careers."

Joe says Paul also was captain of the hoops team, and inherited his athletic prowess from their father Elmer, who pitched the Juneau High School team to the state baseball championship in 1914 under the nickname of "Cocky."

The Hartzheim athletic DNA remains strong – Joe's apartment in Horicon is decorated with photos of his grandsons and granddaughters, and more than a few of them are in football, wrestling and track uniforms.

Paul Hartzheim was a supply sergeant with the 349th Infantry Regiment of the 88th Division. He had been in the Army since 1940. His wife, Reba (who was not from Wisconsin), was living in San Antonio, Texas. It was she who reported to his parents that the War Department had informed her that his plane was missing.

Paul had been in the area newspapers a lot during his athletic career and earlier in the war. In 1944, one of the Madison papers reported a group of 10 area soldiers – including Paul – were in the 349th Regiment, known as the "Kraut Killers," serving in Italy. That nickname was used in the one-column headline. The story said the group "fought across mountainous country to capture Fondi, a key point in the Adolf Hitler line. Below Rome, one platoon ambushed an entire German armored company attempting to flee from Maenza. After envelopment of Valterra, the unit smashed to the south bank of the Arno River."

Another story, from a Fifth Army correspondent, headlined that "Juneau boy helps turn Italian vinery into a supply base," and reported that Hartzheim transformed the place where "the Germans got drunk" into a tightly organized supply area "fixed up like a modern department store. Every item had its place just as it was listed on the table of equipment. Above every article a sign was placed telling exactly what the box contained, even down to the model."

Paul said in the story, "We know those boys in the foxholes are undergoing a terrific strain, so we figure the least we can do is to make sure they get everything they desire."

As for Vincent Popielarski, he was killed in a major attack – one that helped open holes in Germany's vaunted Siegfried Line near the city of Aachen.

At this stage of the war, the 3rd Armored was in the VII Corps (commanded by Maj. Gen. "Lightning" Joe Collins of Normandy fame) of the First Army, under Lt. Gen. Courtney Hodges, also of Normandy fame. The day before Vincent was killed, the First and Ninth Armies, each containing tens of thousands of men, attacked into the Roer River plain east of Aachen. This attack was assisted by 1,200 American bombers and 1,100 British bombers. On the day

Vincent was killed, his First Army captured Gressenich, 16 kilometers east of Aachen. Two days later, British and American forces captured Geilenkirchen, north of Aachen.

The 3rd Armored had been one of the divisions that smashed through at the front of the Breakout in France back in late July, not far from where Andy Popielarski, the Millers, Billie Weiss, and Harvey Hyllested were killed.

Vincent and his wife, Dorothy, had a daughter, Antoinette, who was 2 when he was killed. Her name now is Toni McMasters, and she lives in Berlin in Green Lake County. Her mother remarried when she was 5, to a man who ran a bar in their Milwaukee neighborhood, and the new family moved to Berlin when she was 12. But her name always remained Popielarski.

"The Popielarski family was a beautiful family who kept me in their hearts even though my father was gone, and we still are included in the get-togethers," said McMasters, who in recent years has become the oldest cousin of the clan. "So often I think of my grandparents and can't imagine dealing with the loss of two sons within three months. They were very wonderful people who cherished their faith by going to daily mass and I often remember them sitting with their faithful rosary beads on the loveseat in their living room."

When Toni married in 1963, she had Eddie Popielarski, the only Popielarski boy who came home from the war, march her up the church aisle. She still has the hope chest that her father gave her mother when they got engaged.

The St. Mary's Breeze, the Milwaukee parish newsletter that had reported the deaths of Andy and six other parish boys in its November 1944 issue, featured a large photo of Vincent in the next issue, which ran in January 1945. It also reported one other parish death and two soldiers missing in action. Oddly, it did not note that Andy had been killed previously. Vincent's memorial service was held five days before Christmas.

A year or so passed, a time of grieving, a time of putting lives back together, a time of seeing other soldiers from cities and towns return. Then the government asked families whether their sons should be brought home or should be buried in military cemeteries that were being created in various areas of Europe, North Africa and the Philippines at that time.

In Martin Miller's family, the consensus was that it did not wish to rip open the emotional wounds that still were festering. This was especially the case because of the Aug. 21, 1946, sudden death of 2-year-old Bonnie Damp, the family's first grandchild, who had been born only 16 days after Martin Miller was killed but BEFORE they got the telegrams saying he was missing and then killed. In more than a few ways, the daughter of Pauline Miller Damp and Robert Damp was the little angel sent by God who had helped give the family much happiness. Now her death from lockjaw, going from precocious kid to fatal victim in a matter of only few days, had proven devastating to all, and the family surely wondered why it had received such a cruel, double blow.

Because of these factors, Martin Miller remained forever on the French soil where he died for freedom.

The families of Ken Miller, Andy and Vincent Popielarski, Harvey Hyllested, and Billie Weiss – and many others – also decided that they had grieved too much in 1944 and did not wish to do it all over again, and decided their sons should stay overseas. A total of 93,238 Americans killed in World War II are buried in U.S. military cemeteries around the world, run by the American Battle Monuments Commission.

At the Brittany cemetery, where the Millers and Hyllested are buried, there are 4,410 graves, plus a memorial with the names of 498 missing, while there are 9,386 graves at Omaha Beach, including Andy Popielarski and Weiss, plus 1,557 names inscribed on a memorial to the MIAs. At Henri-Chapelle, where Vincent Popielarski is buried, there are 7,992 bodies and 450 on the MIA wall.

Overall, there are 120 Wisconsin bodies or MIA names at Brittany, 185 at Omaha Beach (Normandy) and 224 at Henri-Chapelle, according to the commission.

Merrill dentist William S. Van Nostrand Sr., father of the POW colonel whose body was never recovered, and thus never had the choice about an overseas burial or Wisconsin burial for his son, died in 1946 at the age of 79 or 80; the ordeal of his son's years of confinement no doubt contributed to his own death. The colonel's mother, Marie, died in 1955. His older brother Peter, an Army corporal, had died while at home in Merrill in November 1941, so this sad news barely would have reached the colonel before the Japanese attack less than a month later. Col. Van Nostrand has a memorial stone at the family plot at Merrill Memorial Park.

The families did not have the bodies of their soldiers, but had plenty of questions about what happened to them. Lucille Miller, in a letter to her in-laws on Oct. 14, 1945, told of one discovery after encountering a soldier who was sent into the 112th Regiment in the second week of August amid dozens of replacements for those who were killed on and around Aug. 1. In other words, he replaced people like her husband Ken, Martin Miller, Andy Popielarski and Billie Weiss, and others replaced Harvey Hyllested in the 110th Regiment.

"Dear Folks:

"Just a few lines .... We had a nice trip and it wasn't too tiring. ...

"Coming up we had a layover at Mpls. and I saw an MP with Ken's insignia on his sleeve. I went and talked with him. He was from the 28th Div. – the 112 Inf. and Co. A. I asked him if he knew Ken and he didn't. He didn't know anyone I named. I told him when Ken was killed and he said he went in as a replacement the second week in Aug. and that the whole division (underlined three times) was made up almost entirely of replacements.

"I told him how Ken was killed taking a hill and he said 'yes, that is now called "Purple Heart Hill."' The division was hit terribly hard there. I asked him why the 28th was never mentioned and he said that was one thing they couldn't understand. They fought entirely alone there. Then they went into the Battle of the Bulge alone, and on to fight at the Siegfried Line, and there the entire Div. was taken prisoner. He said it was awful.

"The young Capt. that Ken liked so much was killed, and so many were injured. It must have been, because of all I named (Ken's friends), he didn't know any at all. I told him how Ken was missing so long and he couldn't understand that because taking that hill was a victory and they pushed the Germans back, unless, he said, it was because there were so many lost there.

I thought this would help. I feel a little better having talked to someone who really knew what he was talking about. I'm glad Kenny got it so quick because the way he talked, this push through France was awful. He (the MP) was so nice to talk to and easy to talk with."

In La Crosse, Marine Cpl. Merlin Mosey's family received a direct account of what happened on Saipan:

"On that day our company landed on the island on a beach that was as you know under quite heavy enemy mortar and artillery fire," Capt. A. Arsenault, Mosey's immediate commander in the 4th Marine Division, said in a letter to the family – the kind of letter-of-condolence that is churned out when things finally calm down and is basically the same to each family except for a description of the specific action, which came in this fashion:

"Your brother (a corporal) was in charge of a machine gun squad, and he led his men to a pre-assigned assembly area and reported to his platoon leader. We set up a defensive position for it was getting dark, but the enemy from his position in the hills could see us, and before we had time to dig adequate foxholes, he placed heavy artillery fire on our area. Cpl. Mosey was hit in the first barrage; and although given immediate medical attention, died in a few moments without ever regaining consciousness."

Army Col. William Van Nostrand's wife received several notes of information and then condolence about his imprisonment in the Philippines.

One of his fellow prisoners on Mindanao, Capt. John J. Morrett of the Air Force wrote to Pidge Van Nostrand on March 28, 1945, to report that he spent months with the colonel in a POW camp and that Van Nostrand was well – as of a year earlier. He had no way of knowing the colonel had been killed nearly three months before the letter was written.

"The last time I saw your husband was on or about March 1, 1944, when I was sent out of the Davos Penal Colony on a work detail," Morrett said. "I have definite information that the remainder of the colony was sent to Manila in June. Some of the men were sent to Japan immediately; others not until some months later. It was my good fortune to escape from the prison ship sunk 7 September 44 off the Zamboanga coast."

(This likely was the Shinyo Maru, traveling from Davao to Manila, and 667 of the 750 men on board were killed.)

Morrett continued: "'Col.' Van as you probably already know was captured on the southern islands and I believe first held at Malay-balay (north central Luzon). At this camp the American prisoners were given very good treatment. In October '42 all the American prisoners from Malaybalay with the exception of the generals and full colonels were moved to the Davao Penal Colony. Treatment was good until the escape in April '43 (he does not give details as to how many escaped). I was moved down from Cabanatuan to the colony in the latter part of October '42 and at this time met 'Col.' Van. As he had been with the 26th Cavalry and I with the 88th F.A. (Field Artillery) Philippine Scouts, both stationed at Fort Stotsenberg, we had quite a bit in common. I also had been a counselor at Camp Minocqua, Wisconsin, and so we had a mutual interest in the Rhinelander district too.

"During the 16 months we were together, 'Col.' Van's health was good, in fact exceptional considering the ration we were made to exist on. His morale of course held up splendidly as you would expect it to. Many of us did some personal gardening in back of the barracks which helped to supplement our daily food considerably. Your husband became quite a proficient farmer passing many hours puttering around a little 8-by-4-foot plot of ground."

Morrett said he conducted Episcopal services because he had been in the seminary for several years before going into the Army, and that Van Nostrand "came consistently each Sunday .... He is a fine man, highly respected by all his fellows and in my opinion, one of the real leaders of men. … He has all the tenacity, spirit and faith to bring him through."

But on Sept. 25, 1945, longtime friend Col. F.W. Barnes from San Francisco sent a very sad letter to Pidge at 529 Madison St. in New Orleans. The words did not come easy, and the news was at least known now. They serve as a fitting epitaph for Van Nostrand, but also extend to all the other men in this book.

"I have had lots of time to think of things to say to you in this letter but I am still without proper words," said the note, which was typed on stationery of the United States Pacific Fleet and Pacific Ocean Areas, headquarters of the commander in chief, and signed "Freddy."

It continued: "But the profound feelings of sadness and shock over hearing of Van's loss are still with me and I find it difficult to believe that anyone as grand as Van is gone. It has made me feel more keenly than ever the futility of what we have just gone through.

"Swell people like Van were meant to live long lives and to help others with their easy-going, unselfish and pleasant ways. You know only too well the ease with which Van made friends and did things that made others love him. He is as irreplaceable in the lives of his friends as he is in the lives of his family.

"I was as certain as you, Jane, that he was coming through his ordeal all right. But it seems that he and others, no matter how patient and courageous they were, had all the odds against them. As a result you have lost one of the finest men who ever lived and I have lost one of my best friends. It must give you much comfort to know that young Bill (the baby who had to be evacuated from Manila at the age of only a few weeks) will inherit from Van all the fine traits of character Van possessed so abundantly."

A handwritten letter of Oct. 7, 1945, gave the grim details of what actually happened on the ship on the fatal day. It came from Tom Dooley of McKinney, Texas, who had been based at Fort Stotsenberg near Manila with Van Nostrand and all the others in happier days.

It began with, "My dear Jane:"

"My group were taken from Kyushu (Jap mainland) to Korea about April 25th of this year and when we boarded the ship at Fukuoka, we found several people from the 26th Cav. When I say we, I mean Johnnie Pugh and myself. Trapnell (no first name was given) and Bill Chandler were aboard (too.)

"Trap and Bill Chandler had been on the Dec. 13 boat (leaving Manila, with Van Nostrand and 1,620 others aboard) and I immediately asked for Van and John Wheeler. Jane – it really hurt me deeply and if you have not heard more – I am sorry but Van is gone.

"You know what I thought of him. It happened on the second ship they were on in Takao Harbor ... when they were hit by dive bombers. All of the survivors who knew Van said he was magnificent during the whole thing, as he was wounded by bomb fragments but kept going on and giving first aid to the wounded and working with them for five hours and suddenly he dropped.

"Jane, he was one of the grandest people I have ever known and you both were so grand to see at Stotsenberg that I know I have lost a true friend.

"I have debated with myself for days about writing this, but I feel that I must and please believe me that only the love for you both prompted me to do so."

Appleton's ties

Bob Rehfeldt and Clara Sprangers honor their relatives who are on the memorial at Appleton West High School. Sprangers, sister of Coast Guardsman Vic Salm, was in the same graduating class as Rehfeldt's distant relative, an Army combat engineer. The memorial lists the approximately 90 names of graduates killed in the war.

Army Pfc.
Gerald Rehfeldt,
killed June 6, 1944.
in Normandy

Coast Guard
Carpenter's Mate
Vic Salm,
killed June 13, 1943

Army Sgt.
Ken Miller,
killed Aug. 1, 1944,
in Normandy

Epilogue:

The ties that bind

The soldiers, Marines, airmen and seamen in this book are MIA or buried overseas, but they live on in many ways. All you have to do is look around, and to think about them and those like them. Some of the stories in this book were found quite by accident or the people were selected at random, which means there are thousands more stories out there — each very poignant and touching and tragic in some way.

Most directly, they live on in their descendants. Col. William Van Nostrand, whose infant son had been evacuated from the Philippines in 1941, is a grandfather of two and a great-grandfather of one, with another to be born in the spring of 2009. Pfc. Vincent Popielarski, whose daughter had been born in 1942, a little more than two years before he was killed in Germany, has two grandchildren and two great-grandchildren. Cmdr. Bertram Prueher had three children, who have blossomed into seven grandchildren and eight great-grandchildren, including one born in January 2009.

Toni McMasters, Popielarski's daughter, has his Purple Heart and keeps it in the hope chest that he gave her mother when they got engaged. Her two children "know he was killed in service, but that's all – because I don't know much more. My daughter said I do look a lot like him," she says. "My wish is to visit his gravesite in Belgium. You still have the feeling of loss every Memorial Day, and you feel so grateful for your freedom."

Prueher, who grew up in Bloomer, had three children when he was killed in 1943, and the youngest, Joseph, who was only a few months old at the time, went on to become a leader on the world military and diplomatic stage. He was a Navy admiral and commander in chief of the U.S Pacific Command, the largest unified command – directing Navy, Army, Air Force and Marine operations in the Pacific and Indian Oceans. Then he was U.S. ambassador to China from 1999 to 2001, under President Bill Clinton.

Bertram Prueher has 15 grandchildren and great-grandchildren, according to Martha Conzelman of Clayton, Mo., one of his daughters. She was only 2 when he was killed; her older sister, Elizabeth, was only 3. So none of them knew their father.

Pidge Van Nostrand, widow of the man killed on a prisoner ship, remarried when her son William S. Van Nostrand III was age 6 or 7, and lived in New Orleans, northern Mexico, Florida, and Texas. She regularly brought young Bill to Merrill in Wisconsin to visit his grandmother and other relatives, said Margaret Van Nostrand of Brownsville, Texas, his second wife.

"All he had were a few photos of his father in uniform holding Bill. That's all he knew of him. He wished he had a Dad … Pidge was always in touch with the military people she knew way back then. He always talked with a sense of pride that his Dad was in the military."

She also said the colonel's son "felt he would die young because so many young men in his family died young." He did, too, of cancer at the age of 53 in 1994.

Margaret said that being interviewed for this book and being told of the books that mention the POWs' ordeal "have given me a new and more realistic picture of what really happened and the awful events that preceded the bombing. Pidge and her mother, Molly, never discussed the negative side of Van's years as a prisoner of war, nor of his death and neither did Bill. They kept the positive memories which helped them deal with this tragedy."

Uniting in memory, 60 years later

In Door County, American Legion Post No. 527 in Sister Bay is named for Billie Weiss, the local boy who was one of the five Wisconsin men killed on Aug. 1 on Hill 210 in France. It is located in the village hall, built in 1941 right by the scenic beach in the town and across the street from the landmark Al Johnson's Swedish Restaurant and its goats on the grass roof. Past the slickly polished wooden floor at the entrance and past the one basketball hoop, just to the left of the stage, a frame hangs on the wall with a photo of Weiss and the newspaper clipping from the Advocate reporting his death.

The post was founded in 1946 and a drawing was held to determine whether it would be named for Billie, his boyhood friend Carl A. Zahn, killed in New Guinea, or one of the other four men from upper Door County killed in the war. Weiss's name was pulled from the hat.

This story was told on the 60th anniversary of the deaths of Weiss, Popielarski, Ken Miller, and Martin Miller by Don Sitte, an officer of the Weiss post. Members and representatives of the four families had traveled from around the state to Menasha for a unique gathering (at the time, the author's research had not yet included Harvey Hyllested, because he was in a different regiment in the 28th Division). We all brought flowers from our homes and from near where the solider lived; Sitte brought ferns from the site of Weiss's house and the flower bed that the boy had made for his parents. Some of the family members were in their 20s, so these men will be remembered for years to come.

Each family discussed their solider, or what older people always said about him, and Sitte represented both the post and Betty Weiss, Billie's sister-in-law, who could not travel so many miles from Door County any more. Three of us who had been to the cemeteries in France discussed how it was so eerie and yet they were happy to see the familiar name of a relative amid all the crosses and Stars of David 4,000 miles from home. Carol Parker told about taking a hat pin that had belonged to Ken's mother and sticking it in the ground at his grave in order to symbolically reunite mother and son.

She agreed it was remarkable that in 1984, Tom Mueller had somehow stumbled upon Ken's grave while becoming, in another part of the cemetery, the first relative to ever visit Martin's grave, and how in her trip to France, she repaid the favor.

Parker reported her Aunt Edith always had said Ken "was nonviolent and would not take other lives as a Christian." Her brother Jim Miller, the youngest boy on his aunt and uncle's porch that morning in October 1944 when the sad news was revealed, got choked up as he said his Uncle Bill (Willis Miller) was "a great big man with a great sense of humor and loved to sing." He could not imagine them being so sad.

Sitte, who wore his Legion uniform, walked up to the photos of the four men and gave a long salute to them, providing the most poignant moment of the luncheon. We then toasted the fallen men with French wine.

Joe Popielarski said he had a vague memory that Andy had been killed by a land mine. Sitte said word among the vets in the Sister Bay post was that Weiss had been killed by a gunshot. Tom Mueller reported that Martin Miller's family also had an Army letter saying a gunshot was responsible, but that an older in-law also recalled that Martin was MIA because his body lay in a minefield for two months before being retrieved. Ken Miller, who likely was in close proximity to Martin, based on being in Company A and being a few feet away from him in the company photo taken during training in Wales, also was MIA for that long. Andy Popielarski's memorial service was Aug. 26, and Weiss's was about the same time – meaning the two Millers basically were on a different timetable.

Joe also said that when the telegram about Andy arrived, the Red Cross people were very nonchalant about it and did not seem to know that they were talking to Andy's fiancée. "She scared the living bejesus out of me," he said of Dolores' hysterical reaction. "It was one of the most telling moments I ever had in my life."

Memorials in hometowns

At Appleton West High School, formerly Appleton High School, a stone memorial has been erected out on the front lawn on Badger Avenue. It contains a plaque with the names of more than 90 graduates who were lost in the war – including Ken Miller from Normandy, Victor Salm from the North Atlantic and Gerald Rehfeldt from D-Day in France. All their stories have been told in this book, and the relatives interviewed also have longtime ties to this very school – Carol Parker of Menasha graduated from there in 1956, along with a classmate named Richard Rehfeldt (no doubt some relative of the man who died on D-Day), and taught English there for two years (her boss had been the stern English teacher of her cousin Ken Miller), Clara Salm Sprangers of Little Chute was a 1942 graduate, and Bob Rehfeldt of Menasha, a distant relative of the Normandy soldier, a 1969 graduate following in the path of all his aunts and uncles who went there. Many siblings and cousins of Rehfeldt, Sprangers and Parker's two brothers also went there.

Clara lived on Meade Street, as did Ken Miller, but many blocks apart – Miller near the heart of town; Clara out on the northern edge.

In fact, Clara and Gerald Rehfeldt were on the very same page, page 34, in the senior photos in the 1942 yearbook. Gerald is in the upper left corner, next to his shirttail relative Robert Rehfeldt, and Clara is in the next row down.

In addition to the memorial rock, another Appleton legacy of the servicemen is that Coast Guardsman Vic Salm was indirectly responsible for three marriages – because his friends met other people with him in the center, according to Sprangers. Those marriages, two in 1942 and one in 1944, bore a total of 23 children and countless grandchildren.

Clara's sister Marie was at a bowling alley on a Sunday in January 1942, and needed another kegler for a game. Vic also was there and retrieved his good friend, Carl Heinritz, who was home on leave from the Navy and was in uniform, to fill out the foursome. That was how the couple met, and they began paying more and more attention to each other as the frames went along. They got married in October of that year in Washington, D.C., where Carl was based.

Marie and Carl went on to have 18 – that's right, 18 – children. It was quite a big strike, courtesy of Vic Salm.

Another of Clara's sisters, Viola, married Vic's best friend, Bill Calmes, in April 1942. The families were neighbors, and Vic and Bill did everything together, from hunting to fishing to sporting to playing around. Along the way, Bill started spending more time with Vi, and the rest is history – five children.

Vic also was responsible for Clara's marriage, in an indirect way. She wore his "football scarf," an award with the school's blue-and-white colors with images of football players, to a dance at the Cinderella Ballroom in Appleton several months after his June 1943 death. "We didn't do much dancing but walked around the hall," Clara said of her girlfriends.

Suddenly, someone snatched the treasured item off her neck and disappeared. It was a bunch of young men doing their flirting, and football scarves were not exactly rare at an event featuring people in high school or a year out of high school, like Clara was. "There was this group of eight guys (who included the guilty party), and the only one I remember was this great big tall guy," she said.

"They didn't know what it meant to me, that's for sure. I was wearing that scarf to honor my brother. It was a treasure. I was just devastated."

A week later, she saw the tall guy again, and asked him where the scarf was. "He said he didn't have it. I told him to look for it."

She was mad but didn't give him hell. The man was Joe Sprangers, and this was the first time she ever talked to her future husband. They got married on Nov. 11, 1944.

All three of Lt. Cmdr. Bertram Prueher's children came back to Bloomer in the summer of 2008 to help dedicate the town's new memorial to all local people who served in the military since the war of 1812. About 2,500 names are on the memorial; the site is not confined to those who died in wars. Prueher's two daughters were born while he was stationed in Panama, and his son was born in Tennessee, but all had come back to Wisconsin for years to see their grandparents, aunts and uncles, and retired Adm. Joseph Prueher still comes back every summer.

"Our dad's parents had a little tavern on Salisbury Lake," Martha Conzelman says of their playground, a 76-acre body of water. The family stayed in a cabin across the lake from the tavern, but the kids were not allowed to row a boat over there by themselves for several years because they were so little. "We children felt a real connection to Bloomer," and when the memorial was created, "we all came for the memorial service and laid the wreath," she said.

Conzelman said their mother's ashes were placed at the Naval Academy in the cemetery columbarium with her father's name on it. But she was surprised to be told that her father's name is on the East Coast Memorial in New York City.

The long-dead men listed in this book are still occasionally in the news, too. In December 2008, the number of Wisconsin MIAs fell by two – Robert Tills of Manitowoc was identified nearly 67 years after he was killed in the Philippines in the Japanese attack that came a few hours after Pearl Harbor, and Air Force Cpl. Richard Grutza of Milwaukee was identified and buried in his hometown 66 years after his bomber crashed in New Guinea.

In both cases, they are on the MIA wall at Manila, but aircraft wreckage was found in recent years, painstakingly recovered, then bone fragments and/or teeth were identified by the military, using DNA technology and scientific analysis worthy of any of the "CSI" television shows.

The story of Tills was described earlier in this book, in the chapter on worst days of the war. He was 23 and was a Navy ensign. Wreckage of his plane was found in October 2007 in Malalag Bay, and one fragment bore the markings "PBY-4," according to the Department of Defense POW/Missing Personnel Office. An interagency team of Americans and the Philippine Coast Guard surveyed the site and recovered human remains, including teeth, and non-biological evidence.

The office announced that Tills had been identified and that he would be buried in March 2009 at Arlington National Cemetery near Washington, D.C.

Grutza, 20, was a member of the 405th Bomber Squadron of the 38th Bomber Group Medium, and was lost on Dec. 5, 1942. The Pentagon office announced in September that it had identified his remains in the wreckage of a B-25 Mitchell bomber, which was found on a jungle mountainside in New Guinea. There were six other men on the plane, which was flying supply missions.

A lasting salute

All these men and women that have been discussed were part of history from long ago.

Richard Grutza, Robert Tills, William and Paul Hartzheim, Martin and Ken Miller, Willis Oftedahl, Vic Salm, Gerald Rehfeldt. Men from 1941, 1942, 1943, 1944, and 1945. Men from the Air Force, Navy, Coast Guard, Army and Marines. Ellen Ainsworth and Eleanor Nelson, members of the Army Nurse Corps.

And they are only the tip of the iceberg of the 3,800 from Wisconsin who are buried overseas, MIA, or lost at sea.

In its final issue dated December 1945, the St. Mary's Breeze, the newsletter of the Popielarski family's church in Milwaukee, ran the photos of all 19 parish men who were killed. The Popielarski family lost two of the 19, Vincent and Andy, thus bearing 10.5 percent of the tragic load for the entire parish.

Father Marion Cieslewicz, parish chaplain, wrote:

"With the deepest sense of gratitude we dedicate this last issue of the Breeze to the glorious memory of these 19 heroes who have paid the supreme sacrifice that we may live as free people.

"Our words and sentiments will be very vain indeed, if we living will not accompany them with action. And so it is for us living, and admiring these heroes, to learn also from them the spirit of sacrifice. They have labored, fought and died for the glory of God and their country, without having a chance to ask us what will their lot be in return.

"Should we then act like a victorious aggressor, who has only one intention to become rich on the spoils of the vanquished; or should we, in the spirit of humility, fall upon our knees with folded hands in prayer, thanking Our Lord for giving us such brave men, and promise to guide our own lives by the great spirit of charity towards God and our country as these 19 heroes from St. Mary's parish and many other thousands have so nobly manifested?"

Now that you are finished reading this book, think about what all these servicemen and women did, and how old they were, or better yet, how old they were not – most of those in this book were in their early 20s; some were only a year out of high school.

Think about their hometowns and how other people in this book also were part of the very fabric of schools and clubs and games in places like Rice Lake, Merrill, Menasha, Racine, Plymouth, Kewaskum, and much more. And then think how they were ripped out of that fabric, first to go to war, followed by death.

Think about what they would have become, had they survived the war and come back to the United States and Wisconsin, and used their talents in their chosen field.

Think about how, as each decade passes, fewer and fewer people actually knew the serviceman, even in their own families.

And let's vow to act now to never forget them, and to always preserve their stories for the future.

We salute them all – with Father Cieslewicz's well-chosen words and these other two grateful epitaphs.

Vive les liberateurs. And all the people of Normandy think as me.

– Jacqueline Sanchez of Bayeux, France, which is near Omaha Beach, to Tom Mueller in a hotel bar in Bayeux

He stands in the unbroken line of patriots who have dared to die that freedom might live, and grow, and increase its blessings. Freedom lives, and through it, he lives – in a way that humbles the undertakings of most men.

– President Franklin D. Roosevelt, in a memorial proclamation sent to families

Other reading

Jones, Meg (2008). Wisconsin native's remains recovered. Navy officer killed hours after Pearl Harbor attack. Milwaukee Journal Sentinel, Dec. 7, page 3B. Story about Robert Tills.

Silvers, Amy Rabideau (2008). 66 years later, soldier finds his way home. WWII gunner's B-25 was lost on mountain in 1942. Milwaukee Journal Sentinel, Dec. 14, pages 1B, 8B. Story about Richard Grutza.

Appendix:

How to make your own search

So what did your relative do in the war? What was his unit's job? What countries, towns and cities were on her trek through Europe or the Pacific? When did he enter the service? What was her official home of record and enlistment data? Who from that city or county was killed?

This book hopefully has inspired you to find out, and the purpose of this appendix is to give you a few basics for the search.

Thanks to Google, it is easier than ever to get going. But that is only a beginning.

If your relative is still alive, this book should serve as a clarion call for you to start getting the basics as soon as possible. Use the old adage, which everyone says over the years but which takes a special effort to get started: "Somebody ought to write this down." Well, you ought to be that somebody, and your descendants 50 years from now will thank you for it.

If it seems to be a giant, intimidating project, start small. Give it a half-hour just to write out the various places where your relative was based, and the years and months involved.

In a couple weeks, give it an hour or two more, to fill out the outline. You will be surprised to discover how fast the ball can get rolling. And view the project as bits and pieces that can be assembled later – a few oral comments, a little research on the Web and in a book, then get a few oral comments based on your book and Web findings, and so on. It can grow and grow, just as most chapters in this book did, from a small nugget of information.

Ask your relative to go through all his pictures and provide a narration for you. Those really unlock the memories. Write some essentials on the backs of the photos, too. Bring a map, because that may further awaken some memories. And hold more sessions, including bringing books from the library with more and more pictures beyond mere tiny snapshots – these will awaken even more memories.

Use a tape recorder if you want to, because that could be pretty priceless in 50 years. But the important thing is to get started – NOW.

Step 1: Check the ABMC database

To find those who died in the war, it has never been easier. Not even 15 years ago, you had to write a letter and ask the American Battle Monuments Commission to search its paper files. Now, just go to www.abmc.com and look for World War II. Then you can search by last name for your serviceman, if he is buried overseas or MIA.

Merchant Marine men are at this site, as are a few civilians, although it is pretty difficult to learn more because for them, the ABMC provides no details beyond date of death and the cemetery or MIA wall.

It is important to note that the search function at the ABMC is very sensitive (in fact, sometimes downright cranky), and although the directions fail to say so, do not capitalize the name. And do not use a comma between the last name and the first name, so your search term should be like this: "hyllested h"

If you capitalize the name and/or use a comma, you are likely to be told the man does not exist.

The search function also yields the serial number of the service person. This can be used in searches at other sites.

When you do find her, the listing will have initials for the name of the cemetery. Go back to the ABMC home page and go to Cemeteries. You will be able to download an information booklet about the cemetery you want, and you can download it with or without pictures. You even can watch an informational video. The booklet gives broad information on the battles in the area and on the design of the cemetery and its monuments.

You also can search the ABMC site via the unit involved, but that can get tricky amid abbreviations and capital letters and the like. However, this does work, and that is how I discovered that my Uncle Martin Miller and Ken Miller, the man whose grave I had found by accident in 1984, were not the only Wisconsin men in the 28th Infantry Division to die in Normandy on Aug. 1, 1944.

Step 2: Official information varies by military service

There is no one, simple way to get information, because the Navy kept records its "Anchors Aweigh" way and the Army did things its "caissons rolling along" way. This means that the "cousins" of each service – the Air Force with the Army, and the Marines and Coast Guard with the Navy – also do it that way.

In the Army / Air Force family, the 1946 booklet lists deaths only by state and county, with no dates and no towns. Finding out someone was from Marathon County, for example, is quite easy, but a person then has absolutely no idea where in that big county he was from. The same trouble came in the chapter of this book on Army Chaplain Capt. Raymond Hansen, who was from Eau Claire County. Eventually, I found on the Web that there is an Army Chaplain Museum at Fort Jackson, S.C., and the officials there had it right in their record: Hansen was from Augusta. I then called a church in Augusta and lucked out because the person who heard the answering machine knew her parents had been married in 1942 by a Rev. Hansen at the Evangelical Church. Things started snowballing at that point.

The story is different for Army nurse 2nd Lt. Eleanor Nelson of Rock County, who died after VJ Day of non-battle injuries and is buried in Hawaii. The Army Nurse Corps' historian could not obtain any information about her hometown or age, even though the corps lost 201 women because of non-battle injuries. Various calls to various places in Rock County yielded nothing, but a dozen or more places – such as schools and churches – could be called if someone were hell-bent on finding an answer.

The booklets, while vital, are not perfect. A member of the Women's Army Corps, Pfc. Alice Pauline McKinney, appears on the list for Wisconsin's Marquette County, but she actually was from

Marquette County in Michigan. It is technically possible she moved from one county to the other for a brief period of time, but the historical society in the Wisconsin county said it had absolutely nothing on her, and an Upper Peninsula researcher, Laraine Koski, who is compiling all of that area's people who served in the war, said there was absolutely no evidence that the WAC had any tie to Wisconsin other than the Army's enlistment record that showed she entered the service via Milwaukee. McKinney is listed as being from Michigan on the MIA wall in Tunisia, and was killed on May 30, 1945. On that day, a plane crashed, killing 18 WACs, among others (www.nooniefortin.com/earlierwars.htm). The C-47 transport plane crashed into the Atlantic off the coast of West Africa. The WACs had been stationed at the Army airfield in Accra, British West Africa (now Ghana), and were en route to new assignments in Europe.

Army 2nd Lt. Ellen Ainsworth of Glenwood City is not even on St. Croix County's list of service people killed in the war, for reasons that have not been determined over the decades. And the Navy list spells one city as "Manasha" in at least one incident, and also spells at least one street name wrong in Madison, my hometown.

The lists are readily available at the National Archives, specifically at www.aad.archives.gov. You also can get them at www.accessgenealogy.com/worldwar.

But another problem is that at both sites, when they were digitized from paper, odd things sometimes happened. The heart of the Milwaukee County Army/Air Force listings (specifically, page 20, spanning some of the letter L, all of M and some of N) were not copied and therefore do not exist. And at accessgenealogy.com, St. Croix County comes up blank. And Polk County is not even on the alphabetical list there.

And despite the best efforts of all the military branches, the homes of some servicemen flat-out cannot be found.

For the Army and Air Force, you might succeed by being able to find recruitment information via the National Archives, in what is called the Electronic Army Serial Number Merged File, ca. 1938 - 1946.

The trouble with that, however, includes the fact that these originated on 9 million computer punch cards, and a healthy number of them were flawed and thus not part of the database. The Archives says in one of the footnotes that it cannot repair them.

But for others, everything works well, and I was able to find enlistment information on my late father (from Dane County) quite easily. The ABMC database has a soldier's serial number, and that can be plugged into the Army form. The form can also be searched via last name, state name and county name – but that requires some patience and use of code numbers.

Another problem is that this database will not have anything on officers, evidently because they do not enlist as officers and thus are given a new serial number when they become officers.

The Merchant Marine Web site of www.usmm.org has a rich amount of information about shipping, ships, and losses. The Coast Guard site of http://www.uscg.mil/top/about/ also has a good amount of history.

Step 3: Some service groups and their alumni are very active; some not at all

For Navy people, it seems that just about every ship has a Web site, whether it is an official site from that service or done by veterans and other interested groups. Submarines, in particular, often seem to have crew lists posted, but the crew of a sub was less than 100, far smaller than the crew of a destroyer or aircraft carrier.

Basic information about any ship's specifications, its armament, its classification (like a model of a vehicle), and its history also are readily available, complete with photos.

Many Marine units have Web sites, and many of those post good articles about histories, but not death lists. One group told me there were so many deaths in World War II and in its other wars since then that finding such information is impossible. Some sites have discussion boards, and some World War II vets participate, but the most frequent users served in the Vietnam War.

Many Army divisions have alumni Web sites, but the number gets far smaller when you go down a size to regiments. But some do. Ditto for the Air Force – in fact, much of the material on specific Air Force men, such as Air Force Staff Sgt. Raymond P. Olson, from Vernon County, in this book is from alumni groups on the Web. Olson is on the West Coast Monument and his ABMC listing says he was in the 29th Bomber Squadron, Heavy. Veterans of the squadron have a Web site that gives a lot of information, some of it specifically about his death.

Some professional researchers would ask whether you should believe information from alumni groups or Wikipedia.com, given that they are not journalists and possibly are not very careful with their facts. Well, my answer to that would be that the alumni were in the fighting, and would know untrue facts when seen. And Wikipedia items are written by individuals who care, and that information often includes what professional item the material came from. If the site seems to be making outlandish claims or things not supported by fact or citations as to where the information came from, you should be a little cautious. If the writing on the site is not very polished and looks like one person doing it all, that is another red flag.

Step 4: Go through address lists of your dead relative – they may be wartime friends

These friends will be wondering what happened, because the veteran has not written to them for some time. They are apt to be tickled pink to be asked to recount their service for the sake of your family.

But don't expect them to be able to talk right off the tops of their heads, or all at once. Give them a warning via mail and then call them once a week, or something like that. Trade photos.

Step 5: Find out what happened on, or right around, the date of death or battle

You can do this via a war chronology book, or on Google, searching first for the date, then a week before and after the date, then that month, etc.

Once you find out what was happening – as I did for the large number of Marine deaths on June 15, 1944, for example – you can gather details, such as in this case about the invasion of Saipan.

The answer may start in an obscure place – for example, I wondered why so many men from Wisconsin were killed on Christmas Eve 1944, and why most of them were from the same infantry regiment. The breakthrough for me was when Google found some sort of site by an Indiana family paying tribute to their relative in that regiment and said he was on a ship that was torpedoed. I then put the name of the ship into Google with the date, and bingo – plenty of information about the Leopoldville.

Of course, connecting a date to your relative's death does not literally mean your man was at that site, but it is a strong indication and can be borne out or disproven by further research.

One important note: Especially for Navy deaths when a body was not recovered, the listed date of death may actually be one year and one day later in the ABMC database. You should check the Pentagon MIA office, too – this often has the right date. The Web address is www.dtic.mil/dpmo/WWII_MIA/MIA_MAIN.HTM.

Step 6: Books

Once you can connect the death to an event, it is a short hop to finding hard, printed data about that event.

If your local library system has its catalog on the Web, you can poke around in there via subject and possibly words in the title to get books that will help you find out more information. University and college libraries certainly are on the Web, and you can search there for material, even if you wind up getting the actual books elsewhere.

Google may lead you to books that are for sale but not in the library – such as ones that were self-published and therefore rare – and these are important clues.

And a favorite of all academic scholars is to find a book and then scour its bibliography for still more resources.

Step 7: Ask historical societies, the local Veterans of Foreign Wars and American Legion, libraries, the Wisconsin Veterans Museum, your State Historical Society, churches, high schools and even cemeteries

Any or all of the institutions on this list may have clues or even the big nugget that you are seeking. Each has been a big help in compiling this book.

Historical societies may have compiled wartime obituaries, or received materials compiled by someone else at the time. The Vernon County Historical Society was able to track down Marine Pfc. Willis Oftedahl's obituary for me, finding it in a donated scrapbook. The Merrill Historical Society gladly assisted in finding the background of Army Col. William Van Nostrand, who died in the Philippines, including information on him in the 1928 high school yearbook.

The name of your serviceman might be a familiar one to the local VFW and Legion, although as the decades have gone by, this is less and less the case. But many years ago, a post historian may well have compiled a list of men and women from the community who were lost in the war, and it may be more than a mere list, too.

Libraries, in smaller towns especially, may have a list of local losses in the war or some ideas on how to find one. You also can get lucky by asking a person well-plugged into the community whether a name is familiar.

The Wisconsin Veterans Museum in Madison has compiled substantial information on its Web site, including lists of various books that it has in its files. It sometimes has more on an individual soldier, but sometimes it might not. I have found some data via this method, but have struck out other times, and look forward to the day when it will get material out of this very book. Similarly, the State Historical Society has large collections and many ideas about where to find more.

If you know the religion of your serviceman, call the parishes in the area involved – you may well find a trail. I did that for Chaplain

Raymond Hansen, as described earlier. While writing another book, I had the name of a Minnesota soldier and a Google search had him listed in a book of members of Calvinist religion from his state. So I searched for churches of that branch in his hometown and left a message with the pastor. He soon called back with the name of the man's sister, although the church had divided into two over the years and she attended the other one. In a short time, I was talking to her.

And Messmer High School in Milwaukee – specifically its fund-raising arm – readily granted access to all its old yearbooks, which I mined for information on 1943 graduate Andy Popielarski, who died little more than a year later as an Army private first class in Normandy.

If your soldier had siblings and they are not buried overseas, they likely are buried at home, as was Col. William Van Nostrand's brother, Peter, who was on the Lincoln County list of dead but not on the ABMC list of foreign burials. I took a guess and figured that, and called the main cemetery in Merrill. When you think about it, getting calls about someone's ancestors is not very unusual at a cemetery.

Step 8: Network

Ask people you know for their ideas. Everyone has a mind that is fertile in some fashion, and you will get more ideas.

Step 9: Use the phone book, or http://whitepages.addresses.com/white_pages.php

This still works – calling people with the same name in the same general area where your soldier came from. It is getting harder and harder, as that generation of people is dying at a pretty good clip. But it was successful in this book when I found a nephew of Coast Guardsman Ray Buddenhagen, by searching for that rather distinctive name in his hometown of Kewaskum. I did not get so cocky as to try calling people named Smith, however, when such a name came up, and I do not recommend that you do so, either.

And of course, names often change on the female side, so this does not work well for them.

Step 10: Is an MIA still an MIA? Not even the ABMC list is updated regularly

If your serviceman was MIA or lost at sea, that is not necessarily still the case. Things change every week, as can be seen in the following recent examples.

In December 2008, the number of Wisconsin MIAs fell by two – Robert Tills of Manitowoc was identified nearly 67 years after he was killed in the Philippines in the Japanese attack that came a few hours after Pearl Harbor, and Air Force Cpl. Richard Grutza of Milwaukee was laid to rest in his hometown 66 years after his bomber crashed in New Guinea. Their cases were discussed in a previous chapter of this book.

In September 2008, three men in a mass grave of unknowns from the battleship USS Oklahoma in Pearl Harbor were identified – and included Navy Fireman 2nd Class Lawrence Boxrucker of Dorchester in Clark County (whose county seat is Neillsville). A total of 429 sailors and Marines on the Oklahoma were killed, and 393 were buried as unknowns in various numbers. The Pentagon MIA office said that in 2003, an independent researcher reported information that he believed could identify one of the unknowns, the military exhumed the casket involved (it is not clear to me how the researcher knew that) and found via DNA and other 21st century techniques that it contained the remains of at least 31 men, including Boxrucker and the other two identified.

Boxrucker was returned to Dorchester for burial in September 2008.

And in February 2008, the office identified three men from a December 1944 plane crash in Germany, including Air Force 2nd Lt. John Lubben of Wisconsin Rapids.

They were the crew of an A-20J Havoc light bomber that was flying from Coullomiers, France, to bomb targets near Wollseifen, Germany. The A-20J was known as the Havoc; built by Douglas Corp. That particular model had a transparent, bomb-aimer's nose. This enabled the aircraft to be used as formation leaders on bombing runs, with solid-nosed A-20Gs dropping their bombs on signal from the leader.

The MIA office said that in 1975, a German company clearing wartime ordnance near Simmerath, Germany, reported it found body parts – and U.S. officials determined they were from three people but could not make identification. The fragments were buried as unknowns in the Ardennes cemetery at Neupre, Belgium. In 2003, the Joint POW/MIA Accounting Command received information correlating the three unknowns with the crew from the A-20J crash. The graves were exhumed in 2005 and identification via dental records and other forensic tools was made in 2008.

Lubben is on the MIA wall at Luxembourg and the others on the MIA wall at Lorraine, and it is not clear why they are separate. The ABMC database gives their deaths as Dec. 13, 1944. All were in the 644th Bomber Squadron, 410th Bomber Group, Light. The three men were reburied at Arlington National Cemetery in April 2008.

The Pentagon office announces several identifications every month, from all wars and all theaters of action. Groups sometimes are large – in April 2008, the office announced that 11 men had been found in the wreckage of a B-24 bomber in New Guinea that crashed on Dec. 3, 1943. The crash site was found in 2004.

The upshot of all of this is that names on MIA walls are not necessarily still MIA. If remains are identified after the wall was built, a rosette is put next to the name.

Step 11: Donate your materials if need be

If the last generation of a family has died, speak up promptly for the fact that those belongings that many may view as "junk to be cleared out" contain invaluable historical material and should be – at the very least – screened by the local historical society. The material on Army Sgt. Ken Miller in this book was very nearly thrown out after his mother died at the age of more than 100, and I asked the family just in the nick of time, basically. The letters that Ken wrote and his mother saved for so long and that family members saved (or better yet, stacked up in the basement) were profound, some of the best that I have ever seen. On the other hand, there are cases like

Pfc. Andy Popielarski who was from a big family. The last sibling died several years ago, and none of the next generation knew where his letters were, nor much information about his brother Vincent who also was killed, nor about his brother Edward, who was in big-time fighting in Europe and survived.

If your relative is still alive, talk to him or her about the future and how it would be a real shame if it got lost, and how there is a clear and present danger that it will be lost. At the very least, see that a giant note is put into such a box saying DO NOT THROW OUT BECAUSE ...

I recommend using colored paper for this big note, because it stands out a lot better than plain white paper.

Step 12: Support your historical society and library

Historical societies provide indispensable material on a community and the state's roots and are repositories of knowledge for all sorts of stories and photographs from all sorts of eras. Ditto for the Wisconsin Veterans Museum. Libraries are essential to the flow of information that makes for an intelligent public, which is vital in a democracy.

Support all of them with your donations, with your patronage and with your own family's records.

Step 13: Get a picture of the grave or the MIA wall, and go there

Your soldier, airman, sailor or Marine may be buried thousands of miles away, but the ABMC will decorate a grave and take a photo, if you send in a request. The floral prices are very reasonable; the wait time until you get the photo may be several weeks or a couple months. You can request a specific day for the flowers and the photo, such as on the day of the soldier's death, his birthday, etc.

As for MIA walls, the ABMC will provide black-and-white photographs of the name involved, but some memorials are not staffed – specifically the East Coast one in New York and the West Coast one in San Francisco.

Above all, some member of your extended family no doubt will be going overseas as some point and ought to detour to this historic point. Believe me, a visit to your relative's cemetery – and finding a familiar name so far away – is unforgettable. The ABMC will escort any family member to the grave or your man's spot on the MIA wall, and the first thing that hits you is how huge the facility is, and how you know one particular person in all of that.

Information about ordering flowers for the graves, and their prices, can be found at www.abmc.gov. Prices vary by size of floral decoration, the season and the location, but generally range from $15 to $50.